GLOBALIZING IN
HARD TIMES

A volume in the series
Cornell Studies in Political Economy
edited by Peter J. Katzenstein

A list of titles in this series is available at
www.cornellpress.cornell.edu.

GLOBALIZING IN HARD TIMES

The Politics of Banking-Sector
Opening in the Emerging World

Leonardo Martinez-Diaz

CORNELL UNIVERSITY PRESS   ITHACA AND LONDON

First published 2009 by Cornell University Press

Printed in the United States of America

Library of Congress Cataloging-in-Publication Data

Martinez-Diaz, Leonardo, 1976–
    Globalizing in hard times : the politics of banking-sector opening in the emerging world / Leonardo Martinez-Diaz.
        p. cm. — (Cornell studies in political economy)
    Includes bibliographical references and index.
    ISBN 978-0-8014-4755-6 (cloth : alk. paper)
    1. Banks and banking, Foreign—Developing countries—Case studies.   2. Banks and banking, International—Developing countries—Case studies.   3. Banks and banking—Deregulation—Developing countries—Case studies.   4. Financial crises—Developing countries—Case studies.   5. Globalization—Economic aspects—Developing countries—Case studies.   I. Title.   II. Series: Cornell studies in political economy.
    HG3550.M37 2009
    332.109172'4—dc22   2009023337

Cornell University Press strives to use environmentally responsible suppliers and materials to the fullest extent possible in the publishing of its books. Such materials include vegetable-based, low-VOC inks and acid-free papers that are recycled, totally chlorine-free, or partly composed of nonwood fibers. For further information, visit our website at www.cornellpress.cornell.edu.

Cloth printing   10 9 8 7 6 5 4 3 2 1

Para Debbie

Why this sudden restlessness, this confusion?
(How serious people's faces have become).
Why are the streets and squares emptying so rapidly,
everyone going home so lost in thought?
Because night has fallen and the barbarians have not come.
And some who have just returned from the border say
there are no barbarians any longer.
And now, what's going to happen to us without barbarians?
They were, those people, a kind of solution.

—Constantine P. Cavafy, "Waiting for the Barbarians," 1904

Contents

Figures and Tables

Preface

I began research for this book in 2004, near the apex of a great "age of capital" that began in the late 1980s. This was an age dominated by American and European financial institutions—commercial and investment banks, insurance companies, and private equity and hedge funds whose vast resources, technical sophistication, and boundless ambition became emblematic of the globalization of finance.

As this book went to press, that age had come to an end. Financial markets crashed. Once-mighty financial institutions in Europe and the United States disappeared or had to resort to government-financed rescues. And the end was not yet in sight. The world's balance of financial power seemed to be changing as well. In the 1990s and early 2000s, it was American and European firms that were making deep inroads into the emerging world's financial sectors, often through mergers and acquisitions. Now, financial firms from emerging-market countries appeared poised to penetrate long-coveted markets in the most advanced economies.

This book sets out to understand how this age of capital was constructed and what political dynamics made it possible. In particular, it tries to explain how and why emerging-market countries removed long-standing barriers to foreign investment, competition, and ownership in the commercial banking sector. At the heart of the political struggles portrayed in this book was an idea: the notion that a country's financial institutions should be controlled by that country's nationals, and that governments should erect regulatory barriers to keep foreigners—"the barbarians"—out. That idea proved remarkably resilient in many countries, and it had purchase even among otherwise committed practitioners of economic liberalism.

The main argument of the book is that in the four emerging-market countries of Mexico, Brazil, South Korea, and Indonesia, it took a banking crisis—a systemic shock—for that idea to be abandoned and for governments to open their banking systems fully to global capital. During noncrisis times, the principle of financial protectionism proved too compelling for emerging-market policymakers, who preferred to engage in gradual, "managed" opening. However, the shock imposed severe resource constraints on governments, rendered them more vulnerable to external pressure, and forced policymakers to liberalize—both in terms of law and practice—in order to regain economic stability and to safeguard their own political survival.

As today's crisis rages across many mature economies, bringing major financial institutions to their knees, the U.S. and other governments will have to deal with a dilemma familiar to policymakers in the countries studied in this book. They will have to decide whether to rescue their ailing institutions with their own (mostly public and mostly borrowed) money, expanding the public debt and the role of the state in the financial system, or to open the door directly to foreign direct investment, sharing with foreigners the financial burden but also the ownership and control over financial resources that come with it. If they choose to open their doors, a political struggle will ensue over the terms of foreign entry, one that will determine who holds power over financial resources in the future. The political battles recounted in this book, far from being historical curiosities, are timely reminders of how other societies have dealt with this difficult dilemma.

I am enormously grateful to Kalypso Nicolaïdis and Valpy FitzGerald, whose guidance and constant encouragement were invaluable. Much credit also goes to Roger Haydon and Peter Katzenstein, whose constructive advice made the revision of this work a very rewarding process. I am also grateful to Ngaire Woods for her many insights, particularly on all things related to the IMF and World Bank. Thanks go also to Andrew Walter for his helpful feedback, to Matias Spektor for his patient reading of early drafts and cheerfully ruthless commentary, and to Julia Guerreiro for her excellent research assistance.

This book owes a debt of intellectual gratitude to the group of distinguished political economists who taught me during my undergraduate years at Northwestern University in the late 1990s. This group includes Ben Ross Schneider, Jeffrey Winters, Meredith Jung-En Woo, and Michael Loriaux. My book is very much in the intellectual tradition of these scholars, who first opened my eyes to the importance of finance in world politics and its role in the exercise of political power.

The multicountry fieldwork required for this project demanded substantial resources. For those, I thank the managers of the Oxford University's Norman Chester, George Webb Medley, and Cyril Foster and related funds, as well as Oxford's Centre for Brazilian Studies and Magdalen College. I thank the Korean Institute for International Economic Policy for its generous support of my fieldwork in Seoul. I am also grateful to Oxford's Global Economic Governance Programme for providing me with a base and the stimulating company of wonderful colleagues during the first half of this project, and to the Global Economy and Development Program at the Brookings Institution for doing the same during the second half.

I am indebted to all the interviewees who participated, including those who preferred to remain anonymous, as well as to librarians, archivists, journalists, bankers, civil servants, and academics who patiently guided me through a maze of banks and bureaucracies in Washington, Jakarta, Seoul, São Paulo, and Mexico City. I am especially grateful to Kyungin Song in Korea; Carlos Augusto Vidotto and the Fundação Getúlio Vargas in Brazil; Gustavo del Ángel Mobarak and Dorothy Walton in Mexico; and Soedradjad Djiwandono, Richard Borsuk, Rena Djunaedi, and Hans Vriens in Singapore and Indonesia.

Last but not least, I thank my parents for their constant encouragement, love, and inspiration.

Acronyms

ABM	Mexican Bankers' Association
AFAS	ASEAN Framework Agreement
ASEAN	Association of Southeast Asian Nations
BACEN	Central Bank of Brazil
Banxico	Bank of Mexico
BB	Banco do Brasil
BBVA	Banco Bilbao Vizcaya Argentaria
BCA	Bank Central Asia
BDN	Bank Dagang Negara
BI	Bank Indonesia
BIBF	Bangkok International Banking Facility
BII	Bank Internasional Indonesia
BIN	Bank Industri Negara
BIS	Bank for International Settlements
BLBI	Bank Indonesia Liquidity Assistance
BNDE/BNDES	National Economic Development Bank (Brazil)
BNI	Bank Nasional Indonesia 1946
BRI	Bank Rakyat Indonesia
CFC	Federal Competition Commission (Mexico)
CEF	Caixa Econômica Federal (Brazil)
CMIT	Committee on Capital Movements and Invisible Transactions (OECD)
CMN	National Monetary Council (Brazil)

CNB/CNBV	National Banking and Securities Commission (Mexico)
CSI	Coalition of Service Industries
DPR	House of Representatives (Indonesia)
EBF	European Banking Federation
EIC	European Insurance Committee
EM	Exposição de motivos
FDI	Foreign direct investment
FEBRABAN	Federation of Brazilian Bank Associations
FIESP	Federation of Industries of the State of São Paulo
FLG	Financial Leaders' Group
FOBAPROA	Fund for the Protection of Bank Savings (Mexico)
FSAL	Financial Sector Adjustment Loan
G7	Group of Seven
G20	Group of Twenty Finance Ministers and Central Bank Governors
GATS	General Agreement on Trade in Services
GATT	General Agreement on Tariffs and Trade
Golkar	"Functional Groups" political party (Indonesia)
HHI	Herfindahl-Herschman Index
HIMBARA	Association of State-Owned Banks (Indonesia)
HSBC	Hong Kong and Shanghai Banking Corporation
IBK	Industrial Bank of Korea
IBRA	Indonesian Bank Restructuring Agency
IMF	International Monetary Fund
IPAB	Institute for the Protection of Bank Savings (Mexico)
IPE	International political economy
ISI	Import-substitution industrialization
KADIN	Chamber of Commerce and Industry (Indonesia)
KDB	Korea Development Bank
KEB	Korea Exchange Bank
KFB	Korea First Bank
KFIU	Korea Financial Industry Union
LOI	Letter of Intent
MFN	Most-favored nation
MOF	Ministry of Finance (Korea)
MOFE	Ministry of Finance and Economy (Korea)
MPR	People's Consultative Assembly (Indonesia)
NAFA	North American Framework Agreement
Nafin	Nacional Financiera (Mexico)
NAFTA	North American Free Trade Agreement
NKP	New Korea Party
NPL	Nonperforming loan

OECD	Organization for Economic Cooperation and Development
PAKTO	Financial reform package of October 1988 (Indonesia)
PAN	National Action Party (Mexico)
PCCC	Capitalization and Loan-Purchase Program (Mexico)
PERBANAS	Association of National Private Banks (Indonesia)
PRD	Party of the Democratic Revolution (Mexico)
PRI	Institutional Revolutionary Party (Mexico)
PROER	Program for Restructuring and Strengthening the National Financial System (Brazil)
PROES	Program of Incentives for the Reduction of the States' Public-Sector Participation in Banking Activity (Brazil)
PSDB	Brazilian Social Democratic Party
Secofi	Ministry of Trade and Industrial Development (Mexico)
SHCP	Ministry of Finance and Public Credit (Mexico)
USTR	United States Trade Representative
WTO	World Trade Organization

GLOBALIZING IN
HARD TIMES

THE POLITICS OF BANKING-SECTOR OPENING IN THE EMERGING WORLD

Financial globalization—the reduction of regulatory and technological barriers that makes possible the unfettered movement of capital across national borders—is one of the most powerful, transformative forces of our time. It has made the global economy more dynamic and more productive, but also more unstable, than in any period since the late nineteenth century. Financial globalization has also challenged the capacity of governments to control financial and monetary variables, throwing into question what it means to be a sovereign state in a world where market participants have vastly enhanced options for circumventing and exploiting gaps in national regulatory frameworks.

Thanks to two decades of scholarship by political economists, today we know a few things about the origins and nature of financial globalization.[1] First, the phenomenon has not emerged spontaneously through the unfolding of unstoppable economic forces; the regulatory framework and institutions that make it possible are the result of conscious political choices, choices that at least in part reflect the interests and power of governments. Second, decisions about when and how to deregulate financial markets have emerged only after a political struggle among domestic and transnational groups, one that has pitted "liberalizers" or "globalizers" against "nationalist" and "protectionist" forces. The contours of financial globalization are

---

1. For surveys of the literature on the political economy of international financial integration, see Andrew Walter, "Understanding Financial Globalization in International Political Economy," in *Globalizing International Political Economy,* ed. Nicola Philips (Basingstoke, U.K.: Palgrave Macmillan, 2005), pp. 141–164, and Benjamin J. Cohen, "Phoenix Risen: The Resurrection of Global Finance," *World Politics* 48:2 (1996), 268–296.

shaped by this process of contestation. Third, it is now clear that however potent the forces promoting financial globalization and however relentless the pressure they exert on governments to adopt open regulatory regimes, considerable diversity remains among national regulatory frameworks. Contrary to theories that predict an inevitable "race to the bottom," the rules and institutions governing finance have not converged around a single standard. Finally, we now know that once the genie of financial globalization is out of the bottle, it is very difficult to put back in, at least in the same bottle. Once implemented, financial openness generates its own political constituencies and alters the political-economic landscape, so that re-regulation can be accomplished only through new instruments and political battles.

These are all important insights, but significant gaps remain in our knowledge of how financial globalization came about and how it has unfolded. The scholarship on financial globalization has tended to focus more on the politics of rule-making (de jure liberalization) and less on how those rules are implemented in practice (de facto liberalization). Also, we do not yet have adequate accounts of the political dynamics that have shaped financial globalization in many developing and "emerging-market" countries, as much of the research on the topic has focused on the most advanced economies of the Organization for Economic Cooperation and Development (OECD). For many emerging-market and developing countries, we do not yet have good answers to the following questions: Why did their governments decide to open their financial systems to foreign capital, after decades of shielding them with protectionist policies? What explains the timing of financial opening? What determined who won the struggle between groups that sought greater openness and those that endeavored to keep the financial system closed? And once a country's financial system was opened to global capital, what determined whether its patterns of financial ownership and control converged with those of other countries or diverged from them?

To address these questions, this book homes in on a particular dimension of financial globalization. It focuses on banking-sector opening, which I define here as legislative and regulatory changes in a particular jurisdiction (the "host" country) that (1) enhance the ability of foreign financial institutions to establish and operate bank branches, subsidiaries, and representative offices in the host country, and (2) expand the capacity of foreign investors to invest in, acquire, control, and operate the host country's indigenous commercial banks.[2] These two types of foreign entry are known as de novo entry and entry by acquisition, respectively. Why focus on this relatively narrow dimension of financial globalization?

---

2. This book is primarily concerned with the commercial banking sector, which is composed of retail and universal banks. Retail banks raise much of their capital by taking deposits from the public and engage in corporate and retail lending whereas universal banks generally have a commercial bank at their core but also provide a range of other financial services. Investment and merchant banks, credit unions, securities firms, insurance companies, pension funds, and other nonbank financial intermediaries are not directly considered here.

Of the various aspects of financial globalization, banking-sector opening is one of the most controversial and politically contested.[3] Even today, most emerging economies have bank-dominated financial systems and relatively underdeveloped securities and insurance markets. Opening securities or insurance sectors to foreign competition usually entails a modest political cost for the government because incumbent firms are small and the financial stakes comparatively low. Opening the banking system to foreign capital, on the other hand, often means confronting large and powerful domestic banks with networks that extend across the whole economy and with strong incentives to retain the flows of rents guaranteed by barriers to entry. For politicians and bureaucrats, banking-sector opening is often an extraordinarily sensitive issue, as it involves ceding to foreigners partial control over a sector long considered to be as strategic to national economic development as oil production or heavy industry. And for foreign investors and financial institutions, banking-sector opening stands as the holy grail of financial-services liberalization, the key to tapping lucrative and underdeveloped retail-banking markets in fast-growing economies. In short, the study of banking-sector opening provides us with a window into some of the most intense political struggles that lie at the heart of financial globalization.

Because banking-sector opening is more heavily contested than other dimensions of financial globalization, and because its politics involve a distinct cast of characters, it makes sense to study the phenomenon separately. Previous studies have tended to cluster banking-sector opening with other strands of financial reform, and the result has been to obscure the particular political factors that underpin the liberalization of commercial banking.[4] For example, Arvid Lukauskas and Susan Minushkin conclude that "the political economy of the various elements of financial opening differs markedly.…Explaining a country's treatment of foreign intermediaries requires consideration of a different set of factors than explaining its policy towards foreign

---

3. There are several other strands to financial globalization. A necessary precursor to financial globalization is domestic financial deregulation, which involves the removal of government controls on banking activity, particularly interest-rate controls and government-directed lending. Stock-market liberalization refers to the removal of constraints on the ability of foreigners to buy and sell securities listed in the local exchange and on the ability of foreign securities firms to establish a presence in a host country. Insurance-sector deregulation refers to the removal of barriers to the ability of foreign insurance companies to establish a presence in a host country and to sell insurance products to host-country nationals.

4. For example, Lukauskas and Minushkin adopted "financial opening" as the dependent variable in their study, a category that included policies covering the capital account, exchange rates, and regulations governing the activities of foreign banks. See Arvid Lukauskas and Susan Minushkin, "Explaining Styles of Financial Market Opening in Chile, Mexico, South Korea, and Turkey," *International Studies Quarterly* 44 (2000), 695–723. Similarly, Haggard and Maxfield tried to explain "financial internationalization," a rubric that bundled together capital account opening, stock-market liberalization, and banking-sector opening. See Stephan Haggard and Sylvia Maxfield, "The Political Economy of Financial Internationalization in the Developing World," *International Organization* 50 (Winter 1996), 35–68. Auerbach, in her study of "financial liberalization," also aggregates several strands of financial reform. See Nancy N. Auerbach, *States, Banks, and Markets: Mexico's Path to Financial Liberalization in Comparative Perspective* (Boulder, Colo.: Westview Press, 2001).

investment in bond or stock markets. Stated another way, theoretical explanations of financial opening that treat it as an aggregate event are flawed."[5]

In geographical terms, this book focuses on four countries that are part of "the emerging world": Mexico, Brazil, South Korea, and Indonesia. All four countries entered the ranks of the world's middle-income countries (and in the case of Korea, high-income countries) relatively late compared with the OECD's most advanced economies. Because most research on banking-sector opening has focused on the advanced economies of Japan, the United States, and Europe, we still know comparatively little about the politics of banking-sector opening in the emerging world.[6] This book is meant to help fill that gap.

Banks, Politicians, and "Barbarians"

Banks have long been objects of special interest to bureaucrats and politicians. They are not only repositories of national wealth but also the pipelines through which the flow of resources to the economy can be regulated for the implementation of monetary policy, the promotion of economic sectors deemed strategic, the financing of government expenditure, the reward of political supporters, and the punishment of political detractors. Control over these financial pipelines has been a priority for virtually all modern governments. As Meredith Jung-En Woo has observed, "at the *core* of state power...is its channeling of the flow of money. No wonder, then, that monetary and financial policy remain the most zealously guarded realms of any state—combined with, of course, centralized control of the military."[7]

Closely tied to this preoccupation with control over finance has been the notion that the commercial banking sector should be under national (rather than foreign) ownership, and that regulatory barriers are necessary to keep the barbarians—as the Greeks used to refer to foreign tribes—out of the realm of national banking. Traditionally, the idea that the banking system should be dominated by locally owned and controlled financial institutions was a matter of national sovereignty. Large national

5. Lukauskas and Minushkin, "Explaining Styles of Financial Market Opening," p. 720.

6. For a seminal work on the politics of banking-sector opening in the advanced economies, see Louis Pauly, *Opening Financial Markets: Banking Politics on the Pacific Rim* (Ithaca: Cornell University Press, 1988). For studies of the politics of financial liberalization in developing and transition countries, see Michael Loriaux et al., *Capital Ungoverned: Liberalizing Finance in Interventionist States* (Ithaca: Cornell University Press, 1997); Paul D. Hutchcroft, *Booty Capitalism: The Politics of Banking in the Philippines* (Ithaca: Cornell University Press, 1998); Diana Thorburn, "The Political Economy of Foreign Banks in Latin America: Mexico and Argentina, 1990–2001," Ph.D. dissertation, School for Advanced International Studies, Washington, D.C., 2004; and Joshua Hjartarson, "Foreign Bank Entry and Financial Sector Transformation in Hungary and Poland," Ph.D. dissertation, University of Toronto, 2005.

7. Meredith Woo-Cumings (Jung-En Woo), *Race to the Swift: State and Finance in Korean Industrialization* (New York: Columbia University Press, 1991), 2.

banks were seen as a badge of self-reliance, modernity, and prestige, not unlike a national airline or oil company, especially in postcolonial countries, where banks had been expropriated from imperial powers along with oil wells, mines, railroads, ports, and other assets seen as vital for national development.

But banking-sector protectionism was also motivated by more than just national glory and prestige. In some cases, domestic private bankers flourished behind protective walls and became a powerful constituency dedicated to keeping foreign competitors out. In other cases, governments adopted state-led development models—import-substitution industrialization in Latin America, *dirigisme* in postwar France, export-led industrialization in East Asia—that called for a significant degree of government control over financial flows and bank lending.[8] Where banks were owned by private financiers rather than by the state, governments preferred to keep the banking sector in the hands of their own nationals in the belief that native financiers—who were embedded in the country's business, social, cultural, and political networks—would be much easier to coax or coerce into cooperating with the government's development plans than foreign bankers, who were both geographically and socially remote and could enlist the support of their own governments if they chose to resist prodding from the host country authorities.

Whatever the underlying motivation, the idea that the commercial banking sector should be controlled by nationals spread quickly around the world after the Great Depression. With the crash of 1929 and the subsequent rise of economic nationalism and protectionism, most countries—developed and developing alike—began to close down what since the late nineteenth century had been a liberal banking regime. Many governments simply stopped issuing licenses to foreign banks or imposed discriminatory regulations. Foreigners were barred from acquiring shares in domestic commercial banks or confronted with limits on how much equity they could hold in local institutions. Gradually, foreign capital was marginalized or pushed entirely out of local banking sectors in dozens of countries. For example, in 1920, 46 of 57 countries covered by one study (81 percent) allowed foreign banks to open branches. By 1980, that number had fallen to 21, down or 37 percent of the original sample. Of the countries that had allowed foreign bank entry in 1920, 24 had closed their banking sectors by 1980, but no country with a closed banking regime in 1920 had opened it sixty years later.[9]

But toward the end of the century, banking-sector protectionism began to wane. First, advanced economies began experimenting with the partial relaxation of

---

8. For a classic treatment of the relationship between the state and banking in "late developers," see Alexander Gerschenkron, *Economic Backwardness in Historical Perspective* (Cambridge, Mass.: Harvard University Press, 1962).

9. Adrian Tschoegl, "Ideology and Changes in Regulations: The Case of Foreign Bank Branches over the Period 1920–1980," in *Political Risks in International Business,* ed. Thomas L. Brewer (New York: Praeger, 1985).

barriers in the 1970s, spurred by what Louis Pauly has called "loose reciprocity." Instead of exchanging access to each other's banking markets on the basis of protracted, concession-by-concession negotiations, the advanced economies opened their markets to each other on the expectation that favorable treatment would be fairly repaid at some undetermined point in the future.[10] The result was gradual, loosely coordinated movement toward more open banking regimes in the major industrialized countries, but it stopped short of total opening. Many advanced economies retained a plethora of formal and informal barriers to protect their banking systems from foreign competition and hostile mergers and acquisitions, barriers that for the most part remain in place.[11]

Then, during the 1990s, developing and transition economies embarked on much more radical experiments in banking-sector opening, unilaterally dismantling the regulatory structures that had protected their commercial banks for decades, often with no realistic expectations of reciprocity. Foreign capital rushed into these countries, usually through the acquisition of domestic banks by foreign investors. The value of financial-sector foreign direct investment (FDI) into developing countries ballooned in the course of a decade and a half—from US$2.5 billion in 1991–1995, to US$51.5 billion in 1996–2000, to US$67.5 billion in 2001–2005.[12] By the end of 2006, almost nine hundred foreign banks had a presence in developing countries, controlling combined assets of some $1.2 trillion and accounting for more than 39 percent of total banking assets in these countries.[13]

Levels of foreign participation varied considerably across regions and countries (see Figures 1.1 and 1.2). Banking sectors in the larger transition economies of Central and Eastern Europe—with the notable exception of Russia—attained some of the highest levels of foreign ownership in the world as German, Austrian, and Italian financial FDI poured in. In Latin America and the Caribbean, the presence of foreign banks grew more moderately, but by 2005, some 35 percent of banking-sector assets were foreign-owned. In developing Asia, the internationalization of banking systems proceeded more slowly, partly because these economies opened later and because some—including China, India, and Malaysia—retain highly restrictive regimes. However, the dominant trend across the developing world is clear: there has been a

---

10. Pauly, *Opening Financial Markets*, pp. 5–6.

11. For example, even though European Union members have very open banking regimes on paper, they also retain a large variety of informal means to prevent the acquisition of local banks by foreign entities. For examples, see "Survey of International Banking," *Economist*, May 19, 2005.

12. Financial-sector FDI is measured here as the value of cross-border mergers and acquisitions in which developing-country banks were the target. Dietrich Domanski, "Foreign Banks in Emerging Market Economies: Changing Players, Changing Issues," *BIS Quarterly Review* (December 2005), p. 70, and World Bank, *Global Development Finance: Financing the Poorest Countries* (Washington, D.C.: World Bank, 2002), p. 65.

13. World Bank, *Global Development Finance: The Role of International Banking* (Washington, D.C.: World Bank, 2008), p. 86.

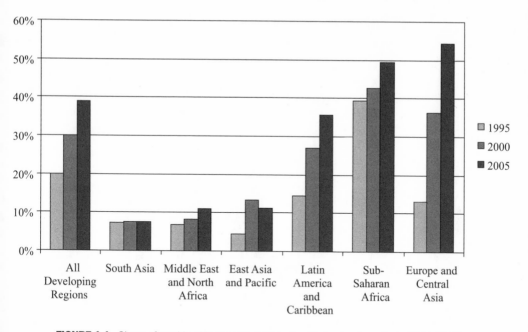

FIGURE 1.1. Share of total banking assets held by foreign banks, by region, 1995–2005.

Note: Foreign banks are those in which foreign shareholders hold 50 percent or more of total capital.
Source: World Bank staff estimates based on data from Bankscope.

dramatic increase in foreign participation in domestic banking, marking a historic break with the preceding half-century.

Explaining Banking-Sector Opening

How can we explain the rapid decline of banking-sector protectionism in emerging-market countries? Drawing on the vast literature on the politics of regulatory reform, I identify four potential drivers of banking-sector opening: external pressure, domestic power shifts, ideational change, and changing political survival priorities. These four drivers generate four hypotheses about the causes of banking-sector opening, and they provide the analytical framework of this book. Next I explain the logic behind each hypothesis and outline the kinds of evidence needed to test it empirically.

External Pressure

One possibility is that banking-sector opening is the product of political pressure by external actors. According to this hypothesis, developed-country governments,

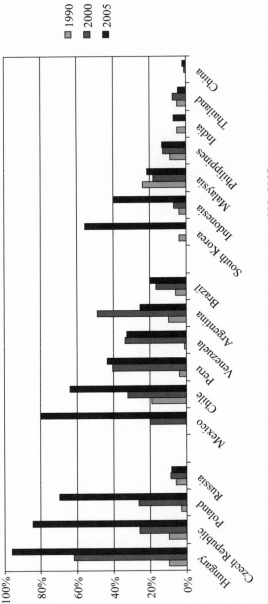

FIGURE 1.2. Percentage of total banking system assets held by foreign banks, 1990–2005.

Source: Based on data from Hawkins and Mihaljek, "The Banking Industry in the Emerging Market Economies: Competition, Consolidation, and Systemic Stability: An Overview," p. 25 and Bank Regulation and Supervision Database, World Bank.

major global banks, and international financial institutions apply a mix of structural power and political pressure to cajole or coerce governments into dismantling protectionist barriers.[14] Foreign investors and multinational corporations use their ability to "shop around" for the most permissive regulatory environment and the threat to migrate to other jurisdictions in order to influence domestic regulations, forcing regulatory convergence in a so-called race to the bottom.[15] Similarly, international financial institutions use the power they derive from lending to governments to withhold resources from them to bring about policy change.[16] These institutions can mobilize not only their own resources but also those of bilateral donors and the private sector through the "catalytic role" of their lending, bringing to bear considerable leverage on recipient states when negotiating policy conditionality.[17]

What kinds of empirical clues should we look for to determine whether external pressure is responsible for a particular case of banking-sector opening? We would expect to find (1) evidence of domestic resistance to the kind of opening advocated by the external actor presumed to be exerting the pressure. We should also be able to identify (2) forums, negotiations, or communications in which external actors pressed for opening by, for example, promising rewards for liberalization or threatening punishment for continued closure. Finally, we should observe (3) the timing of the banking-sector opening to be proximate but subsequent to the purported application of external pressure.

Domestic Power Shifts

A second potential explanation turns on shifts in the relative power of domestic groups. In these accounts, reform is what occurs when "liberalizers" in the domestic

---

14. Structural power refers to the influence a firm enjoys by virtue of its position in the economic structure of a country or locality. This position allows the firm to exercise influence by threatening to withhold investment, move to a different jurisdiction, or otherwise reallocate the resources it controls.

15. See, for example, Henry Laurence, *Money Rules: The New Politics of Finance in Britain and Japan* (Cambridge: Cambridge University Press, 2001); David M. Andrews, "Capital Mobility and State Autonomy: Toward a Structural Theory of International Monetary Relations," *International Studies Quarterly,* 38 (1994), 193–218; Paulette Kurzer, *Business and Banking: Political Change and Economic Integration in Western Europe* (Ithaca: Cornell University Press, 1993); and Thomas Oatley, "How Constraining Is Capital Mobility?" *American Journal of Political Science* 43 (October 1999), 1003–1027.

16. See, for example, Miles Kahler, "Orthodoxy and Its Alternatives: Explaining Approaches to Stabilization and Adjustment," in *The Politics of Economic Adjustment: International Conflicts and the State,* ed. Stephan Haggard and Robert Kaufman (Princeton, N.J.: Princeton University Press, 1992), pp. 33–61; Ngaire Woods, *The Globalizers: The IMF, the World Bank, and Their Borrowers* (Ithaca: Cornell University Press, 2006); and Barbara Stallings, ed., *Global Change, Regional Response: A New International Context of Development* (New York: Cambridge University Press, 1995).

17. The empirical evidence on the magnitude of the catalytic role is mixed. The literature suggests that its effect is stronger in low-income countries and that IMF lending is more likely to attract official bilateral aid flows than private capital flows. See Dani Rodrik, "Why Is There Multilateral Lending?" NBER Working Paper No. 5160, 1995, and Graham Bird and Dane Rowlands, "Do IMF Programmes Have a Catalytic Effect on Other International Capital Flows?" *Oxford Development Studies* 30:3 (2002), 229–249.

political sphere are empowered relative to protectionist interests. The story here is one of rent-seeking domestic interests—bankers, in our case—who lobby their governments for protection and are able to "buy protection" in exchange for financial or political support.[18] Government officials are assumed to have no preferences other than to stay in office. Their behavior is driven by the need to maximize political contributions and support, and they react to interest-group pressure accordingly. Over time, the bankers' lobbying capacity erodes because of some exogenous shock, because of changes in the structure of the industry, or because the sector becomes sclerotic and inefficient, leading to falling profits. Domestic bankers at that point can no longer afford the payments needed to buy protection, and without a domestic bargain between bankers and politicians to underpin it, protectionism crumbles. This type of argument has been used to explain banking-sector opening in handful of developing countries.[19]

For this explanation to be persuasive, we should observe several things. First, we should uncover evidence that (1) incumbents in the banking industry favor continued protection and actively lobby for it, and (2) groups favoring liberalization are present in the political system. We should also be able to show that (3) the groups favoring opening were initially frustrated by protectionist interests in early attempts at liberalization and (4) a gradual decline or a shock weakened protectionist interests by eroding their sources of structural and lobbying power. Finally, we should uncover evidence that (5) the advocates of opening took advantage of their position of relative strength to implement more liberal banking policies.

Ideational Change

A third hypothesis explains banking-sector opening as the product of a shift in policymakers' ideas, particularly in their causal beliefs.[20] Opening occurs when bankers or politicians change their beliefs about the merits of banking-sector protectionism and conclude that the potential benefits of opening outweigh the costs and risks.[21] This can happen when decision makers learn from foreign models,[22] interact with

---

18. For a classic version of this argument in a more general form, see Gene M. Grossman and Elhanan Helpman, "Protection for Sale," *American Economic Review* 84:4 (September 1994), 830–850.

19. See Gabriella Montinola and Ramón Moreno, "The Political Economy of Foreign Bank Entry and Its Impact: Theory and a Case Study," Federal Reserve Bank of San Francisco, Working Paper No. PB01–11, October 2001. See also Thorburn, "Political Economy of Foreign Banks."

20. The term "causal beliefs" comes from Judith Goldstein and Robert Keohane, who define causal beliefs as "beliefs about cause-effect relationships that derive authority from the shared consensus of recognized elites." See Goldstein and Keohane, eds., *Ideas and Foreign Policy: Beliefs, Institutions, and Political Change* (Ithaca: Cornell University Press, 1993), p. 10.

21. For a version of this argument applied to banking-sector opening, see Hutchcroft, *Booty Capitalism,* and the Australian and U.S. cases in Pauly, *Opening Financial Markets.*

22. Kurt G. Weyland, ed., *Learning from Foreign Models in Latin American Policy Reform* (Baltimore: Johns Hopkins University Press, 2004), and Weyland, "Theories of Policy Diffusion: Lessons from Latin American Pension Reform," *World Politics* 57 (January 2005), 262–295.

communities of experts (epistemic communities),[23] or make policy mistakes that force them to revise their understanding of liberalization and its potential consequences.[24] A more common mechanism involves changes in the leadership of a political party or government that bring to power policymakers or technocrats espousing different ideas than their predecessors.[25]

Two kinds of evidence are crucial if this hypothesis is to be credible.[26] We should observe (1) the opening of the banking sector to be proximate but subsequent to a change in leadership that brought to power decision makers with more liberal causal beliefs about banking-sector regulation than their predecessors. Ideally, we should be able to document the new leadership's beliefs *before* their coming to power. Alternatively, we should perceive (2) the opening to be proximate but subsequent to evidence of change in policymakers' causal beliefs that is consistent with banking-sector opening. This change should be closely associated in time with events that could plausibly trigger such learning, including a major shock, recognized policy errors, or a regional shift to a similar model of liberal banking.

Changing Political Survival Priorities

Like the second hypothesis, this one relies on the assumption that government decision makers—both elected and appointed—have a strong preference for staying in office, for political survival. However, policy change in this case is explained by a shift in policymakers' preferences, not their relative power. In this story, a change in the economic or political environment persuades policymakers that favoring liberalization is the best way to overcome some immediate challenge to their political survival. Policymakers do *not* change their causal beliefs about the merits of banking-sector opening; the reordering of their preferences takes place in spite, not because of, their causal beliefs. This hypothesis is different from the "domestic power shift" explanation because it is not about the collapse of a

---

23. Peter M. Haas, "Introduction: Epistemic Communities and International Policy Coordination," *International Organization* 46 (Winter 1992), 1–35.

24. See Anne Krueger, "Trade Policy and Economic Development: How We Learn," *American Economic Review* 87:1 (1997), 1–22; Thomas Biersteker, "The 'Triumph' of Liberal Economic Ideas in the Developing World," in Stallings, *Global Change, Regional Response,* pp. 174–196; and Kathryn Sikkink, "Development Ideas in Latin America," in *International Development and the Social Sciences,* ed. Frederick Cooper and Randall Packard (Berkeley: University of California Press, 1997), pp. 228–256.

25. On the role of "neoliberal technocrats" in policy reform, see John Williamson, ed., *The Political Economy of Reform* (Washington, D.C.: Institute for International Economics, 1994); Jorge I. Domínguez, ed., *Technopols: Freeing Politics and Markets in Latin America in the 1990s* (University Park, Pa.: Pennsylvania State University Press, 1997); and Valpy FitzGerald and Rosemary Thorp, eds., *Economic Doctrines in Latin America: Origins, Embedding, and Evolution* (London: Palgrave Macmillan, 2005).

26. On the methodological challenges of showing the causal impact of ideas, see Peter Hall, ed., *The Political Power of Economic Ideas: Keynesianism across Nations* (Princeton, N.J.: Princeton University Press, 1989), chap. 14.

bargain between politicians and incumbent firms; it is about politicians acting out of fear of swift retribution by the electorate if they do not embrace liberalization in the short run as a quick-fix solution to financial ills.

To show that this dynamic is at work, we would expect to see evidence that (1) the government or the ruling party was perceived by itself and others to be in a position of high political vulnerability in the period immediately preceding the opening; that (2) policymakers identified specific threats to their political survival and came to believe that those threats could be mitigated if they embraced banking-sector liberalization; and that (3) the timing of opening was proximate and subsequent to this realization. At the same time, we should find evidence that policymakers' causal beliefs did not shift.

Research Strategy

This book does not seek to develop a general theory of banking-sector opening. The more general application of its insights is considered in the last chapter, but the book's aim is more modest: it is to understand the process through which the commercial banking sector was liberalized in four countries that are important in their own right because of their weight in the global economy. Because case-study methods are the best instruments we have to study processes, the book relies on four detailed case studies to explore the origins and dynamics of banking-sector opening.[27] It draws on archival research, including newly declassified materials, and on extensive interviews with key decision makers to test systematically each of the four hypotheses described above through a method known as process tracing. Process tracing involves splitting up the policymaking process into small steps, or microdecisions, and looking for observable evidence at each step.[28] Every effort was made to relate this microhistory to the macroeconomic and macropolitical events in each country.

As part of the process-tracing exercise, I conducted seventy interviews with key decision makers in Mexico, Brazil, Indonesia, South Korea, and the United States (a complete list of interview subjects is found in Appendix 1). Interviewees include five former finance ministers, five former central bank governors, one deputy central bank governor, one deputy finance minister, four heads of foreign banks, top banking regulators, legislators, International Monetary Fund (IMF) and World Bank staff and executive directors, and trade negotiators. The interviews were used

---

27. On the strengths and limitations of case study methods, see John S. Odell, "Case Study Methods in International Political Economy," *International Studies Perspectives* 2 (2001), 161–176.

28. Andrew Bennett and Alexander L. George, "Case Studies and Process Tracing in History and Political Science: Similar Strokes for Different Foci," in *Bridges and Boundaries: Historians, Political Scientists, and the Study of International Relations,* ed. Colin Elman and Miriam Fendius Elman (Cambridge, Mass.: MIT Press, 2001), p. 144.

to complement, rather than replace, the documentary record. However, in places where essential documents do not exist or remain classified, more weight was placed on the interviews.

Why Mexico, Brazil, Indonesia, and South Korea?

To understand the timing and dynamics of banking-sector opening, I chose as cases countries that engaged in banking-sector opening but also share certain economic and political characteristics. These similarities create a semicontrolled environment that allows us to screen out numerous factors that could also affect the dynamics of banking-sector opening. Mexico, Brazil, South Korea, and Indonesia are particularly well suited for this study because they are similar in four respects.

First, these countries have historically shared a common position in the global political and economic hierarchy. Described in the 1970s as "late developers" or members of the "semiperiphery" and in the 1990s as "emerging markets," they are part of a relatively small group of countries whose diversified economies and high incomes have set them apart from the much larger group of poor countries still dependent on commodity exports and agriculture. At the same time, these countries are not part of the club of "early developers" or "core" economies: their GDPs have historically been too low, they have been debtor rather than creditor nations, they have been net recipients of foreign aid and investment, and they have been followers rather than leaders in technology and product innovation. Politically, they have had fewer policy instruments and less freedom to set rules and shape outcomes in the global economy than the states with the most advanced economies.

To be sure, the four countries have diverged in the past two decades. South Korea, in particular, experienced superior rates of economic growth, so that by the mid-1990s, it crossed the World Bank's definitional threshold to become a "high-income country" in per capita terms. In absolute terms, Brazil, Mexico, and South Korea have economies of roughly equal size, as shown in Table 1.1. Indonesia remains the smallest of the four economies, and its per capita GDP puts it toward the bottom of the "middle income" category. However, its large population (the fourth largest in the world), strategic location, and considerable natural resources have secured its status as a key emerging market. In terms of trade, Mexico, South Korea, and Indonesia are relatively open economies, with exports accounting for over 30 percent of their GDPs. Brazil, by contrast, has always been a more closed economy.

Second, Mexico, Brazil, South Korea, and Indonesia have gone through similar political evolutions. All four have traditions of strong central governments and presidencies. In Brazil, South Korea, and Indonesia, military dictatorships took the reins of power in the 1960s and kept them in their grip for decades. In Mexico, political power became concentrated, from the late 1920s onward, in the hands of a single political party and a very powerful civilian president. Subsequently, all four countries underwent a transition to democracy, Brazil and South Korea first, in the

Table 1.1 Selected indicators, 1996 and 2006

	YEAR	BRAZIL	SOUTH KOREA	MEXICO	INDONESIA
Population (millions)	1996	163.8	45.5	92.6	195.5
	2006	189.3	48.4	104.2	223.0
GDP (current	1996	774.9	557.6	332.9	227.4
US$, billions)	2006	1,067.5	888.0	839.2	364.8
GDP per capita	1996	3,377	9,707	5,064	878
(constant 2000 US$)	2006	4,044	13,865	6,387	983
Exports of goods and	1996	7.1	27.9	32.1	25.8
services (% of GDP)	2006	14.7	43.2	31.9	30.9

Source: World Development Indicators, World Bank.

second half of the 1980s, and Mexico and Indonesia in the second half of the 1990s. In all four, legislatures and civil society groups emerged as active players in domestic politics during and after the transition.

Policymakers in all four countries also held similar notions about the role of the state in the economy. After the Second World War, the four countries adopted state-led development models, but in contrast to the command economies of the Communist bloc, they also allowed for extensive private-sector participation in the economy. While the precise mix of public and private ownership varied in each country, their financial systems were all dominated by banks rather than securities markets, and their governments all engaged in similar kinds of "financial repression," imposing controls on interest rates, directing lending to specific sectors, and adopting highly protectionist banking regimes. Also, in all four countries, foreign- (usually U.S.) trained technocrats with liberal ideas came to occupy senior positions in economic policymaking during the 1980s and 1990s.

Finally, Mexico, Brazil, South Korea, and Indonesia were similarly perceived by global financial institutions, private-sector banks and investors, and developed-country governments in terms of their economic significance and their business potential. This similarity is important because the amount of external pressure brought to bear on a country to persuade it to liberalize can vary enormously, depending on how urgently foreign investors want to enter a market. In the 1990s, Mexico, Brazil, South Korea, and Indonesia were all explicitly identified by the U.S. government and private sector as ranking among the ten most important markets in the developing world for U.S. business interests.[29] Leading European financial-services

29. In the mid-1990s, after an extensive review of 130 economies, the Clinton administration included Mexico, South Korea, Brazil, and Indonesia on its list of ten "Big Emerging Markets"—the developing countries expected to offer the greatest business potential to U.S. private-sector firms in the subsequent two decades. The other "Big Ten" emerging markets were Argentina, South Africa, Poland,

companies also included the four countries on their list of twenty "key markets," so designated because of their special significance to the European financial community in the context of the General Agreement on Trade in Services (GATS) financial-services negotiations.[30] In parallel, the four countries were designated "systemically significant" by the world's leading governments and were among the ten emerging economies invited by the G8 to establish the Group of Twenty Finance Ministers and Central Bank Governors (G20), an exclusive forum for discussion "among countries whose size or strategic importance gives them a particularly crucial role in the global economy."[31] Since November 2008, the group has started to meet at the head-of-state level and aspires to replace the G7/G8 as the informal steering committee of the global economy.

The Argument

This book argues that in Mexico, Brazil, South Korea, and Indonesia, banking crises were critical triggers for de jure and de facto banking-sector opening, and that these shocks were a necessary, if not always sufficient, condition for opening. In all the cases, it was a banking crisis that forced policymakers to reappraise their banking access policy and created opportunities for domestic and transnational groups favoring opening to push very liberal policies through the political system. The origins of the banking crises varied from case to case; in Brazil, the causes of the shock were internal, while in the other three cases, the shocks were at least partly sparked by external events. Yet they all had a similar effect in triggering opening. In three of the four cases, the banking crisis was accompanied by a capital account crisis, a large and sudden reversal of net private capital flows. The capital account crises served as catalysts of opening, magnifying the leverage external actors could bring to bear in their attempts to open the banking sector.

The importance of the banking shock as a "critical juncture" in banking-sector policy emerges clearly from all the cases. A critical juncture is "a period of significant change, which typically occurs in distinct ways in different countries and which is hypothesized to produce distinct legacies." Critical junctures trigger patterns of

---

Turkey, India, and China. See U.S. Department of Commerce, "The Big Emerging Markets," *Business America* 115:3 (1994), 4–6.

30. The key markets were selected based on the following criteria: WTO membership, financial-services markets of significant size, and significant barriers to trade in financial services still in place. The other key markets were Argentina, Chile, Colombia, Czech Republic, Egypt, Hungary, India, Malaysia, Pakistan, Philippines, Poland, Singapore, South Africa, Thailand, Turkey, and Venezuela. "Barriers to Financial Services Trade in Key Markets (First Revise)," document prepared by British Invisibles, a U.K. lobby group, for the Financial Leaders Working Group, June 9, 1997.

31. Press release of G7 finance ministers' meeting, "Finance Minister Paul Martin Chosen as Inaugural Chairperson of New Group of Twenty," September 25, 1999. The other six countries were Saudi Arabia, South Africa, Argentina, India, China, and Turkey.

historically discontinuous change, and they "dislodge" existing structural or institutional patterns.[32]

In all four countries, political forces advocating banking-sector opening had been at work prior to the banking crises. Since at least the late 1980s, the U.S. government had been actively pressuring the governments in question to open their banking markets. World Bank and IMF advisers had counseled them to deregulate their financial systems and to reduce barriers to foreign entry. The OECD extracted from Mexico and South Korea pledges to dismantle capital controls that interfered with banking services as a condition for accession. At the same time, liberal technocrats sitting atop the finance ministries and central banks of Mexico, Brazil, South Korea, and Indonesia were busy liberalizing much of the economy, removing tariffs on goods, controls on portfolio investment, and restrictions on foreign investment in the nonfinancial sector.

But these liberalizing forces failed to secure meaningful opening of the four countries' banking sectors. By 1994, Mexico, Brazil, South Korea, and Indonesia retained strict limits on whether and how many representative offices, branches, and subsidiaries foreign banks could establish, as well as when and where they could open them.[33] The amount of banking-sector assets that could be owned by foreigners was tightly capped. In Mexico—even after the North American Free Trade Agreement (NAFTA) had opened almost all sectors of the economy to U.S. and Canadian competition—foreigners could hold no more than a tiny fraction of the banking system's total assets and were forbidden from acquiring or merging with large Mexican banks. The Brazilian authorities declared an outright freeze on all foreign entry into the banking sector at 1988 levels, which were very modest. Indonesia, which was rapidly becoming an exporting powerhouse and FDI magnet, capped the permissible number of foreign-bank branches and barred foreigners from purchasing controlling stakes in large Indonesian banks. And South Korea, which in 1994 was at the doorstep of the OECD and of high-income-country status, prohibited all foreign entry through subsidiaries, retained tight limits on foreign-bank branching, and capped the amount of shares that individual investors could own in a domestic bank at 4 percent, keeping acquisitions of domestic banks off limits to foreigners.

---

32. See Ruth Berins Collier and David Collier, *Shaping the Political Arena: Critical Junctures, the Labor Movement, and Regime Dynamics in Latin America* (Princeton, N.J.: Princeton University Press, 1991), p. 29.

33. Representative offices handle foreign-market-related financial transactions on behalf of a client, but they do not engage in retail banking and may sometimes be restricted to non-income-generating activities. A branch office is an integral part of the parent bank; it can lend and borrow on the basis of the parent's full capital base and credit rating. Foreign branches cannot fail unless the parent bank also fails. Branch offices typically participate in wholesale and money markets, arrange loans for local and foreign clients, and deal in the capital markets. A bank subsidiary is separately incorporated from the parent bank and is independently capitalized. Therefore, it can fail even if the parent bank remains solvent.

The banking regimes changed markedly with the banking crises. With the crises, managed opening—gradual, controlled, and limited opening—was replaced by improvised opening—unplanned, rapid, and extensive liberalization. In all cases, de novo foreign entry was allowed through both branches and subsidiaries, and foreigners were allowed to acquire controlling shares in domestic commercial banks. The sequence of banking-sector opening was similar in the four countries: it flowed from managed opening, to banking crisis and critical juncture, to a period of improvised opening (see Table 1.2).

Crises as Triggers of Reform

That crises can trigger reform is not a novel idea.[34] Scholars of political economy have advanced the "crisis-causes-reform" hypothesis before, postulating that policy change must be *perceived* and *decided on* as a result of the crisis, not merely that the implementation of reform happened to coincide with the crisis.[35] Skeptics have countered that crisis-based explanations are both tautological and nonfalsifiable. Tautological, argues Dani Rodrik, because "reform naturally becomes an issue only when policies are perceived not to be working. A crisis is just an extreme case of policy failure. That reform should follow crisis, then, is no more surprising than smoke following fire."[36] And nonfalsifiable because crises that do not trigger policy reform can always be characterized as "not severe enough" or even defined as non-crises, while events that produce reform are automatically identified as crises.

However, the hypothesis can be salvaged from these objections, for two reasons—one empirical and one theoretical. The empirical point is that although smoke always follows fire, reform does not always follow crisis. In a study of economic policy reforms undertaken by seventeen governments in thirteen countries suffering from balance-of-payments crises in the 1980s, Joan Nelson and her colleagues concluded that the nature, causes, and severity of the crises had "little clear relation to the timing of policy response" in many of their cases.[37] Instead, they found that other factors, such as electoral cycles, policymakers' perceptions, and domestic political support of the chief executive, were much better predictors of whether a country undertook extensive structural reform.

---

34. Multicountry studies of crisis and policy reform include Joan Nelson, ed., *Economic Crisis and Policy Choice: The Politics of Adjustment in the Third World* (Princeton, N.J.: Princeton University Press, 1990); Peter A. Gourevitch, *Politics in Hard Times: Comparative Responses to International Economic Crises,* (Ithaca: Cornell University Press, 1986); and Williamson, *Political Economy of Reform.*

35. Allan Drazen and William Easterly, "Do Crises Induce Reform? Simple Empirical Tests of Conventional Wisdom," *Economics and Politics* 13 (July 2001), 130–131.

36. Dani Rodrik, "Understanding Economic Policy Reform," *Journal of Economic Literature* 34 (1996), 27.

37. Nelson, *Economic Crisis and Policy Choice,* p. 326.

Table 1.2 Sequence of banking-sector opening in the case countries

	Managed opening	Banking shock	Critical juncture	Improvised opening
MEXICO	• Banking regime closed in practice since the 1940s; de jure closure in 1965 • Managed opening through NAFTA, 1991-92	1994–96	Executive and legislature consider key reforms in 1995 and 1998; adopt total de jure opening through legislation	Major bank acquisitions by foreigners authorized in 2000–2001
BRAZIL	• 1988 constitutional ban froze foreign participation in the banking sector • Managed opening implemented to assist state-bank privatization	1995–96	Executive announces strategy to overrule constitutional ban on foreign participation; signals key shift in enforcement of regulation	Major bank acquisitions by foreigners authorized in 1997, 1998, and 2000
INDONESIA	• System closed de facto since 1970 • Managed opening in 1988 and 1992 to help reduce the public sector's role in banking	1997–98	Executive and legislature consider key reform in 1998; adopt total de jure opening through legislation	Major bank acquisitions by foreigners authorized in 2002-4
SOUTH KOREA	• Foreign banks invited into Korea in 1967, but with stringent restrictions • Managed opening in 1996 as part of OECD accession	1997–98	Executive and legislature consider reform measures in December 1997; total de jure opening adopted through legislation	Major bank acquisitions by foreigners authorized in 1999–2004

The second point is theoretical. Allan Drazen and William Easterly write that the *magnitude* of the deterioration in the status quo necessary to trigger reform is what makes the hypothesis meaningful: "if we interpret the crisis hypothesis as arguing that reform follows (or is much more likely to follow) only *extremely* bad economic situations, but not 'medium' bad situations, then the hypothesis becomes both non-trivial and falsifiable."[38] In our case, all four countries suffered from banking-sector distress in previous years, yet these "medium" bad situations did not lead to banking-sector opening. The distinction between banking distress (a "medium" bad situation) and a banking crisis (an extremely bad situation) is critical to understanding the dynamics of reform.

To avoid falling into the circularity trap ("crisis causes reform and a crisis is that which causes reform"), we need a clear, a priori definition of crisis. Distinguishing between banking distress and banking crisis is not a straightforward matter, but today there is broad agreement on the elements that must be present for a situation to be termed a banking crisis. Tomás J. T. Baliño and V. Sundararajan define a banking crisis as "a situation in which a significant group of financial institutions have liabilities exceeding the market value of their assets, leading to runs and other portfolio shifts, collapse of some financial firms, and government intervention."[39] In contrast, an episode of mere banking distress is defined as one in which particular banks lose reserves but not the system as a whole.[40] A banking crisis, then, involves banking-system decapitalization that is *systemic* in nature, either engulfing a large number of financial institutions in the system or affecting a small number of large, systemically significant institutions. In this book, I adopt a widely accepted definition of banking crisis: an episode in which the ratio of nonperforming assets to total assets exceeds 10 percent, the cost of the rescue operation is at least 2 percent of GDP, the problems of the banking sector result in the nationalization of major banking institutions, and bank runs take place or emergency measures such as bank holidays, deposit freezes, or generalized deposit guarantees are enacted by regulators.[41] As Table 1.3 shows, the four cases all experienced shocks that fall well within this definition. Three of the four crises were "twin" crises—simultaneous banking and capital account crises.[42]

---

38. Emphasis in original. Drazen and Easterly, "Do Crises Induce Reform?" p. 131.

39. V. Sundararajan and Tomás J. T. Baliño, eds., *Banking Crises: Cases and Issues* (Washington, D.C.: IMF, 1991), p. 3.

40. George J. Benston and George G. Kaufman, "Is the Banking and Payments System Fragile?" *Journal of Financial Services Research* 9 (December 1995), 209–240.

41. Asli Demirgüç-Kunt and Enrica Detragiache, "The Determinants of Banking Crises in Developing and Developed Countries," *IMF Staff Papers* 45 (March 1998), 91.

42. A capital account crisis is defined as a sudden reversal of net private capital flows. A more precise definition is a decline in the ratio of net private capital flows to GDP of at least 3 percent from the previous year and of at least 2 percent from two years before. Marcos Chamon, Paolo Manasse, and Alessandro Prati, "Can We Predict the Next Capital Account Crisis?" paper presented at the 7th Jacques Polak Annual Research Conference, International Monetary Fund, November 9–10, 2006.

Table 1.3   Banking crises in the four case countries

COUNTRY	DATE OF BANKING CRISIS	NPLS (AS % OF TOTAL LOANS)	FISCAL AND QUASI-FISCAL COST AS % OF GDP	LARGE-SCALE NATIONALIZATION OF BANKS?	RUNS OR EMERGENCY MEASURES?
Mexico	1995–95	11	20	4 of the top 10 banks taken over by the government	Runs, blanket deposit guarantee extended
Brazil	1994–96	15	5–10	3 of the top 10 private banks taken over by the government, as well as the 2 largest state banks	Runs
Indonesia	1997–98	65–75	50–55	9 of the top 10 private banks taken over by the government or closed down	Runs, blanket deposit guarantee extended
South Korea	1997–98	30–40	34	2 of the top 10 banks taken over by the government	Blanket deposit guarantee extended

Source: Glen Hoggarth, Ricardo Reis, and Victoria Saporta, "Costs of Banking System Instability: Some Empirical Evidence," *Journal of Banking and Finance* 26 (2002), 830, and author's calculations.

Pathways to De Jure Opening

Crises can trigger reform through at least four channels, which mirror the hypotheses presented earlier in this chapter. A crisis can magnify the leverage of external actors by heightening a country's dependence on external financial resources. This dependence allows foreign actors to push for opening more effectively than they could before the shock. A crisis can also induce opening by changing the balance of power among domestic groups, strengthening liberalizers at the expense of protectionist interests. Third, a crisis can bring about ideational change by forcing policymakers to revise their beliefs about how the world works. Finally, a crisis can change political survival priorities, forcing policymakers to adopt reform because they perceive this to be their best option for holding on to power.

This book shows that the combination of channels through which banking and capital account crises led to de jure banking-sector opening varied in each case. In Mexico, the banking crisis helped change the beliefs of legislators about the merits of opening (ideational change). In Brazil, a banking shock persuaded the Cardoso administration to open the system in order to protect the government's economic plan and to safeguard the president's prospects for reelection (changing political survival priorities). Political survival was also critical in Indonesia, where an embattled president saw opening as the only way to prevent economic collapse and secure his political future. Finally, in both Korea and Indonesia, twin crises magnified the power of external actors, bringing about an opening of the banking system (external pressure). In all four cases, a banking shock was a necessary driver of de jure opening, but in the Korean case, it was not sufficient; there the capital account crisis also played a key crucial by giving the IMF the leverage to push reform through despite considerable domestic opposition.

The Politics of Implementation

Crisis triggered de jure opening, but once the immediate effects of the shock subsided, domestic politics reasserted themselves. The aftermath of the crisis was a system-defining period in all four countries, as large segments of the domestic banking system were suddenly up for sale to the highest bidder and the system's structures of ownership and control became open to radical restructuring. Thus, government bureaucrats, politicians, domestic bankers, and local industrialists mobilized alongside foreign capital to shape the process of de facto opening to their advantage. In three of the four cases—Mexico being the exception—the result of this struggle was to slow down or limit the degree of foreign entry, and in two of them, to drive a wedge between foreign *ownership* and foreign *control* of domestic banks.

While all four countries embraced similar policies during the phase of de jure opening, the politics of implementation ensured that in the postcrisis, structures of bank ownership and control in each country diverged significantly. In Mexico, the banking sector essentially became an extension of the global networks of major international banks, fully owned and controlled by foreign institutions. In Brazil, ownership and control remained largely in the hands of the government and private domestic banks, with a few major banks fully owned and controlled by foreign banks. Ownership and control in most major Indonesian banks became fragmented, as foreigners were forced to share with domestic investors and sometimes with the government the equity ownership and management control of each institution. Finally, the equity in most large Korean banks came to be owned by foreigners, but restrictions on individual equity holdings ensured that ownership and control were divided: while the banks were mostly foreign-owned, the management remained Korean.

Plan of the Book

This book proceeds as follows. Chapter 2 sets the stage by describing and analyzing the behavior and motivations of external advocates of banking-sector opening. In particular, it examines how international financial institutions, major international banks, and foreign governments pursued relentlessly, but ultimately with modest success, the opening of commercial banking in the emerging world. Chapters 3, 4, 5, and 6 contain case studies on Mexico, Brazil, Indonesia, and South Korea, respectively. Each chapter provides a brief overview of the historical context in each country and analyzes the anatomy of de jure and de facto banking-sector opening before, during, and after the banking crises. Finally, chapter 7 draws conclusions from the case studies, discusses the postcrisis divergence of banking structures in each country, and explores how the findings of this book may be generalized to other cases.

2

THE FRUSTRATED QUEST
TO GLOBALIZE BANKING

During the late 1980s and 1990s, a diverse group of actors began to work toward a common goal: the elimination of barriers to foreign participation in the banking sectors of large emerging economies. The group included the Bretton Woods institutions (the World Bank and the International Monetary Fund), some of the largest American and European financial institutions, their home governments, and their countries' trade negotiators. Their motivations were different; the Bretton Woods institutions peddled liberalization in the name of sound financial policy and economic growth, foreign banks did so with an eye to raising profits through overseas expansion, and their home governments and negotiators did so to secure the best terms possible for their national financial-services firms. Their preferred channels for promoting liberalization were also different; the Bretton Woods institutions employed policy advice, loan conditionality, and influential research; foreign banks turned to lobbying their own governments; and the home governments used multilateral trade negotiations and sometimes direct government-to-government lobbying. These actors did not act in concert, but they were keenly aware of each other's agendas and together shaped an international environment in which developing countries faced significant pressure to adopt more liberal banking regimes.

Yet for all their political power, financial resources, and determination, these global players were able to secure surprisingly little banking-sector opening in major emerging markets before the mid-1990s. Their efforts were frustrated by several factors: bad timing, strong resistance from developing-country governments, and ineffective attempts to influence the intellectual environment. Pressures from these global actors would not generate deep opening until they converged with banking crises in the second half of the 1990s. This chapter explains why.

The Search for New Markets

In the early 1980s, the leading advanced-economy banks—large financial-services firms based in the United States, Europe, and Japan—began to experience strong and growing competitive pressures in their home markets. This was not a temporary trend but part of a deep transformation of the international banking industry, brought about by regulatory and technological change, the growing disintermediation of finance, and the emergence of nonbank rivals.[1] Bank profits stagnated or fell. German and British banks saw their return-on-assets ratios remain roughly flat, while French banks experienced a pronounced decline in profitability (Figure 2.1). In Japan, return-on-assets ratios briefly turned negative in the mid-1990s and then sank deep into the red after 1996. Only U.S. banks experienced robust growth in profitability in the early 1990s, but after 1993, profits stagnated for the rest of the decade.

To reverse the trend of declining or stagnating profitability, the advanced economies' leading banks resorted to a variety of strategies: consolidation, the generation of fee income, and cross-border expansion. In practice, only a handful of institutions chose to expand across borders. These tended to be large and relatively efficient institutions, both in absolute terms and relative to their developing-country rivals.[2] To be sure, the global banks that chose cross-border expansion had different motivations and strategies for doing so, but what most of them had in common is that they were not looking to penetrate new markets for the traditional reason—to follow abroad multinational corporations from their own countries and help them finance their operations in a foreign market. Instead, the banks sought to enter foreign *retail*—rather than only wholesale—banking markets, aiming to compete directly with domestic banks, attract deposits, and serve the masses, rather than simply cater to a handful of multinationals and the local rich. With the decline of Japanese banks, U.S., British, and Spanish financial institutions emerged as the most active institutions in cross-border expansion in the 1990s. The key players included the U.S.-based Citigroup and Bank of America, the British banks HSBC and Standard Chartered, the Dutch bank ABN Amro, and the Spanish duo of Banco Santander and Banco Bilbao-Vizcaya (BBVA).[3]

---

1. The term "disintermediation" refers to the erosion of the role of banks as middlemen between depositors and borrowers. This happens when new financial products and markets allow borrowers and lenders to transact directly with each other, as they can in securities markets.

2. For example, a study of 2,500 banks based in twenty-nine OECD countries found that the size and relatively superior efficiency of a bank are key determinants of its decision to expand abroad. See Dario Focarelli and Alberto Franco Pozzolo, "The Patterns of Cross-Border Bank Mergers and Shareholdings in OECD Countries," *Journal of Banking and Finance* 25 (2001), 2305–2337.

3. On the different strategies of major international banks, see Adrian E. Tschoegl, "Financial Crises and the Presence of Foreign Banks," Financial Institutions Center Working Paper 03-35, Wharton School of Business, December 5, 2003; David P. Baron and David Besanko, "Strategy, Organization, and Incentives: Global Corporate Banking at Citibank," *Industrial and Corporate Change* 10:1 (2001); Mauro

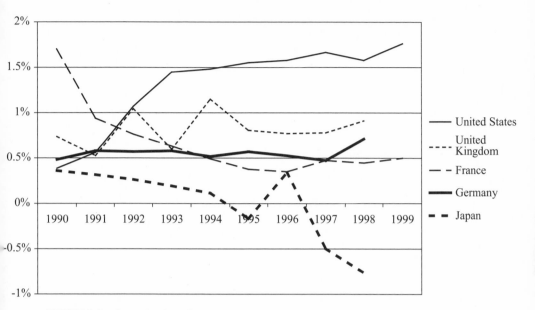

FIGURE 2.1. Pretax bank profits as a percentage of average assets, selected countries. *Source:* Based on data from G-10, "Report on Consolidation in the Financial Sector," Data Annex B.

In order to penetrate the highly protected banking sectors of emerging economies, the major international banks first needed to persuade host-country governments to adopt more liberal banking regimes. To do so, they lobbied their home governments to exert government-to-government pressure on the host-country authorities, either bilaterally or through multilateral trade-in-services talks, especially in the context of the General Agreement on Trade in Services (GATS) negotiations.

The most politically active were U.S. financial-services firms, organized under the U.S. Coalition of Service Industries (CSI). The CSI was formed in 1982, but the GATS negotiations reenergized its agenda in the 1990s. Meanwhile, European banks and insurance companies joined forces with their American counterparts by establishing the Financial Leaders Group (FLG), a transatlantic industry group created in 1996 to harmonize positions and to coordinate U.S. and European lobbying efforts in the context of the GATS talks. U.S. and British firms formed the core of the group,[4] but the European Banking Federation (EBF) and the European Insurance

---

F. Guillén and Adrian E. Tschoegl, "At Last the Internationalization of Retail Banking? The Case of the Spanish Banks in Latin America," Working Paper 99-41, Financial Institutions Center, Wharton School of Business, September 1999; and Adrian E. Tschoegl, "'The World's Local Bank': HSBC's Expansion into the US, Canada, and Mexico," *Latin American Business Review* 5:4 (2005), 45–68.

4. The FLG was chaired jointly by Andrew Buxton, chairman of the U.K.-based Barclays Bank, and Ken Whipple, president of the U.S.-based Ford Financial Services.

Committee (EIC) also joined. Combining forces with the European financial community through the FLG was an American idea, one the Europeans welcomed. From Europeans' perspective, the FLG presented an opportunity to engage American business leaders and to temper their overly optimistic expectations of the GATS negotiations.[5]

Opening through Trade Talks: The GATS

The General Agreement on Trade in Services—negotiated under the Uruguay Round of the General Agreement on Tariffs and Trade (GATT) and in force since January 1995—was the first major international agreement to set rules for the liberalization of services, including financial services. For the advanced-economy banks and their governments, these negotiations represented a historic opportunity to shake loose protectionist barriers in some of the world's most promising banking markets.

The GATS financial-services negotiations took place in two rounds. The first began with the completion of the GATS framework in December 1993 and culminated with the breakdown of the talks and the signing of an Interim Agreement on Financial Services in July 1995. The second round began in 1996 and culminated with the signing of the Financial Services Agreement in December 1997. As the world's largest market and home to some of the most competitive banks in the world, the United States became the central player and most forceful advocate of financial liberalization at the GATS financial-services negotiations.[6]

Throughout the GATS talks, U.S. negotiators consistently pursued three core objectives, formulated in close cooperation with the U.S. financial community.[7] They sought to secure for American financial-services firms the right to establish a local commercial presence in foreign markets and to acquire full-majority ownership of domestic financial institutions in those markets. In addition, the negotiators aimed to protect ("grandfather") the existing rights of U.S. firms already present in those countries and to ensure that U.S. firms would enjoy full national treatment, which meant they would be treated by host-country authorities in the same way as host-country financial institutions. In terms of tactics, U.S. negotiators wanted to retain the United States' long-standing guarantee of unconditional

5. Stephen Woolcock, *The Liberalization of Financial Services,* European Policy Forum, London, October 1997, p. 33.

6. The U.S. Treasury was in charge of the negotiations on banking and securities for the U.S. government, while the Office of the United States Trade Representative (USTR) was the lead agency on insurance.

7. "Statement by Lawrence H. Summers, Deputy Secretary of the Treasury on the WTO Agreement in Financial Services," RR-2111, U.S. Treasury, December 13, 1997.

most-favored-nation (MFN) status for all and to strive for a multilateral agreement, as long as other nations gave up the right to discriminate against U.S. firms.[8]

Geographically, Washington's strategy was centered on key Asian countries that were of greatest value to the U.S. financial-services industry. Because the negotiations operated on the basis of a cumbersome request-offer mechanism,[9] the number of countries the U.S. government was willing and able to negotiate with at any given time was limited. For example, in the second round of negotiations (1995–1997), the United States limited its negotiations to twenty-four countries, even though sixty-four participated in the negotiations.[10] This prompted U.S. negotiators to concentrate their efforts on the largest markets and the most recalcitrant governments. Chief among the U.S. Treasury's priorities was to open South Korea's financial markets, which in the words of one U.S. negotiator "offered the most attractive opportunities for U.S. firms of the countries that could be realistically expected to respond to pressure."[11] Second-tier priorities included Indonesia, Thailand, and Malaysia. Washington had already pursued intensive trade negotiations with Mexico on banking services in the context of the North American Free Trade Agreement, and U.S. officials were hopeful that Brazil's ongoing negotiations with its Mercosur neighbors would also offer opportunities for U.S. banks already with a presence in Brazil's South American neighbors to penetrate the Brazilian market.

One of the U.S. Treasury's major challenges during the negotiations was to persuade the governments of emerging economies that financial-services liberalization was not a back-door attempt to pry open their capital account, exposing their economies to hot-money flows and financial instability. As another U.S. official put it, "Treasury needed to convince these policymakers that foreign financial institutions would not be fronts for George Soros."[12] In mid-1996, the U.S. Treasury sent a letter to all major developing-country governments participating in the negotiations, assuring them that Washington was not trying to force capital account opening under the guise of free trade in financial services, and that the timing of capital account liberalization was an issue for them to decide on their own.[13] Meanwhile, at the talks, U.S. negotiators focused on securing commitments through the so-called Mode 3, a type of opening under the GATS protocol that placed relatively low

---

8. Testimony of Treasury Undersecretary for International Affairs Lawrence H. Summers before the House Committee on Banking, Finance, and Urban Affairs, U.S. House of Representatives, February 1, 1994.

9. Under the request-offer mechanism, countries request offers from each other on a bilateral basis, and then those countries receiving the requests make counteroffers, launching the negotiation. These bilateral agreements are then "multilateralized" at a later stage.

10. Interview with Whittier Warthin, director, Office of Financial Services Negotiations, U.S. Treasury, March 4, 2005, Washington, D.C.

11. Warthin interview.

12. Interview with Mary Lundsager, former deputy assistant secretary for trade and investment policy, U.S. Treasury, March 8, 2005, Washington, D.C.

13. Lundsager interview.

demands on capital account opening while allowing the entry of foreign financial institutions.

In June 1995, the initial round of talks collapsed, and a new deadline was set for December 31, 1997.[14] With the clock ticking, U.S. negotiators intensified their efforts to secure concessions. To ratchet up the pressure, the negotiators adopted a broad exemption that allowed the U.S. government to deny MFN status to any country that did not make adequate GATS commitments, but in July 1995, they backed down, guaranteeing MFN status for all if an acceptable multilateral agreement could be reached by December 1997. At the same time, Washington launched a "diplomatic offensive," deploying top United States Trade Representative (USTR) and Treasury officials to lobby governments in Singapore, Seoul, Manila, Bangkok, Kuala Lumpur, New Delhi, Tokyo, and Jakarta.

Unfortunately for U.S. trade negotiators, the last round of the talks coincided with the early stages of the Asian financial crisis, which began with a currency crisis in Thailand in May 1997. By the time U.S. officials arrived in Bangkok on August 27, the Thai government had abandoned its currency peg, watched the value of its currency plunge, and sought emergency financing from the IMF. The currencies of Malaysia, Indonesia, and the Philippines had also come under attack. Invoking the crisis, Thai officials refused to make further commitments on financial services.[15] U.S. negotiators returned to Washington empty-handed, at least in terms of banking services, though they were more successful obtaining concessions from Asian countries in the insurance and securities sectors.

The Financial Services Agreement (FSA) was signed in December 1997 by ninety-one countries. Despite triumphalist public statements, the U.S. government and private sector accepted the outcome with disappointed resignation. The only countries that agreed to bind fully liberal commitments in all modes of banking-service provision were small and marginal economies such as Kenya, Mozambique, Haiti, and Panama.[16] Most Eastern European countries, which were already open to European firms under EU directives, bound full commitments in commercial presence, allowing foreign entrants. Numerous African countries, as well as the smaller Latin

---

14. The talks collapsed in part because of opposition from U.S. insurers. U.S. insurance companies were furious with USTR when they discovered late in the negotiations that U.S. banking and securities firms, whose negotiations were being handled by Treasury, had secured more attractive commitments—often from the same countries—than they had. In response, the insurers, through the CSI, "revolted" and put considerable pressure on USTR to walk away from the final agreement. Confidential interview with former U.S. Treasury official, Washington, D.C., 2005.

15. "Thailand Not Ready to Liberalize Finance Sector," Xinhua News Agency, June 16, 1997.

16. "Bound" commitments cannot be made more restrictive without reentering into negotiations with the country's trading partners. Binding commitments can function as a locking-in device and as a signal that the government is willing to guarantee a certain level of treatment. Similarly, countries that bound below the status quo signaled that they were not prepared to guarantee the prevailing treatment, reserving for themselves the right to tighten restrictions in the future if deemed appropriate.

American economies, also fully liberalized their regimes in terms of commercial presence.

However, most emerging economies of strategic interest to U.S. and European firms bound their banking-sector commitments at or below the levels that existed before the GATS negotiations, as shown in Table 2.1. Countries that bound at or below the status quo included the important markets of Brazil, Indonesia, Thailand, South Korea, and Japan; only Mexico and Malaysia made and bound new banking-sector commitments. I explain in more detail the motivations behind the commitments of Mexico, Brazil, Indonesia, and South Korea in the in-depth case studies. As the table also shows, many of the same countries that declined to open their banking sectors also made commitments that exceeded the status quo in the less politically sensitive insurance and securities industries. With the end of the GATS negotiations in December 1997, the liberalization process on which advanced-economy banks had pinned many of their hopes ended with a whimper.

The underwhelming results of the negotiations were related to two factors: the weak structure of the GATS framework and the timing of the negotiations. Although the GATS was inspired by the GATT, its liberalization mechanisms were decidedly weaker. In contrast to the GATT, national treatment under the GATS was not an automatic right but a negotiable status, and MFN status could be made subject to reservations limited, in theory, to ten years. Also, the GATS worked on the basis of "positive lists": governments would choose the service sectors or subsectors, without a mandatory minimum, in which they intended to make commitments. This system generated much less pressure for liberalization than the GATT's "negative list" approach, in which the assumption was that *all* sectors would be liberalized, and governments would list only the exceptional sectors they intended to keep protected.[17]

There were two additional complications. Because the financial-services talks were not completed by the time the Uruguay Round came to a close, they were separated from talks on trade in goods, which effectively turned them into single-sector negotiations. Thus, negotiators could not strike cross-sectoral bargains; developing countries could not offer to open their banking sectors in exchange for market access to sectors of greater interest to them, such as European agricultural markets. This left developing countries with the unappealing prospect of exchanging access to their own banking markets—which were highly vulnerable to foreign competition—for access to American or European banking markets, where their banks could not realistically compete. Also, because free trade in financial services requires a degree of capital convertibility, the negotiations invariably became talks

---

17. The GATS did include a memorandum of agreement on financial services, which offered countries the option of adopting a "negative-list approach" to liberalization through which they could commit to broad market-opening principles and list only the sectors they would keep closed. However, only OECD countries (except Mexico, South Korea, and Poland) accepted this option by 1998.

Table 2.1 Market-access commitments under the FSA, February 1998

NATURE OF COUNTRY'S GATS COMMITMENTS	BANKING	INSURANCE	SECURITIES
Exceeded status quo	Malaysia	Brazil	Brazil
	Mexico	Indonesia	Indonesia
		Japan	South Korea
		South Korea	Malaysia
		Philippines	Philippines
		Mexico	
Status quo	Argentina	Chile	Argentina
	Brazil	India	Thailand
	Chile	Thailand	
	India		
	Indonesia		
	Japan		
	South Korea		
	Thailand		
Less than status quo	Philippines	Malaysia*	Chile
			India

Source: Wendy Dobson and Pierre Jacquet, *Financial Services Liberalization in the WTO* (Washington, D.C.: Institute for International Economics, 1998), p. 93.

*Based on a comparison of practice in February 1998 (up to 100 percent foreign ownership on a case-by-case basis) with Malaysia's commitment (up to 51 percent foreign ownership) in December 1997.

over the politically sensitive issue of capital account opening as well.[18] The second round of the GATS coincided with the onset of the Asian financial crisis, which ensured that emerging markets lost their appetite for any new commitments involving foreign capital inflows.

Opening through Conditionality: The Bretton Woods Institutions

The International Monetary Fund and the World Bank were vocal advocates for removing barriers to the flow of capital across borders, particularly in the 1990s. Their power to bring about policy change derived from their capacity to provide

---

18. Conscious of this, the architects of the GATS framework left plenty of room for flexibility on how much capital account opening the GATS would demand of its members. Articles XI and XII of the agreement, as well as a footnote to Article XVI, left the precise capital-convertibility obligations required by the agreement vague. In addition, a so-called "prudential carve-out" allowed members to impose restrictions on trade in financial services if the restrictions were meant to safeguard the integrity of the financial system or to protect consumers.

countries with financing in exchange for policy reforms and to influence the intellectual environment in which policies are debated and decided. Starting in the 1980s, the Bank and the Fund actively promoted financial-sector reform in general and banking-sector opening in particular. But while both institutions are often portrayed as having promoted the same mix of "Washington consensus" policies, in reality they took different approaches to banking-sector opening and should therefore be examined separately.

The World Bank

The World Bank's advocacy of banking-sector opening was closely tied to a larger objective—the privatization of state-owned financial institutions. Privatization was regarded as the cure for what the Bank's staff saw as the pathologies of government ownership of financial institutions: inadequate competition, inefficiency, and the allocation of credit based on political and other nonmarket considerations. For the Bank, pushing the state out of the business of banking became a priority. During the 1990s, bank restructuring and privatization came to dominate the institution's financial-sector operations. Of 280 Bank operations with financial-sector components between 1993 and 2003, almost 70 percent included reforms aimed at bank restructuring and privatization.[19] Bank privatization was pushed by staff with such zeal that an internal Bank review concluded that "there are cases where Bank lending, in pursuit of reducing the role of government as owner of banks, has been overly focused on privatization as an end in itself, and too little focused on the ultimate objective of having well-managed banks whose owners have incentives to both manage risks and realize returns."[20] In this context, any measures that facilitated the purchase of government-owned banks by private investors—including opening the banking sector to foreign investment—were to be supported.

How successful was the World Bank as an advocate of banking-sector opening? I examine this question in detail as it relates to Mexico, Brazil, Indonesia, and South Korea, but here it is worth examining the Bank's own analysis of its entire project portfolio. An internal evaluation of financial-sector projects examined the Bank's record in twenty-three countries over the 1985–1996 period. In general, the evaluation found the Bank's success rate in financial-sector reform wanting: overall performance was deemed satisfactory in 52 percent of the countries.[21] Bank programs

---

19. World Bank, *OED Review of Bank Assistance for Financial Sector Reform* (Washington, D.C.: Operations Evaluation Department, World Bank, July 22, 2005), p. 14. Three large projects accounted for over half the total commitments for financial-sector reform. These were a Banking Sector Restructuring and Privatization Project in Pakistan and two loans to finance the privatization of two state-owned banks in Brazil.

20. World Bank, *OED Review of Bank Assistance,* p. 24.

21. World Bank, Operations Evaluation Department, *Financial Sector Reform: A Review of World Bank Assistance,* Report No. 17454, vol. 1 (Washington, D.C.: World Bank, March 6, 1998), p. 14.

were found to be particularly weak at promoting competition, an area that included the reduction of barriers to foreign entry into the banking sector. Of the twenty-three countries in the sample, the majority had financial sectors with levels of competition judged by the World Bank to be unsatisfactory (see Table 2.2).[22] In nine of these countries, the Bank used its policy instruments—loan conditionality—to promote competition in the financial system, including the removal of barriers to foreign participation in the banking sector. Program design was not a problem; eight of the nine reform packages in which conditionality was used were judged by the evaluators to have been "hits"—they were well designed to improve initial conditions. However, the evaluation found that only in three cases were the reforms actually implemented by the recipient governments, and thus conditionality failed to achieve the desired policy change two-thirds of the time.

Notably, the countries that implemented the Bank's proposed reforms were Indonesia, Mexico, and Pakistan, a group that includes two of the cases in this study. However, as I show in the chapters on Mexico and Indonesia, it was domestic ideational change and IMF pressure, respectively, that induced these governments to implement the reforms, rather than the World Bank's activities. Thus, even if we adopt a charitable interpretation of the data, the World Bank's record in promoting banking-sector opening before the second half of the 1990s was modest.

The International Monetary Fund

The IMF's advocacy of banking-sector opening was rooted in two larger objectives. The first was the Fund's controversial promotion of capital account liberalization through policy advice and conditionality.[23] From 1990 to 2002, Fund staff explicitly provided advice on capital account liberalization to at least eighteen member countries, thirteen of which were under an IMF program at some point during that period.[24] Sometimes this advice touched on barriers to the entry of foreign investment into the banking system. Second, like the World Bank, the Fund saw the promotion of banking-sector opening as an instrument to increase banking-sector efficiency.[25]

---

22. The data cited in this paragraph are contained in the second volume of the study: Nicolas Mathieu, *Financial Sector Reform: A Review of World Bank Assistance* (Washington, D.C.: World Bank, 1998).

23. On the Fund's role in capital account liberalization, see Joseph P. Joyce and Ilan Noy, "The IMF and the Liberalization of Capital Flows," East-West Center Working Paper No. 84, Economics Series, August 2005; IMF, Independent Evaluation Office, "The IMF's Approach to Capital Account Liberalization," April 20, 2005; Ralf J. Leiteritz, "Explaining Organizational Outcomes: The International Monetary Fund and Capital Account Liberalization," *Journal of International Relations and Development* 8 (2005), 1–26; and Rawi Abdelal, *Capital Rules: Institutions and the International Monetary System* (Cambridge, Mass.: Harvard University Press, 2007).

24. IMF, "IMF's Approach," p. 49.

25. For a clear exposition of the Fund's thinking on the issue, see address by Michel Camdessus at the Annual Meeting of the Union of Arab Banks, New York, May 20, 1996.

Table 2.2 Outcomes of World Bank programs for promoting financial-sector competition, 1985–1996

COUNTRY	STARTING YEAR OF PROGRAM	DEGREE OF COMPETITION IN THE FINANCIAL SECTOR BEFORE PROGRAM	WORLD BANK POLICY INSTRUMENTS USED TO PROMOTE COMPETITION?	WAS POLICY PACKAGE WELL DESIGNED?	WERE PRESCRIBED POLICIES IMPLEMENTED?
Egypt	1992	Unsatisfactory	No	Miss	No
Ghana	1988	Unsatisfactory	No	Miss	No
Bolivia	1987	Unsatisfactory	No	Miss	No
Chile	1986	Satisfactory	No	Hit	No
Senegal	1987	Unsatisfactory	No	Miss	No
Tanzania	1992	Unsatisfactory	No	Miss	No
Tunisia	1988	Unsatisfactory	No	Miss	No
Turkey	1986	Unsatisfactory	No	Miss	No
Venezuela	1990	Unsatisfactory	No	Miss	No
Kenya	1989	Unsatisfactory	No	Miss	No
South Korea	1985	Satisfactory	No	Hit	No
China	1993	Unsatisfactory	No	Miss	No
Malaysia	1987	Satisfactory	No	Hit	No
Cote d'Ivoire	1992	Unsatisfactory	No	Miss	No
Bangladesh	**1990**	**Unsatisfactory**	**Yes**	**Hit**	**No**
India	**1995**	**Unsatisfactory**	**Yes**	**Hit**	**No**
Indonesia	**1988**	**Unsatisfactory**	**Yes**	**Hit**	**Yes**
Malawi	**1991**	**Unsatisfactory**	**Yes**	**Hit**	**No**
Mexico	**1989**	**Unsatisfactory**	**Yes**	**Hit**	**Yes**
Morocco	**1986**	**Unsatisfactory**	**Yes**	**Hit**	**No**
Pakistan	**1989**	**Unsatisfactory**	**Yes**	**Hit**	**Yes**
Philippines	**1989**	**Satisfactory**	**Yes**	**Overkill**	**No**
Poland	**1991**	**Unsatisfactory**	**Yes**	**Hit**	**No**

Source: Based on data from Nicolas Mathieu, *Financial Sector Reform: A Review of World Bank Assistance* (Washington, D.C.: World Bank, 1998), pp. 10 and 14-16.

Note: Boldface indicates countries in which the Bank used loan conditionality to promote financial competition; shading indicates the countries in which prescribed policies were implemented.

Compared with the Bank, the IMF was less active in promoting banking-sector opening through conditionality before 1997. By the mid-1990s, the World Bank had been thinking seriously about banking-sector reform for at least six years; the Fund would not devote significant intellectual resources to this area until after the 1997–1998 Asian financial crisis. But this does not mean that the Fund was entirely inactive. IMF activity in this area began in the transition economies of Eastern Europe in the early 1990s, especially in Hungary and Poland.[26] In its 1991 Letter of Intent

---

26. See Hjartarson, "Foreign Bank Entry and Financial Sector Transformation."

with the Fund, for example, the Hungarian government committed to encouraging foreign participation in the banking sector.[27] Fund Executive Directors argued that foreign-bank entry would "spur the modernization of domestic banking practices" in Eastern Europe.[28] The Fund provided similar advice in other regions. A 1995 technical assistance report for China recommended that Beijing eliminate restrictions on the ability of foreign banks to operate in the domestic market in order to enhance the efficiency of the foreign-exchange market.[29] That year, Costa Rica also agreed to facilitate the establishment of foreign-bank outlets as part of its commitments with the Fund.[30]

The Fund's overall record is not easy to assess, as no systematic evaluation of this issue is available and there are few cases to analyze. Costa Rica, Hungary, and Poland all embraced liberal banking regimes in law and in practice, but two of those countries were also under considerable pressure to comply with the financial-services-liberalization requirements of European Union directives, so it is difficult to determine whether the Fund's role in these cases was decisive. Meanwhile, the Fund's advice to China went unheeded.

The Tide Shifts: The Late 1990s and Beyond

In terms of advancing the cause of liberal banking regimes, the fortunes of the Bretton Woods institutions took a marked turn for the better in the late 1990s. Another internal evaluation of the Bank's financial-sector lending programs analyzed a sample of fifty-one countries—including borrowers as well as nonborrowers—over the 1998–2003 period. The study found circumstantial evidence to suggest that the Bank's record in promoting liberal banking regimes had improved. The evaluation found that, on average, countries that had borrowed from the multilateral institution reduced restrictions on the activities of foreign banks whereas nonborrowers tended to increase them.[31] Also, the evaluation found that in the twenty-five countries that did not borrow from the Bank, foreign participation in the banking system increased by two-thirds during the period studied whereas in borrowing countries, it increased by more than 100 percent.[32]

It is hard to attribute causation based on this data. First, the data is about de facto, not de jure, opening since it measures foreign participation, not the relaxation of regulatory restrictions. This is only an indirect measure of opening because the

---

27. IMF, "IMF's Approach," p. 32.

28. IMF, *IMF Annual Report 1996—World Economic Outlook*, September 27, 1996, p. 27.

29. IMF, "IMF's Approach," p. 32.

30. IMF, Press Release No. 95/59, "IMF Approves Stand-By Credit for Costa Rica," November 29, 1995.

31. World Bank, *OED Review of Bank Assistance*, p. 64.

32. Ibid. For similar results, see World Bank, Independent Evaluation Group, *IEG Review of World Bank Assistance for Financial Sector Reform* (Washington, D.C.: World Bank, 2006), p. 70.

volume of foreign entry depends on other factors aside from the banking regime. Also, no effort was made to control for other factors that could affect banking-sector opening. In addition, there is probably a selection-bias problem, given that countries that seek loans from the Bank are more likely than nonborrowers to share the Bank's diagnoses and approaches to economic problems, and therefore more likely than nonborrowers to engage in banking-sector opening in the first place. Finally, the evaluation's headline results were largely driven by nine transition economies in the borrowing-country group, several of which were outliers because they experienced extraordinary levels of foreign-bank entry in the 1990s. Opening in many of these Eastern Europe outliers had at least as much to do with European Union accession as it did with World Bank borrowing. But even if we put aside these problems with the data, what is striking here is the dramatic rise in foreign participation in *all* the countries examined—borrowers and nonborrowers alike—which suggests that there were powerful liberalizing forces at work in addition to World Bank lending programs.

For the IMF, the change was more straightforward. A series of crises in emerging economies, starting with the Mexican crisis in 1994–1995, provided the Fund with new opportunities to lend and to promote banking-sector opening. Mexico's 1995 agreement with the IMF included commitments to open the banking sector, as did South Korea's 1998 Letter of Intent with the Fund.[33] Similar measures were included in the Letters of Intent of Thailand and Indonesia, both signed in 1997.[34] Small economies under IMF programs made similar commitments. Georgia and Bolivia committed to scaling back barriers to the entry and operation of foreign financial institutions, and Ethiopia and the Ukraine committed to banking-sector opening as well.[35] References to banking-sector opening—both in the Fund's policy advice and in the policy commitments of the Fund's client countries—peaked in 1997–1998.

Of course, simply because governments included in Fund documents some provisions liberalizing their banking regimes is not proof that they would not have adopted such policies without an IMF program, or that they did so under Fund coercion, or indeed that they actually implemented the reforms. Such an assessment requires a finer-grained analysis, which I provide in subsequent chapters. Nevertheless, it is clear that the conditions under which the IMF could exert pressure on governments to liberalize their banking regimes proliferated after the late 1990s.

---

33. "Mexico: Letter of Intent and Memorandum of Economic Policies," January 26, 1995, and "Korea: Letter of Intent," February 7, 1998, Annex A.

34. "Thailand: Letter of Intent and Memorandum of Economic Policies," August 14, 1997, and "Indonesia: Letter of Intent and Memorandum on Economic and Financial Policies," October 31, 1997.

35. See "Georgia: Enhanced Structural Adjustment Facility Policy Framework Paper, 1998–2000," July 10, 1998; "Bolivia: Enhanced Structural Adjustment Facility Policy Framework Paper, 1998–2001," August 25, 1998; "Ethiopia Letter of Intent: Memorandum on Economic and Financial Policies," December 31, 2001; and "Ukraine Letter of Intent: Memorandum on Economic and Financial Policies," August 11, 1998.

Opening through Ideas: The Fund and Bank as an Intellectual Force

What role did the Bretton Woods institutions play as intellectual actors? To what degree were they able to disseminate ideas supportive of banking-sector opening, to change policymakers' causal beliefs, and to use, as Ngaire Woods calls it, the power to persuade?[36] Two things are striking about the international financial institutions' attempts to shape the intellectual environment. First is how late their research on the subject began to appear relative to the wave of banking-sector opening sweeping across many countries. Second, and somewhat ironically, once the Bretton Woods institutions began to think deeply about banking-sector opening and to produce research on its implications, the results of those studies undermined the institutions' confidence in the policy, forcing them to retreat from assertive proselytizing.

The Knowledge Gap

Before the year 2000, there was little a policymaker sitting in Mexico City, Brasilia, Jakarta, or Seoul could read to help him or her to get traction on important policy questions related to banking-sector opening, such as: How will the allocation of credit change if foreign banks are allowed to enter the market? Will the entry of foreign capital and institutions make the domestic banking sector more competitive and more efficient, without destabilizing the financial system in the process? How will foreign-controlled banks behave during financial crises? Will they be agents of financial stability or transmission belts for financial shocks?

When the advanced economies began to experiment with banking-sector opening in the 1970s and 1980s, a trickle of academic research on foreign-bank entry began to appear. Initial writings focused on the factors driving banks to expand beyond their home countries,[37] and others examined the theoretical efficiency-enhancing qualities of foreign-bank entry.[38] Later work began exploring the impact of foreign-bank entry on the financial systems of specific countries, but most of this work was descriptive (and often based on poor data) rather than analytical.[39]

In the 1990s, the theoretical debate grew more heated. In a 1993 paper, Joseph Stiglitz expressed strong skepticism of the purported benefits of banking-sector

---

36. Woods, *Globalizers*.

37. See, for example, Lawrence G. Goldberg and Anthony Saunders, "The Determinants of Foreign Banking Activity in the United States," *Journal of Banking and Finance* 5 (March 1981), 17–32.

38. See Ingo Walter and H. Peter Gray, "Protectionism and International Banking: Sectoral Efficiency, Competitive Structure, and National Policy," *Journal of Banking and Finance* 7 (December 1983), 611–614.

39. See, for example, Joydeep Bhattacharya, "The Role of Foreign Banks in Developing Countries: A Survey of the Evidence," Cornell University (mimeo.), 1994, and H. Cheng, ed., *Financial Policy and Reform in Pacific-Basin Countries* (Lexington, Mass.: Lexington Books, 1986).

opening, arguing that foreign-bank entry would undermine the control developing-country authorities needed to exercise over the financial system.[40] In response, Ross Levine, an economist at the World Bank, argued forcefully for the theoretical benefits of the banking-sector opening, including better and more financial services, stronger regulation, and better access to international capital.[41] In 1997, Joe Peek and Eric Rosengren published one of the very first empirical articles on the sensitive question of foreign banks and financial stability.[42] But beyond these writings, there was little else to substantiate strong support or outright rejection of banking-sector opening in developing countries. It was at this time that many governments began to open their banking sectors to foreign capital.

The knowledge gap that existed when these critical decisions were made had two important consequences. In the absence of strong empirical research, advocates of banking-sector opening—particularly the Bretton Woods institutions and the U.S. Treasury—based their spirited defense of the idea on an analogy with the liberalization of trade in goods, an area where the empirical record was more robust.[43] Reducing barriers to trade in goods increased competition, forced inefficient producers out of the market, and induced significant increases in productivity. Dismantling barriers to trade in banking services was assumed to have the same consequences.

Second, the knowledge vacuum meant that developing-country policymakers were forced to rely on a variety of other sources of knowledge when making decisions. They drew, to different degrees, on ideology, on advice from other governments, on anecdotal evidence, on analogies of their own, and in the end, on gut instinct. As we will see, especially in the case of Mexico, the knowledge gap led to the proliferation of divergent viewpoints not only between governments but also within them; disagreement emerged even among technocrats with similar backgrounds and world views.

Mobilizing Knowledge in Support of Opening

As important middle-income countries began to open their banking sectors to foreign capital in the late 1990s, academics, government agencies, and the Bretton Woods institutions rushed to produce research that would allow them to understand and promote further liberalization in the developing world.[44] Much of the initial wave of

---

40. Joseph Stiglitz, "The Role of the State in Financial Markets," in *Proceedings of the World Bank Annual Conference on Development Economics* (Washington, D.C.: World Bank, 1993).

41. Ross Levine, "Foreign Banks, Financial Development, and Economic Growth," in *International Financial Markets,* ed. E. B. Claude (Washington, D.C.: AEI Press, 1996).

42. Joe Peek and Eric S. Rosengren, "The International Transmission of Financial Shocks: The Case of Japan," *American Economic Review* 87 (September 1997), 495–505.

43. See Camdessus, address.

44. For surveys of this literature, see John Hawkins and Dubravko Mihaljek, "The Banking Industry in the Emerging Market Economies: Competition, Consolidation, and Systemic Stability; An Overview,"

research at this stage appears to have been aimed at giving reformers in developing countries the intellectual ammunition to push for financial opening at home. In the short space of time between 1998 and 2001, a wide array of studies appeared using a variety of methodologies to study the relationship between foreign-bank entry and financial stability,[45] the lending behavior of foreign banks,[46] and the impact of foreign-bank entry on banking-sector efficiency and competition.[47]

Overall, this emerging body of literature painted a very positive picture of the impact of banking-sector opening. Foreign-bank entry appeared to generate increasing competition and efficiency in most domestic banking systems. However, the evidence was still fragmentary, based on single cases or on large-n studies using data from the early to mid-1990s, before most foreign entry took place.[48] But despite its shortcomings, advocates of banking-sector opening used the newly published research to marshal support for the policy. The World Bank was aggressive in its interpretation of the research. In its 2001 report, *Finance for Growth: Policy Choices in a Volatile World,* the Bank articulated a detailed position on banking-sector opening for the first time. The Bank's reading of the empirical literature was staunchly optimistic: "There are clearly some potential drawbacks to excessive reliance on just a few foreign financial institutions, especially if they come from just one country....Nevertheless, despite the growing presence of foreign-owned financial intermediaries, it is difficult to find any hard evidence for the proposition that admitting foreign firms has adverse

---

BIS Paper No. 4, August 2001, and George Clarke et al., "Foreign Bank Entry: Experience, Implications for Developing Economies, and Agenda for Further Research," *World Bank Research Observer* 18 (Spring 2003), 25–59.

45. Major studies on this question include Jennifer S. Crystal, B. Gerard Dages, and Linda S. Goldberg, "Does Foreign Ownership Contribute to Sounder Banks in Emerging Markets? The Latin American Experience," Federal Reserve Bank of New York, May 29, 2001; Joe Peek and Eric S. Rosengren, "Collateral Damage: Effects of the Japanese Bank Crisis on Real Activity in the United States," *American Economic Review* 90 (March 2000), 30–45; and Asli Demirgüç-Kunt, Ross Levine, and Hong G. Min, "Opening to Foreign Banks: Issues of Stability, Efficiency, and Growth," in *Proceedings of the Bank of Korea Conference on the Implications of Globalization of World Financial Markets,* December 1998.

46. See, for example, George Clarke, Robert Cull, and María Soledad Martínez Peria, "Does Foreign Bank Penetration Reduce Access to Credit in Developing Countries? Evidence from Asking Borrowers," World Bank Policy Research Working Paper 2716, November 2001; Allen N. Berger, Leora F. Klapper, and Gregory F. Udell, "The Ability of Banks to Lend to Informationally Opaque Small Businesses," *Journal of Banking and Finance* 25 (2001), 2127–2167; and Adolfo Barajas et al., "The Impact of Liberalization and Foreign Investment in Colombia's Financial Sector," *Journal of Development Economics* 63 (2000), 157–196.

47. Important work in this area includes George Clarke et al., "The Effect of Foreign Entry on Argentina's Domestic Banking Sector," World Bank Policy Research Working Paper 2158, August 1999, and Stjin Claessens, Asli Demirgüç-Kunt, and Harry Huizinga, "How Does Foreign Entry Affect the Domestic Banking Market?" *Journal of Banking and Finance* 25 (2001), 891–911.

48. For example, the most ambitious and most cited study of this period, by Claessens et al. (2001), used data for eighty countries covering the period 1988–1995. For a critique of these this and other studies, see Pierre-Richard Agenor, "Benefits and Costs of Financial Integration: Theory and Facts," Policy Research Working Paper 2699, World Bank, October 2001.

consequences for the economy as a whole."[49] The Bank concluded that "an open-door policy to the admission of qualified and reputable foreign financial firms seems overwhelmingly to be the best policy, and one that could have a strongly favorable impact on growth."[50]

The IMF was more conservative. After the Asian financial crisis in 1997–1998 dealt a severe blow to its reputation, the Fund grew more cautious with anything that smelled of imprudent advocacy of capital account liberalization. In contrast to its advice before the crisis, after 1998 Fund staff began to highlight the potential adverse effects of foreign bank entry on the stability of host countries' financial systems. In 2000, an IMF survey of the literature was careful to point out the remaining knowledge gaps: "The evidence to date on the effects of foreign bank entry suggests that the competitive pressures created by such entry lead to improvements in banking system efficiency, but it is still unclear whether a greater foreign bank presence contributes to a more stable banking system and a less volatile supply of credit."[51]

Meanwhile, the U.S. Treasury's discourse on banking-sector opening incorporated the familiar arguments about the expected benefits and stressed the positive contributions that foreign banks can make to domestic banking systems. The potential risks of foreign bank entry were never voiced explicitly, although the benefits of strong regulation and supervision of banks were usually highlighted in the same speeches. Surprisingly, the Treasury's unqualifiedly optimistic discourse on banking-sector opening remained unchanged even after the Asian financial crisis.[52] Treasury's message was usually sprinkled with references to World Bank studies on the positive effects of foreign-bank entry.[53]

Toward a More Nuanced View

Beginning in 2002, two factors led to a significant change in the intellectual environment and the tone of the discourse. First was the Argentine currency and banking crisis of 2001–2002. Argentina had a long tradition of liberal banking, one of the most open banking regimes in the developing world, and one of the highest levels

49. World Bank, *Finance for Growth: Policy Choices in a Volatile World* (New York: Oxford University Press for the World Bank, 2001), p. 165.

50. Ibid., p. 169.

51. IMF, *International Capital Markets: Developments, Prospects, and Key Policy Issues* (Washington, D.C.: International Monetary Fund, September 2000), p. 152.

52. See, for example, "Repairing and Rebuilding Emerging Market Financial Systems," remarks by Lawrence H. Summers to the Federal Deposit Insurance Corporation's International Conference on Deposit Insurance, Washington, D.C., September 9, 1998; "Riding the Storm: Latin America and the Global Financial Market," remarks by Lawrence H. Summers to the Council of the Americas, Washington, D.C., May 3, 1999; and Testimony of John B. Taylor before the House Small Business Committee, U.S. House of Representatives, October 24, 2001.

53. See "Russian Integration in the Global Financial System," remarks by Randal K. Quarles to the US-Russia Banking Conference, Washington, D.C., April 15, 2005.

of banking-sector foreign participation in Latin America. For advocates of banking-sector opening, Argentina was a role model they hoped would be emulated by other emerging economies.[54]

Yet during the country's crushing financial crisis, some of the most important anticipated benefits of a large foreign-bank presence failed to materialize.[55] Foreign-bank portfolios proved to be just as vulnerable to shocks as those of local banks, and several major foreign banks, including Crédit Agricole and Scotiabank, abandoned their Argentine branches and subsidiaries in the midst of the crisis. Others were persuaded to stay, but only under considerable pressure from the Argentine authorities. Advocates of liberal banking were quick to point out that foreign banks had left only in extreme crisis conditions and in the midst of strong antiforeign sentiment. However, the damage was done, and the episode was noted with concern by policy-makers in other middle-income countries. This was the first time that foreign banks' crisis behavior had been tested since the wave of foreign-bank capital that started in the mid-1990s.

The second factor was the appearance of a new generation of research on the impact of foreign investment in the banking sectors of developing countries. These studies, published between 2002 and 2006, used more sophisticated methodologies and drew on better, newer, and more relevant data. They produced a more nuanced picture of the effects of foreign bank entry, one that made facile conclusions for or against liberal banking regimes hard to sustain.

The claim that foreign-bank entry increases competition and efficiency largely survived the new wave of scrutiny,[56] but the degree to which these developments translate into lower costs for borrowers was found to depend on a host of initial conditions, such as banking-sector concentration.[57] Not surprisingly, researchers found that foreign banks react to macroeconomic shocks in complex ways, and that their willingness to inject liquidity or retrench during a crisis depends on the nature of the shock and on the business orientation of the foreign bank.[58] Particularly sobering

---

54. Indeed, its "role-model" status in banking-sector-access policy was one of the main reasons the U.S. Treasury was keen to include Argentina in the G20 (Group of Twenty Finance Ministers and Central Bank Governors), which was created in 1999. Confidential interview with former U.S. Treasury official.

55. See Marco del Negro and Stephen J. Kay, "Global Banks, Local Crises: Bad News from Argentina," *Federal Reserve Bank of Atlanta Economic Review* (Third Quarter 2002), 1–18.

56. One of the best and most sophisticated studies found that in developing countries, foreign banks' share of the banking market is negatively and significantly correlated with interest-rate margins, over-head costs, and loan provisions. See Alejandro Micco, Ugo Panizza, and Mónica Yañez, "Bank Ownership and Performance," Inter-American Development Bank Working Paper 518, November 2004.

57. Robert Lensink and Niels Hermes, "The Short-Term Effects of Foreign Bank Entry on Domestic Bank Behaviour: Does Economic Development Matter?" *Journal of Banking and Finance* 28 (March 2004), 553–568, and María Soledad Martínez Peria and Ashoka Mody, "How Foreign Participation and Market Concentration Impact Bank Spreads: Evidence from Latin America," World Bank Policy Research Working Paper 3210, February 2004.

58. Arturo Galindo, Alejandro Micco, and Andrew Powell, "Loyal Lenders or Fickle Financiers: Foreign Banks in Latin America," Inter-American Development Bank Working Paper 529, December 2005,

were the results of research on the impact of foreign banks in low-income countries. There even the efficiency-enhancing effects of foreign-bank entry observed elsewhere failed to appear, and in many poor countries credit to the private sector actually contracted as foreign-bank entry grew.[59]

As a result, the World Bank moderated its rhetoric on the benefits of banking-sector opening. In 2002, the Bank retreated from its more aggressive *Finance for Growth* position. In its 2002 issue of *Global Development Finance,* Bank staff made reference to the usual expected benefits of banking-sector opening but also discussed the risks of shock transmission and warned developing countries that they should screen foreign entrants carefully before allowing them into the market.[60] By 2008, the Bank had arrived at an internal consensus: "The increased presence of foreign banks has generated substantial economic benefits to some developing countries," but "like globalization in general, the increased role of foreign banks can also expose developing countries to certain macroeconomic risks."[61]

Meanwhile, the IMF retreated from banking-sector opening in Fund conditionality and policy advice. As the U.S. alternate executive director at the IMF put it in 2005: "The Fund's focus has been on the competitiveness of the banking sector, but not on pushing for the opening of the market directly.... The issue has not been discussed by the Board, as there have been no crises lately. It [banking-sector opening] is neither viewed as a panacea nor as a problem."[62] In short, the shift in the intellectual environment had cooled any delusions that banking-sector opening would be an easy cure for the maladies plaguing developing-country banking systems.

In the early 1990s, a group of international actors coalesced around the goal of promoting liberal banking regimes in the developing world. I have argued that despite their considerable resources and ambition, these actors were largely unable to bring about significant banking-sector opening in major emerging economies until the late 1990s. Weaknesses in the structure of the GATS, poor timing of the negotiations, and considerable resistance from developing-country governments account for the modest achievements of all this advocacy. Also significant was that the Bretton Woods institutions' attempts to shape the intellectual environment

---

and Enrica Detragiache and Poonam Gupta, "Foreign Banks in Emerging Market Crises: Evidence from Malaysia," IMF Working Paper WP/04/129, July 2004.

59. See Enrica Detragiache, Poonam Gupta, and Thierry Tressel, "Finance in Lower-Income Countries: An Empirical Exploration," IMF Working Paper WP/05/167, August 2005, and Enrica Detragiache, Thierry Tressel, and Poonam Gupta, "Foreign Banks in Poor Countries: Theory and Evidence," IMF Working Paper WP/06/18, January 2006.

60. World Bank, *Global Development Finance: Financing the Poorest Countries* (Washington, D.C.: World Bank, 2002), pp. 66–69.

61. World Bank, *Global Development Finance: The Role of International Banking* (Washington, D.C.: World Bank, 2008), p. 82.

62. Interview with Mary Lundsager, alternate executive director for the United States, International Monetary Fund, Washington, D.C., March 8, 2005.

came too late, and when they came, they did more to undermine these actors' assertive pursuit of openness than to advance it.

These shortcomings had one important implication that I take up in the rest of this book. The weakness of external influence in the late 1980s and first half of the 1990s afforded developing-country governments the political space they needed to engage in managed opening—space to experiment with gradual, controlled, and limited opening. Also, in the absence of expert consensus on the merits of banking-sector opening, this intellectual vacuum was filled by ideas from a variety of other sources, including ideology and analogy. The tide began to change decisively in the second half of the 1990s, when pressure from the advocates of globalization converged with banking and capital account crises.

3

MEXICO

Liberal Ideas in a Crisis Environment

Of the four countries in this book, Mexico undertook the most radical exercise in banking-sector opening. Compared with Brazil, South Korea, and Indonesia, Mexico had the longest and most consistent tradition of banking-sector protectionism: from the end of liberal finance in the 1930s to the eve of liberal resurgence in the late 1980s, its banking sector was one of the most closed in the emerging world. Yet in the course of the decade running from 1992 to 2002, Mexico's banking regime shifted from highly protectionist to totally open, and its banking sector moved from one held entirely by private domestic bankers to one of the most highly internationalized banking systems in the world.

This chapter attempts to understand what drove Mexico's dramatic transition to liberal banking, as well as the political forces that conditioned the process. I trace the evolution of de jure and de facto opening through three administrations, from Mexico's early and reluctant steps toward liberalization in the early 1990s, to the foreign acquisition of most major financial institutions in the early 2000s. The story that emerges is one in which exogenous ideational change—in the form of a new president with liberal ideas—was the catalyst of reform, while the trigger that made the opening possible was the banking crisis that began in late 1994 and lasted until at least 1996. The crucial factor that overcame the last bastion of financial protectionism in the Mexican congress was the deteriorating state of the country's banks, which when combined with changes in the composition of the relevant congressional committees, allowed the government to persuade key legislators of the merits of liberalizing the banking regime. Interestingly, the Mexican case shows that external pressure (in this case from the U.S. government), rather than being a catalyst for opening, actually slowed it down and made the process more politically contentious.

The chapter proceeds in four parts. It begins with a brief analysis of the historical evolution of Mexico's banking structure and a discussion of the relations between the state and private bankers. The second part examines Mexico's experiment with managed opening in the context of NAFTA, a phase of negotiated but ultimately limited opening. The third part examines the capital account and banking crisis of 1994–1995 and Mexico's shift to total de jure opening. The final section is dedicated to the politics of implementation.

Mexican Banking: Concentrated, Private Oligopoly

Historically, the Mexican banking system has been characterized by two qualities that have proved remarkably resilient over time: a high degree of concentration and domination by the private sector.[1] Mexico's highly concentrated banking structure dates back to the regime of Porfirio Díaz (1876–1910), whose financial policies entrenched the dominant positions of two very large private institutions, the Banco Nacional de México (Banamex) and the Banco de Londres, México, y Sudamérica (BLMS). By the end of the Porfirian period, the two banks held just over half the system's assets.[2] In exchange for their considerable privileges, these institutions—and especially Banamex, which became a "semi-official superbank" with a monopoly on lending to the federal government—financed the state, making the creation of large public banks largely unnecessary.[3]

The Porfiriato also marked the apogee of liberal finance in Mexico and the high point of foreign participation in Mexican banking. On the eve of the Mexican Revolution in 1910, foreign capital held a commanding share of bank capital. Foreigners held controlling stakes in twenty-eight of the fifty-two financial institutions then operating in Mexico and controlled 76 percent of the system's capital.[4] The Díaz regime, particularly in the 1880s, was openly welcoming of foreign capital,

---

1. For useful histories of Mexican banking, see Robert L. Bennett, *The Financial Sector and Economic Development: The Mexican Case* (Baltimore: Johns Hopkins University Press, 1965); Eduardo Turrent Díaz, *História del Banco de México* (Mexico City: Banco de México, 1982); Russell N. White, *State, Class, and the Nationalization of the Mexican Banks* (New York: Crane Russak, 1992); and Hilda Sánchez Martínez, "El sistema monetario y financiero mexicano bajo una perspectiva histórica: El Porfiriato," in *La banca: Pasado y presente,* ed. José Manuel Quijano (Mexico City: CIDE, 1983), pp. 15–92.

2. Sánchez Martínez, "El sistema monetario," p. 89.

3. For an argument on the government's motivations for building this financial structure, see Noel Maurer, *The Power and the Money: The Mexican Financial System, 1876–1932* (Stanford, Calif.: Stanford University Press, 2002).

4. White, *State, Class,* p. 19. The French were preeminent, controlling almost half of all foreign-held bank capital (they held much of Banamex's and BLMS's capital, for example). North American and British interests trailed behind with 18 and 11 percent of foreign participation, respectively.

granting foreign banks generous regulatory treatment and allowing them to establish branches throughout the country.

After the Revolution (1910–1917) and the fall of General Díaz, the government became committed to the gradual indigenization of financial capital. Foreigners (with the exception of Citibank) were gradually squeezed out of the Mexican financial system. Regulatory norms issued in 1932 tightened central bank control over foreign banks and placed onerous guidelines on their capital and deposits; most foreign banks left soon afterward. The government would further tighten restrictions on foreign capital in 1965, barring any kind of foreign entity from participating directly or indirectly in the capital of domestic financial institutions.

Between 1950 and 1980, the Mexican economy experienced rapid growth, and its banking system grew faster than the economy as a whole. Although Mexico's banking laws required the separation of institutions providing different types of financial services, bankers cobbled together financial conglomerates, bringing separately incorporated asset-management, leasing, and insurance companies under the same roof. Concentration increased steadily; the number of banks controlling 75 percent or more of the system's resources fell precipitously from forty-two in 1950 to six in 1979.[5]

Collaborative relations between bankers and the government began to unravel as the state's ability to regulate the financial system began to erode. In the 1970s, private banks learned to bypass the government's directed-lending regulations by using interbank lending to transfer funds within the same conglomerate. Government efforts to control credit allocation were increasingly frustrated by bankers' speculative activities, regulatory evasion, and facilitation of capital flight. By 1980, the central bank had lost the ability to regulate the flow of credit in the financial system.[6] In frustration, President López Portillo nationalized Mexico's commercial banks in September 1982 and embedded the measure in a constitutional amendment so that the nationalization could not be easily reversed by future administrations.[7] The move seriously damaged government relations not only with the financial sector but also with the private sector more widely.[8]

During the "technocratic revolution" of President Carlos Salinas de Gortari (1988–1994), the structures of financial repression in Mexico were dismantled, and

5. María Elena Cardero et al., "Cambios recientes a la organización bancaria y el caso de México," in Quijano, *La banca*, p. 197.

6. Auerbach, *States, Banks, and Markets*, p. 36.

7. For an insider's account of the bank nationalization, see Carlos Tello, *La nacionalización de la banca en México* (Mexico City: Siglo Veintiuno Editores, 1984). See also R. Hernández Rodríguez, *Empresarios, banca, y estado: El conflicto durante el gobierno de José López Portillo* (Mexico City: Miguel Angel Porrúa Editores, 1988), and Gustavo A. del Angel-Mobarak et al., *Cuando el estado he hizo banquero* (Mexico City: Fondo de Cultura Económica, 2005).

8. Roderic A. Camp, *Entrepreneurs and Politics in Twentieth-Century Mexico* (New York: Oxford University Press, 1989), p. 132.

the government moved to reprivatize the banks and encourage foreign investment in the banking sector. The government created in 1990 a new type of bank shares with no voting rights, known as "C-series" shares, which could be purchased by foreign investors. Crucially, the Salinas administration pushed through the congress a constitutional amendment reversing the 1982 bank nationalization. Mexico's commercial banks were then swiftly sold back to the private sector in 1991–1992, and the owners of brokerage houses that had flourished during the stock-market boom of the 1980s came to own fifteen of the country's eighteen commercial banks.[9] After reprivatization, the system remained highly concentrated: in terms of assets, the top three banks—Banamex, Bancomer, and Serfín—accounted for just under half the system's total assets in 1994.[10]

What kind of political influence did Mexican bankers enjoy vis-à-vis the state? Because of the government's heavy dependence on private capital and the highly concentrated structure of the banking industry, the owners of Mexico's biggest banks historically enjoyed a great deal of policy influence. This influence stemmed partly from the bankers' ability to threaten to withhold capital and engage in capital flight, but also from their privileged position in the intricate web of financial-industrial links connecting banks and *grupos*—Mexico's large, diversified, family-owned conglomerates.[11] These financial relationships meant that Mexico's top bankers were uniquely positioned to act as interlocutors and mediators between the government and the nonfinancial private sector, a role that was much valued by the government.[12] For this reason, the bankers had the government's ear on more than just banking and monetary-policy issues: they had influence in virtually all areas of economic policy.

Mexico's private bankers cultivated their lobbying capabilities as well. With the encouragement of the finance ministry, the Mexican Bankers' Association (Asociación de Banqueros Mexicanos, or ABM) was established in 1928, providing the bankers with a vehicle for coordinating policy and communicating with the government.[13] The ABM interacted regularly and directly with cabinet members and top executive-branch officials. Given the legislature's weak policy role and the

9. Elvira Concheiro Bórquez, *El gran acuerdo* (Mexico City: Ediciones Era, 1996), p. 101. On the rise of the *bolseros*, see Susan Minushkin, "*Banqueros* and *Bolseros*: Structural Change and Financial Market Liberalization in Mexico," *Journal of Latin American Studies* 34 (2002), 915–944.

10. Pablo Graf, "Policy Responses to the Banking Crisis in Mexico," in "Bank Restructuring in Practice," BIS Policy Paper No. 6, Bank for International Settlements, August 1999, pp. 179–180.

11. On the financial links connecting banks and *grupos*, see Jorge Basave Kunhardt, *Los grupos de capital financiero en México (1974–1995)* (Mexico City: Instituto de Investigaciones Económicas, UNAM, y Ediciones El Caballito, 1996), and Rafael La Porta et al., "Related Lending," NBER Working Paper 8848, March 2002.

12. Camp, *Entrepreneurs and Politics*, p. 175.

13. Sylvia Maxfield, *Governing Capital: International Finance and Mexican Politics* (Ithaca: Cornell University Press, 1990), p. 42.

nonexistent degree of electoral competition before the mid-1980s, the ABM never saw the need to engage legislators seriously.

The power of the private banking community was decisively broken with the bank expropriation in 1982 and only partially reconstituted with privatization the 1990s. The banking elite that emerged in 1992 was in some ways weaker than its pre-1982 predecessor; the new bankers were a politically inexperienced group, and the old links between banks and business groups had been disrupted. In addition, the bureaucracy under President Salinas was highly insulated from private-sector influence. Key decisions, such as deregulating the financial system in 1989, reprivatizing the banks, and negotiating the opening of Mexican banking markets through the North American Free Trade Agreement were led by the powerful finance ministry (Secretaría de Hacienda y Crédito Público, or "Hacienda"), behind closed doors and with little input from outside groups. The bank regulators of the National Banking Commission (first CNB and later CNBV) were under Hacienda's direct line of authority. Compared with central banks in Indonesia, Brazil, or South Korea, the Mexican central bank (Banxico) was more independent from the finance ministry, but when Banxico and Hacienda clashed on major policy questions, Hacienda tended to prevail.[14]

Experimenting with Managed Opening (1992–1993)

Mexican policymakers began to experiment with banking-sector opening in the context of the North American Free Trade Agreement (NAFTA). The Mexicans negotiated bilaterally with the world's largest economy and most powerful government, one that was keenly interested in opening the Mexican banking market to U.S. firms. Yet Mexican negotiators managed to secure an extremely conservative and limited liberalization schedule in their own experiment in managed opening.

Policymakers' Beliefs and the NAFTA Debate

The top tier of the administration of Carlos Salinas de Gortari (1988–1994) was a cohesive group of U.S.-educated economists who shared a strong belief in the growth-generating capacity of free markets and international economic integration.[15] A politically sophisticated group, the Salinas technocrats saw economic

---

14. For a comparative analysis of central bank independence in Mexico, South Korea, and Brazil, see Sylvia Maxfield, *Gatekeepers of Growth: The International Political Economy of Central Banking in Developing Countries* (Princeton, N.J.: Princeton University Press, 1997).

15. The career paths, beliefs, and policies of Mexican technocrats have been studied extensively. See, for example, Sarah Babb, *Managing Mexico: Economists from Nationalism to Neoliberalism* (Princeton,

liberalization not only as a means of to generate wealth but also as a vehicle to rejuvenate a political system that was undergoing a crisis of legitimacy. Salinas had been elected in 1988 amid widespread and credible allegations of systematic electoral fraud. Meanwhile, Salinas's party, the PRI, had been suffering from a secular decline in its share of the vote since the 1970s but had not yet lost control of either the congress or the executive.

Sold as "social liberalism," Salinas's vision was a kind of *perestroika* with little *glasnost*—a liberal restructuring of the economy with just enough political opening to give the party that had ruled Mexico since the 1920s a new lease on life by defusing the crisis of legitimacy it faced.[16] The intuition was that opening political space would allow civil-society and pro-democracy pressures to dissipate, while integration with the global economy would help generate the economic growth necessary to satisfy the demands of Mexico's middle classes and many of its poor. The PRI's political opposition would be left with little discontent on which to build.

Following this vision, President Salinas decided in early 1990 to pursue a comprehensive free-trade agreement with the United States and Canada, one that would substantially reduce or eliminate trade barriers in most sectors of the economy, including financial services.[17] On the eve of the NAFTA negotiations, which were launched in June 1991 and concluded fourteen months later in August 1992, Mexican policymakers paused to consider how far they were prepared to go in the negotiations on banking.

The Salinas team decided to put financial services on the NAFTA negotiating table from the start, for two reasons. First, the group believed that some degree of banking-sector opening was necessary to transform Mexican banks into modern, efficient sources of growth-enhancing credit. Guillermo Ortiz, then deputy secretary of finance and later finance secretary and central bank governor, noted that "the opening of the financial system was conceived as a tool to complement the other reforms undertaken in the [financial] sector. Only by facing external competition would Mexican financial intermediaries ensure the productive sector access to financial resources at internationally competitive interest rates."[18] Second,

---

N.J.: Princeton University Press, 2001); Miguel Angel Centeno, *Democracy within Reason: Technocratic Revolution in Mexico* (University Park: Pennsylvania State University Press, 1997); José Córdoba Montoya, "Mexico," in Williamson, *Political Economy of Reform*, pp. 232–284; and Stephanie R. Golob, "'Making Possible What Is Necessary': Pedro Aspe, the Salinas Team, and the Next Mexican 'Miracle,'" in Domínguez, *Technopols*, pp. 95–143.

16. For an exposition of Salinas's notion of social liberalism, see Carlos Salinas de Gortari, *México: Un paso difícil a la modernidad* (Mexico City: Plaza & Janés, 2000), chap. 10.

17. For an account of how the Salinas administration was able to overcome traditional government resistance to a free trade agreement with the United States, see Stephanie R. Golob, "Beyond the Policy Frontier: Canada, Mexico, and the Ideological Origins of NAFTA," *World Politics* 55 (April 2003), 361–398.

18. Guillermo Ortíz Martínez, *La reforma financiera y la desincorporación bancaria* (Mexico City: Fondo de Cultura Económica, 1994), p. 170 (my translation).

the Mexicans understood that financial services—a high-value sector for U.S. and Canadian companies—could be exchanged for concessions in sectors valuable to Mexican industry and agriculture. According to Mexico's top NAFTA negotiator, banking was a valuable negotiating chip that Mexico needed to put on the table at the beginning of the talks.[19]

How far should Mexico go in terms of opening the banking sector to U.S. investment? Strong liberals in trade-in-goods liberalization and privatization, key members of the Salinas team were more conservative when it came to banking-sector opening. Hacienda carried the most weight in this debate, as it was tasked by Salinas with negotiating NAFTA's financial-services chapter. Hacienda's view was that banking-sector opening should be both gradual and limited, a view that was based on two causal beliefs. The first was that rapid opening would lead to bank failures and jeopardize the future of financial-sector reform. According to Ortiz,

> the benefits of opening the financial sector would hardly materialize if the opening was undertaken abruptly. The ambitious reforms of the Mexican financial sector launched recently needed a chance to consolidate....Because of this, it was essential to find a balance between two conflicting objectives: on one hand, to use the opening of the financial system as an instrument for its modernization, but at the same time, to avoid putting at risk the reform process as a whole. This is why the opening of the financial system was conceived as a gradual process, with the purpose of minimizing the risk of bank failures before the reforms could consolidate. Gradualism was, then, a principle to be followed in the unilateral opening first implemented in the reforms of 1989–1990, as well as in the negotiation of NAFTA's chapter on financial services.[20]

The second causal belief was that excessive foreign participation would undermine the Mexican authorities' capacity to regulate the banks through informal channels, or moral suasion, as it is often called. A member of the negotiating team put it this way:

> As for myself and the other finance negotiators in NAFTA, we did not see bank protection as a question of protecting our sovereignty. We wanted the three largest banks to be always in Mexican hands, for the purpose of management and control....I need to be able to sit down with the owner of Banamex, Mr. Hernández, who is my friend, who pays taxes, whose kids go to school here, who owns other businesses here, who is a Mexican. I need to be able to tell him that he needs to support me in any number of different situations—for example to support government initiatives and pacts, and particularly in crisis situations. When the owner of the bank is Mexican, we in the government have

---

19. Correspondence with Jaime Serra Puche, former secretary of commerce and industry and head of Mexico's NAFTA negotiating team, January 4, 2006.

20. Ortíz Martínez, *La reforma financiera*, pp. 170–171 (my translation).

more elements of control. When the owner is [then Citibank CEO] John Reed, who is not a personal friend, whose family lives in the US, who doesn't have other businesses here, I cannot negotiate with him to elicit his support the way I can with Mr. Hernández.[21]

President Salinas himself agreed with both these ideas and was always explicit about the need to balance opening and financial control: "I pointed out that we should open the banking sector to foreign investment but retain restrictions to protect certain strategic aspects: we were not going to leave the Mexican payments system in international hands."[22]

The Salinas technocrats' beliefs drew on British and Canadian thinking on the matter. According to a senior Banxico official, the Canadian's strategy—which allowed foreign-bank entry but kept the largest banks in domestic hands—became the cornerstone of the Mexican strategy.[23] The Salinas technocrats also claim to have been influenced by British policymakers, who reportedly warned them that transferring control of the largest banks to foreigners would undermine moral suasion and other methods of informal bank regulation.[24]

Washington's Frustrations

I do not recount here the details of the financial-services negotiations, which has been done elsewhere, but focus only on the outcome.[25] Despite intense lobbying by U.S. banks interested in wholesale banking in Mexico and in the bourgeoning cross-border remittance market, the NAFTA negotiations produced disappointing results for the American and Canadian financial communities. Under the final agreement, banks incorporated in the United States and Canada were allowed to engage in de novo expansion in Mexico and to purchase equity in Mexican banks, subject to a complex web of caveats and restrictions.[26] No individual foreign institution could hold more than 1.5 percent of the banking system's total net capital for a six-year transition period (1994–2000). This limitation effectively barred foreign

---

21. Confidential interview, qtd. in Kristin Johnson Ceva, "Business-Government Relations in Mexico since 1990: NAFTA, Economic Crisis, and the Reorganization of Business Interests," in *Mexico's Private Sector: Recent History, Future Challenges,* ed. Riordan Roett (Boulder, Colo.: Lynne Rienner, 1998), pp. 132 and 153–154.

22. Salinas de Gortari, *México,* p. 116 (my translation).

23. Interview with Ariel Buira, former deputy governor, Bank of Mexico, Washington, D.C., February 28, 2005.

24. Buira interview and Salinas de Gortari, *México,* pp. 441–442.

25. See Sylvia Maxfield, "Capital Mobility and Mexican Financial Liberalization," in Loriaux et al., *Capital Ungoverned,* pp. 92–119.

26. For an analysis of the implications of the final agreement on the Mexican banking sector, see Ignacio Trigueros, "The Mexican Financial System and NAFTA," in *Mexico and the North American Free Trade Agreement: Who Will Benefit?* ed. Victor Bulmer-Thomas, Nikki Craske, and Mónica Serrano (London: Macmillan, 1994), pp. 43–57.

acquisition of most domestic banks, as there were only two banks in Mexico whose capital amounted to 1.5 percent or less of the system's total when the NAFTA was ratified.[27] In addition, foreigners as a group could control no more than 8 percent of the system's net capital in 1994, with the cap rising by one percentage point every year until it stopped at 15 percent in 2000.[28]

At the end of the transition period, in December 1999, all these caps would be lifted, with three important qualifications. The Mexican government could invoke a one-time, three-year freeze on foreign participation if the foreigners' share exceeded 25 percent of the system's net capital. Also, foreign participation in individual Mexican banks would be limited to 30 percent of common stock, indefinitely. And third, foreign banks were permanently forbidden from acquiring Mexican banks if the acquisition put the purchaser's total share of the system's aggregate capital above 4 percent. This restriction ensured that the controlling stakes in Mexico's largest banks—all of which accounted for more than 4 percent of the system's aggregate capital—would remain always in the hands of Mexican nationals.[29]

How did the Mexican negotiators manage to get away with such little opening? According to a close observer of the negotiations, the key was Mexico's insistence on linking concessions in financial services with access to U.S. and Canadian markets in other sectors, particularly agriculture.[30] U.S. negotiators strongly opposed this linkage, but the Mexicans refused to back down. In the end, the U.S. financial community could not muster enough political muscle at home to push through the concessions needed to meet Mexican demands.

When it came to selling NAFTA at home, the Salinas government enjoyed a high degree of autonomy both from the legislature and from domestic bankers. The executive prevented the Chamber of Deputies (where the opposition held 45 percent of the seats) from providing any input on the agreement and limited the debate to the Senate, where the president's party held 60 of the 64 seats. Congressional ratification of the treaty has been described as a formality at best.[31] At the same time, private Mexican bankers were not directly involved in the debate because the government

---

27. Stephen Haber, "Mexico's Experiments with Bank Privatization and Liberalization, 1991–2003," *Journal of Banking and Finance* 29 (2005), 2329.

28. For details, see Annex VII of the NAFTA treaty text.

29. Mexican negotiators imposed other types of restrictions on the operations of foreign banks in addition to caps on participation. Foreign intermediaries were allowed to establish subsidiaries but not branches. This effectively raised the cost of entry to foreign banks, as subsidiaries have to be individually capitalized while branches do not. Foreigners were also forbidden from issuing subordinated debt during the transition period, and the Mexican government retained the right to implement prudential measures and to restrict trade in services to protect the balance of payments.

30. Hermann von Bertrab, *Negotiating NAFTA: A Mexican Envoy's Account,* Washington Paper 173 (Westport, Conn.: Praeger, 1997), p. 65.

31. For an account of the marginalization of the congress during the NAFTA ratification, see Adolfo Aguilar Zínser, "Authoritarianism and North American Free Trade: The Debate in Mexico," in *The Political Economy of North American Free Trade,* ed. Ricardo Grinspun and Maxwell A. Cameron (London: Macmillan, 1993), pp. 205–216.

was in the midst of reprivatizing the banks as the trade negotiations were unfolding. The bank privatizations (June 1991 to July 1992) and the NAFTA negotiations (November 1991 to August 1992) overlapped, even though the decisions for each were made independently.[32] Thus, there was no real "banker's lobby" to advocate protection at this stage.

Joining the OECD

As part of President Salinas's plan to globalize Mexico and modernize its image, the Mexican government sought to join the Organization for Economic Cooperation and Development (OECD). Salinas formally conveyed Mexico's intention to apply for membership in an address to the members of the OECD Council in July 1992. Mexico's application was noteworthy, as the organization had admitted no new members in over twenty years.

OECD accession would directly impact Mexico's banking-sector-access policies. All OECD members are required to comply with the Code of Liberalization of Capital Movements, which calls for the removal of restrictions on cross-border capital movements, including those related to financial services.[33] Compliance with the code would require loosening restrictions on foreign-bank entry into the Mexican market, on how much money they could bring in, and on whether investors from OECD countries could purchase stakes in local financial institutions. Accession was made all the more challenging for Mexico because the OECD's members had decided that new members would have to abide by the code's provisions on capital movements *as they stood at the member's time of entry,* rather than give new members a lengthy grace period to comply. The organization's older members, on the other hand, had taken years to come into compliance with the code.

Compared with the NAFTA negotiations, OECD accession process was a decidedly less constraining option in terms of banking policy. Unlike the NAFTA, the OECD code does not have the status of an international treaty; the code is a collection of voluntary rules enforced through peer pressure.[34] There are no explicit sanctions if members violate their commitments under the code, other than the impractical "nuclear option" of expelling the member from the organization. (Under the NAFTA, violation of the rules would result in arbitration and retaliatory trade measures.) In addition, OECD members can take exceptions to the code by lodging reservations. On provisions affecting politically sensitive short-term capital flows, members are allowed to reintroduce reservations, even if they have withdrawn

---

32. Thorburn, *"Political Economy of Foreign Banks,"* p. 136.

33. OECD members must also comply with the Code of Current Invisibles Operations and the OECD Declaration on International Investment and Multinational Enterprises.

34. Technically, the code is a decision of the OECD Council. It is not considered by most scholars to constitute international law. See Abdelal, *Capital Rules,* p. 89.

them in the past. If members face serious balance-of-payments difficulties or other kinds of emergencies, they can resort to a range of loopholes. Finally, a member may invoke a general derogation from the code, the so-called safety valve, though this measure has been used sparingly. Fortunately for the Mexican negotiators, the OECD's original members have historically lodged plenty of reservations to the code in matters concerning financial services. This diluted peer pressure and gave the Mexicans more arguments to demand flexibility at the negotiating table.[35]

Compared with Korea—whose own experience with OECD accession I examine later on in this book—Mexico's negotiations in Paris were short.[36] In terms of banking, Mexico conceded nothing beyond the status quo pre-NAFTA; all restrictions remained in place, and foreign investors could hold only up to 30 percent of a bank's ordinary stock through "C-series" shares.[37] The key point of contention was whether Mexico would extend NAFTA's more liberal terms to other OECD members. To appease the OECD's Committee on Capital Movements and Invisible Transactions (CMIT), Mexico agreed to do so in principle, starting in early 1998.[38] Mexico became the twenty-fifth member of the OECD in May 1994, but its entry into the club of rich countries imposed no obligations that seriously threatened its experiment with managed opening.

Crisis and Critical Juncture (1994–1998)

Nineteen ninety-four was one of the most turbulent years in modern Mexican history. The Zapatista uprising in January of that year, combined with two high-profile political assassinations, including that of the ruling party's presidential candidate, led to political and economic chaos not seen in Mexico since the 1920s.[39] With the death of the PRI candidate, President Salinas lost the traditional privilege of hand-picking his successor, and a man he never intended to become president—the

---

35. For example, as of 1996, the members of the European Union had lodged a total of fifty-two reservations relating to cross-border capital transactions and related financial services. Seven EU countries accounted for more than 80 percent of these reservations. On a per-country basis, the United States and Japan have taken on more reservations than EU countries, on average. National Institute of Economics and Research, "Capital Market Liberalization: Summary," Single Market Review Series, European Commission, August 1996, p. 5.

36. Abdelal, *Capital Rules,* p. 110.

37. On the terms of Mexico's accession, see "Declaración del Gobierno de los Estados Unidos Mexicanos sobre la aceptación de sus obligaciones como miembro de la Organización de Cooperación y Desarrollo Económicos," April 14, 1994.

38. Pierre Poret, "Mexico and the OECD Codes of Liberalisation," *OECD Observer* 189 (August/September 1994), 39–43.

39. For informative accounts of the political events of 1994, see Andres Oppenheimer, *Bordering on Chaos* (New York: Little, Brown, 1996), and Jorge G. Castañeda, *Sorpresas te da la vida: México 1994* (Mexico City: Aguilar Nuevo Siglo, 1994).

former education minister and campaign manager for the assassinated candidate—was chosen as the PRI's candidate for the presidency.[40] The PRI won the 1994 elections easily, and Ernesto Zedillo was sworn in on December 1, 1994. These events, plus the financial crisis that erupted that December, produced a critical juncture in which Mexican policymakers were forced to contemplate significant change to their country's banking regime.

Mexico's Banking Shock

The sudden loss of confidence precipitated by the political events of 1994 and herding behavior in the currency markets led to a sell-off of peso-denominated assets and to enormous downward pressure on the peso, quickly outstripping central bank reserves. The authorities devalued the peso by 15 percent on December 20 and allowed the currency to float two days later. The value of the peso continued to decline rapidly, with ruinous consequences, as a large amount of Mexican public and private debt was in short-term, dollar-linked securities known as *tesobonos*. To slow the capital outflow, the central bank raised interest rates drastically, reaching 80 percent in the first quarter of 1995. This put enormous pressure on banks' balance sheets, which were weak and vulnerable even before the devaluation. The capital account crisis soon became a banking crisis, triggering a deep economic contraction.[41]

The devaluation and interest-rate increase affected the banking sector almost immediately. Already on January 5, projections for 1995 showed that the devaluation had increased the (declared) foreign currency–denominated liabilities of Mexico's banks by 47 percent in the first few days of the year.[42] The most affected banks included two of the largest, Banamex and Serfin. Meanwhile, the Mexican government faced *tesobono* repayments of at least US$50 billion in 1995.[43]

---

40. On Zedillo's nomination process, see Jorge G. Castañeda, *Perpetuating Power* (New York: New Press, 2000), pp. 115–129.

41. For analyses of the causes of the Mexican financial crisis, see Sebastian Edwards and Moisés Naím, eds., *Mexico 1994: Anatomy of an Emerging-Market Crash* (Washington, D.C.: Carnegie Endowment for International Peace, 1997); Francisco Gil-Diaz and Agustin Carstens, "One Year of Solitude: Some Pilgrim Tales about Mexico's 1994–1995 Crisis," *American Economic Review* 86 (May 1996), 164–169; and Guillermo A. Calvo and Enrique G. Mendoza, "Petty Crime and Cruel Punishment: Lessons from the Mexican Debacle," *American Economic Review* 86 (May 1996), 170–175. For analyses of the vulnerabilities of the Mexican banking system, see José Antonio Murillo, "La banca después de la privatización: Auge, crisis y reordenamiento," in del Angel-Mobarak et al., *Cuando el estado he hizo banquero*, pp. 247–290; William C. Gruben and Robert McComb, "Liberalization, Privatization, and Crash: Mexico's Banking System in the 1990s," *Federal Reserve Bank of Dallas Economic Review* (1st quarter, 1997), 21–30.

42. Marcos Chávez, "Aumenta 47% su deuda en dólares; Pérdidas por 3 mil 176 mdnp," *El Financiero*, January 5, 1995, p. 8.

43. Nora Lustig, "Mexico in Crisis, the US to the Rescue: The Financial Assistance Packages of 1982 and 1995" (mimeo.), January 1997, p. 25.

The decision to open the banking sector to foreign participation was one of the very first concrete reforms announced by the Zedillo administration. On January 2, 1995, a little over a week after the start of the crisis, the media reported that the government had decided to open the banking sector to foreign participation,[44] and the following day, the government announced that foreigners would be allowed to own "up to 100 percent" of equity in Mexican banks.[45] Two weeks later, the president sent draft legislation to the congress to this effect.[46]

President Zedillo's proposal was a radical departure from the NAFTA formula, as it expanded the permissible ownership of voting shares in domestic banks. The nonvoting "C-series" shares, which had been created by Salinas in 1990 to encourage foreign investment, would be eliminated, and foreign investors would be allowed to purchase "B-series" shares—voting stock constituting up to 49 percent of common stock (see Table 3.1). In addition, the proposal gave individual investors—foreign or national—the right to own up to 20 percent of a bank's common stock. These two provisions were designed to encourage the purchase of minority shares by foreign investors in Mexican banks.

Crucially, however, the president's bill also contained a provision that granted Hacienda the power to authorize foreigners to purchase *any* amount and class of shares necessary to turn a Mexican bank into a fully owned subsidiary of the purchasing institution. This provision was meant to encourage "savior" foreign banks to absorb Mexican banks whole, ensuring the much faster recapitalization of troubled institutions than the purchase of minority stakes. If approved, the proposal would give Hacienda full discretion over when to authorize foreign participation and how much foreign capital would be allowed to enter the sector, without predetermined limits.

Political Survival and Causal Beliefs

How can we explain the government's decision to adopt full de jure opening so early in the crisis? Political survival was not President Zedillo's major preoccupation. The "accidental president" had never coveted his office and was less attached to its powers and to the ruling party than his predecessors. Indeed, on taking office, President Zedillo voluntarily relinquished key extraconstitutional powers that

---

44. Stephen Fidler and John Ridding, "Foreigners to Own Mexico banks," *Financial Times,* January 2, 1995, p. 3.

45. William Acworth, "Mexico Weighs Action to Urge Foreign Banks," *American Banker* 5 (January 9, 1995), 2, and Georgina Howard et al., "Prepara Hacienda una mayor apertura financiera; Autorizará México 100% de participación extranjera en intermediarios nacionales," *El Financiero,* January 4, 1995, p. 7.

46. Draft law amending the Law Regulating Financial Groups, the Law of Credit Institutions, and the Securities Market Law, January 16, 1995; presented by the Federal Executive to the Chamber of Deputies on January 17, 1995.

Table 3.1 President Zedillo's 1995 proposal

TYPE OF BANK SHARES	VOTING POWER?	COMPOSITION OF TOTAL BANK STOCK	STATUS QUO IN 1994	ZEDILLO'S PROPOSED REFORM
A series	Yes	Up to 51% of paid-in capital	Can be acquired by the government, development banks, and Mexican individuals only	Can be acquired by the government, development banks, and Mexican individuals only
B series	Yes	Up to 49% of paid-in capital	Can be acquired by those who can acquire A-series shares and by Mexican companies whose bylaws prohibit any capital ownership by foreigners	Can be acquired by those who can acquire A-series shares, by Mexican companies, and by any foreign individuals or companies (not governments)
C series	No	Up to 30% of paid-in capital	Can be acquired by those who can acquire A- and B-series shares and by any Mexican entity and any foreign (nongovernmental) individual or company	Disappear
L series	Limited*	Up to 30% of paid-in capital	Can be acquired by Mexicans and foreigners	Can be acquired by Mexicans and foreigners; banks can issue them for up to 35% of common stock

Source: Author's summary based on draft legislation.

*Holders of L-series shares could vote only on matters relating to mergers or the liquidation, breakup, or dissolution of the bank, as well as the cancellation of stock.

Mexican presidents had appropriated over time.[47] Zedillo would not be running for reelection either, as Mexican presidents may serve a single six-year term, and in any event, his position was not in jeopardy. In contrast to Salinas, President Zedillo won the 1994 elections by a substantial margin—just over 50 percent of the vote, a full 24 percentage points ahead of his closest rival—and the process was not tainted by credible allegations of fraud. Both houses of congress were controlled by his party,

47. Luis Rubio, "Coping with Political Change," in *Mexico under Zedillo,* ed. Susan Kaufman Purcell and Luis Rubio (Boulder, Colo.: Lynne Rienner, 1998), p. 14.

and the electorate was too frightened by the political and economic turmoil to want to destabilize the political system further.

More significant than imperatives of political survival were President Zedillo's causal beliefs, two in particular. First, the president believed that banking-sector opening would help recapitalize a banking system that was already bankrupt or quickly heading toward bankruptcy. This was already manifestly clear to the government and to financial analysts in December 1994, after the devaluation of the peso. Eliminating all ceilings on foreign investment would allow the banking authorities maximum flexibility to decide which banks should be recapitalized with foreign resources and sold off, if necessary. Second, in contrast to the Salinas team and consistent with his instinctive suspicion of the concentration of power in Mexico's political economy, Zedillo believed that banking-sector opening would induce salutary structural change and foster efficiency in the banking system. In a 1997 speech, the president made both motives clear: "one of the first legislative acts I supported when the crisis hit was to increase the permissible levels of foreign participation in our banks, because we knew that we would need that external capital to restore its capital base, but also to ensure that our banks would have renewed technological performance and capacity, not only to overcome the crisis, but also so they could position themselves better during the recovery."[48]

That Zedillo held these beliefs had been clear at least since he was minister of planning and budget in the early 1990s. Salinas recalls that when the cabinet debated the issue of banking-sector opening in preparation for the NAFTA negotiations, a member of the cabinet proposed ceilings on FDI in certain sectors, including banking. In his memoirs, Salinas notes:

> Zedillo affirmed, uncompromisingly, that he favored total opening, as the purchase of firms was a fact of life in all countries and that we needed more capital than Mexico could generate internally. It was an extreme position that did not get traction. I pointed out that we should open the banking sector to foreign investment but maintain restrictions to protect certain strategic aspects: we were not going to leave the Mexican payments system in international hands....Years later, as president, Zedillo would make his proposal to open completely Mexican banks to foreign capital a reality.[49]

Salinas's recollection is no doubt self-serving, but it is also consistent with the fact that President Zedillo's ideas about the banking system stood in sharp contrast with those of his predecessor's economic team. In deciding to open the banking sector completely, Zedillo overruled his own finance minister and veteran of the Salinas administration, Guillermo Ortiz. As we have already seen, Ortiz was a strong

---

48. Speech delivered at the 60th convention of the Mexican Bankers' Association, Cancún, Mexico, March 1997 (my translation).

49. Salinas de Gortari, *México*, p. 116 (my translation).

believer in gradual opening, and he reportedly advised the president against total opening in December 1994. Ortiz lost the argument.[50]

Mexico and the World Bank

The Bretton Woods institutions were active participants in Mexican economic policymaking in the late 1980s and early 1990s. Mexico had been one of the World Bank's most important borrowers and clients since the 1950s, receiving a total of US$21 billion worth of loans from the Bank by 1994—some 10 percent of the institution's total commitments since 1948.[51] After the 1982 debt crisis, when stabilization became top policy priority, the Mexican government looked primarily to the IMF for guidance, but once the economy stabilized and technocrats moved into the government with President de la Madrid (1982–1988), the Bank regained its position as the leading source of policy advice and lending, particularly in trade liberalization and agricultural policy. When Salinas became president in 1988, the ties between the Mexican technocrats and World Bank grew even closer.[52]

Financial-sector reform would test the limits of this close and collaborative relationship. Mexico–World Bank cooperation reached its high point in financial-sector policy with a 1989 Financial Sector Adjustment Loan (FSAL), which assisted the Mexican authorities with domestic financial deregulation. Mexican policymakers had come to the conclusion that deregulation was needed to mobilize domestic resources and to prepare for the eventual privatization of the banks. The World Bank's Mexico team, which for years had been advocating an end to financial repression, was delighted to participate, and the loan was deemed a success. But to the Bank's disappointment, once the final tranche of the loan was disbursed in 1990, the Mexican government informed the Bank that its financial-sector advice and assistance would no longer be required.[53] Consequently, the Bank disengaged from financial-system monitoring during the critical years of 1992–1993. A Bank evaluation would later conclude, "The inadequate high-level attention to the financial system during 1992–93 was by far the most serious omission in the Bank's agenda in Mexico during the period under review [1989–2000]."[54]

Once the crisis exploded, the Bank quickly reengaged with a US$1 billion Financial Sector Restructuring Loan to help Mexico regain international confidence and to help restructure its insolvent banks, but the harmonious relations had vanished.[55]

---

50. Interview with José Sidaoui, deputy governor, Bank of Mexico, Mexico City, April 5, 2005.

51. World Bank, Operations Evaluation Department, "World Bank Relations with Mexico," *OED Précis* No. 71, June 1994, p. 1.

52. Woods, *Globalizers*, p. 96.

53. World Bank, Operations Evaluation Department, "Mexico Country Assistance Evaluation," Report No. 22498, June 28, 2001, p. 11.

54. Ibid.

55. On the World Bank's role and perspective on the 1994–1995 crisis, see Shahid Javed Burki, "A Fate Foretold: The World Bank and the Mexican Crisis," in Edwards and Naím, *Mexico 1994*.

Bank staff and Mexican authorities clashed over a variety of crucial policy issues, including the role of foreign participation in the banking sector.[56] These disagreements proved irreconcilable, and the Bank soon pulled the plug on the loan, canceling disbursement of the loan's second tranche in June 1996.[57] The fiasco was not only due to policy disagreements; the Bank admitted to "poor management in its staffing and relationships at the working level."[58] A Mexican official was more blunt, recalling that the Bank team lacked professionalism and that its constant infighting badly damaged its credibility in the eyes of the Mexican authorities.[59]

In sum, once the Mexican government pushed the World Bank out of financial-sector reform in 1990, its influence in this policy area declined dramatically. The Bank's near-total disengagement and its disastrous reengagement after the crisis ensured that the influence it enjoyed in other policy areas did not extend into financial-sector policy. Although Mexico's decision to open its banking sector was one the Bank supported in principle, its adoption cannot be understood as the product of World Bank persuasion or coercion.

Mexico and the IMF

The IMF became deeply involved in shaping Mexican economic policy after the 1982 debt crisis, when the Fund designed Mexico's macroeconomic stabilization plan. As was the case with the World Bank, the Fund's relationship with the Mexican authorities greatly benefited from the country's "technocratic revolution," and in the 1990s, the IMF was providing Mexico with advice on exchange-rate, debt-management, and monetary policy issues. Banking-sector opening, however, was not on the Fund's agenda at this time.

Fund conditionality made a relatively late appearance in the Mexican crisis of 1994–1995.[60] Although the IMF sent a team to Mexico in late December 1994, the Mexican authorities chose not to pursue a standby arrangement at that point for fear that it would be interpreted by the markets as a sign of weakness.[61] The U.S. Treasury apparently did not support an IMF package at this stage, either.[62] Thus, the first international rescue package for Mexico did not involve the IMF. In late December, the Mexican finance secretary, Jaime Serra Puche, traveled to Washington, where he met with U.S. Treasury officials. On January 2, 1995, the U.S. Treasury announced an

---

56. World Bank, "Mexico Country Assistance Evaluation," p. 11.

57. The key report that documents the details of the FSAL's failure remains classified; the author's request for declassification was denied.

58. World Bank, "Mexico Country Assistance Evaluation," p. 11.

59. Confidential interview with former senior banking regulator, Mexico City, 2005.

60. For a background of the Fund's role in the crisis, see Claudio M. Loser and Ewart S. Williams, "The Mexican Crisis and Its Aftermath: An IMF Perspective," in Edwards and Naím, *Mexico 1994*.

61. Lustig, "Mexico in Crisis," pp. 27–28.

62. Interview with Claudio Loser, director of the IMF's Western Hemisphere Department (1994–2002). Washington, DC, July 31, 2007.

US$18 billion emergency-assistance package for Mexico.[63] The package was based on an expanded version of the North American Framework Agreement (NAFA), an April 1994 accord between the United States, Canada, and Mexico that created swap arrangements to provide emergency liquidity. The "NAFA-plus" initiative did not contain policy conditionality.

However, once it became clear that this arrangement would not be enough to restore confidence, the IMF was called in. On January 6, Managing Director Camdessus announced that the IMF would begin negotiations with the Mexican authorities. The Fund agreed to give Mexico access to US$7.6 billion, but most of the package's financial muscle was to come from the U.S. government in the form of US$40 billion in loan guarantees. When the U.S. Congress blocked the proposal, the Clinton administration used its executive power to extend Mexico a US$20 billion credit line in a controversial move that did not require congressional approval.[64]

Conditionality was contained in to two separate agreements. First was the understanding between the Mexican authorities and the IMF. In their January 26, 1995, Memorandum of Economic Policies outlining their commitments with the Fund, the Mexican authorities stated that they had "proposed legislation to permit greater foreign participation in the banking system than envisaged under the NAFTA agreements."[65] The agreement with the U.S. government, signed nearly a month later on February 21, was based on the terms already negotiated with the Fund and used very similar language. It stated, more directly, that "the Government...will permit greater foreign participation in the banking system than envisaged under the NAFTA."[66]

How crucial was IMF and U.S. government pressure as a trigger for banking-sector opening? The timing of events does not support the external pressure hypothesis. Negotiations with the IMF began on January 6, but they followed, not predated, President Zedillo's initial decision to open the banking system on January 2 and the official press release promising foreign participation of "up to 100 percent" on January 3. This timing is corroborated by the director of the IMF's Western Hemisphere Department, who negotiated with the Mexicans and recalled that the provision on banking-sector opening "was not an IMF initiative, but one brought to the table by the [Mexican] authorities."[67] Fund conditionality must have surely strengthened the

---

63. In the package announced January 2, the U.S. government agreed to enlarge short-term swap lines to a total of US$9 billion. The remaining US$9 billion consisted of credit lines from other governments and commercial banks arranged through the Bank for International Settlements.

64. For details, see Robert Rubin and Jacob Weisberg, *In an Uncertain World: Tough Choices from Wall Street to Washington* (New York: Random House, 2003), pp. 22–24.

65. "Mexico: Letter of Intent and Memorandum of Economic Policies," January 26, 1995, p. 7. This document remains confidential but was shown to me by an anonymous source.

66. "Framework Agreement between the United States and Mexico for Mexican Economic Stabilization," February 21, 1995, Annex C, section 10.

67. Loser interview.

resolve of Mexican policymakers to push for opening, but President Zedillo's liberal instincts and the imperatives of bank recapitalization were the main forces propelling the reform forward *before* the Fund and the U.S. Treasury had a chance to bring their leverage to bear.

Ironically, Washington's involvement in the Mexican rescue had a boomerang effect on the Zedillo administration's liberalization plans. Rather than strengthen the president's hand in the domestic arena, the agreement with the United States provoked a nationalist backlash in the Mexican congress, where legislators denounced U.S. imperialism and bullying. Members of the left-wing Party of the Democratic Revolution (PRD) labeled the conditions in the Framework Agreement "unacceptable," and soon after, the president of the Fiscal Affairs Commission of the Chamber of Deputies announced that legislators from the PRI and the right-of-center National Action Party (PAN) had agreed on the need to impose caps (or "locks," in the preferred Spanish term) on foreign participation in the banking sector.[68] In other words, external pressure promoted closure rather than opening at this stage.

Foreign banks that already had operations in Mexico adopted a dual response. On one hand, they welcomed the president's proposal, arguing that 100 percent foreign participation would be "the salvation" of many Mexican banks.[69] But at the same time, seventeen of the eighteen foreign banks that had been authorized in 1994 to establish subsidiaries in Mexico under NAFTA rules postponed the opening of new outlets until at least June 1995.[70] The foreign banks' unwillingness to commit to future investment regardless of what policies were adopted by the government undermined whatever leverage they could have exercised at this time to press for further opening.

Bargaining with Bankers and Legislators

President Zedillo's proposal to open the banking sector met with fierce congressional resistance at a time when the executive's power was dissipating rapidly. Opposition came not only from the PRD, which included the president of the Senate's Commission on Credit Institutions, but also from key members of the ruling PRI, including the presidents of both the Senate's Fiscal Affairs and Public Credit Commission and its Commission on Foreign Affairs.[71]

---

68. Víctor González and Gerardo Flores, "El capital foráneo no afectará el sistema de pagos," *El Financiero,* January 21, 1995, p. 4.

69. Georgina Howard and Gerardo Flores, "Chase Manhattan, la excepción; pospone proyectos la banca extranjera hasta julio," *El Financiero,* January 6, 1995, p. 6.

70. Ibid.

71. Salvador Rico, "Aceptarán banqueros el control extranjero de la banca; eficiencia, el requisito: ABM," *El Financiero,* February 25, 1995, p. 7.

The legislators made three significant changes to the president's proposal. To encourage foreign investment without surrendering management control over Mexican banks, they increased the amount of "L-series" shares that could be issued by banks up to 40 percent of total common stock. L-series shares could be bought by foreigners but conferred only limited voting power. A second change empowered the finance ministry to authorize foreign acquisitions of Mexican banks, but foreigners—collectively or individually—could acquire no more than 20 percent of the equity of any bank whose net capital exceeded 6 percent of the system's aggregate net capital. This provision effectively protected the three largest institutions—Banamex, Bancomer, and Serfín—from foreign takeovers. And third, aggregate foreign participation was capped at 25 percent of the system's total net assets. The Chamber of Deputies approved the amended bill by a wide margin (372 to 34), and it sailed through the Senate as well.[72]

Was the Mexican congress acting just on behalf of Mexican bankers seeking to preserve their privileges, or were the parliamentarians driven by ideas and motives of their own? The evidence supports the latter hypothesis. At the behest of the Senate's Commission on Credit Institutions, an extraordinary meeting was organized on January 15, 1995, to bring together the leadership of the Mexican Bankers' Association (ABM) with fifteen senators and six deputies from the leading political parties. This was the first time in modern Mexican history that bankers and legislators met to discuss policy without officials from the executive branch present. Entirely unaccustomed to dealing with legislators, the bankers were reportedly puzzled and somewhat bemused by the meeting; the bankers had traditionally regarded these politicians as irrelevant in financial policymaking.[73]

To the legislators' considerable surprise, the bankers did not demand protection from foreigners but instead declared themselves untroubled by the prospect of banking-sector opening. They expressed support for the President Zedillo's initiative. "It is preferable to have an efficient domestic banking sector, even if it is run by foreigners, than an inefficient domestic banking sector that is managed by Mexicans," the ABM's vice-president was quoted as saying at the meeting.[74] This view, however, reflected the preferences of the ABM's leadership—the owners of Mexico's largest banks—not those of the rest of the banking community.[75] Mexico's top bank owners apparently believed that their institutions would survive the crisis, and that even if the government removed restrictions on foreign participation, Banamex and Bancomer would remain safe from foreign

72. Senado de la República, *Diario de los debates,* No. 3, January 17, 1995.

73. See, for example, the comments of Senator Mauricio Fernández Garza, Senado de la República, *Diario de los debates,* No. 10, January 27, 1995, p. 16.

74. Salvador Rico and Georgina Howard, "Acelerada apertura financiera despreocupa a la banca nacional," *El Financiero,* January 25, 1995, p. 1.

75. The ABM was headed by the presidents of either Bancomer or Banamex without interruption from 1992 to 1997.

takeovers.[76] The big bankers were probably also keen to avoid antagonizing the president, knowing that their fate during the crisis would partly depend on maintaining good relations with the executive. The rest of the ABM's membership was less confident. The directors of Mexico's medium-sized banks dismissed the statements of the ABM's leadership as unrepresentative of the majority of bankers. They also complained (anonymously) that some bankers had been excluded from the ABM meeting with legislators.[77]

Unlike the big bank owners, key legislators had serious misgivings about banking-sector opening.[78] They worried that foreign-bank entry would facilitate capital outflows and undermine monetary control, particularly if foreign subsidiaries were allowed to accept dollar-denominated deposits. Foreign-bank entry could not be guaranteed to improve efficiency or competition, they argued. A senator expressed concern over "monopolistic competition among large foreign entities, which would act, less and less, in response to domestic market conditions and more in response to external interests and conditions."[79] Legislators were also concerned that foreign control of Mexican banks would not necessarily translate into more or cheaper credit for Mexican firms.

In the end, President Zedillo relented. "Zedillo's priorities were not there," remembers the president of the Fiscal Affairs Commission of the Chamber of Deputies. "His priorities were saving the country, stabilizing the fiscal situation, adjusting the value-added tax. For him, the 'locks' were part of a larger political negotiation."[80] Domestic politics did make a difference, but not in the sense that rent-seeking interest groups blocked banking-sector opening. Rather, total opening was blocked by senators and deputies who, acting on the basis of their own causal beliefs, used the legislature's newfound veto power.

The Search for Fresh Capital

As the debate over banking-sector opening unfolded, the capital base of Mexico's banks eroded rapidly. The system's capital-asset ratio fell from 9.3 percent in end-1994 to below 8 percent two months later.[81] Banks needed to increase loan-loss

---

76. Rico, "Aceptarán banqueros," p. 7.

77. Georgina Howard, "Divide a banqueros eventual control del sistema de pagos," El Financiero, January 26, 1995, p. 9.

78. See the comments of Senators Guillermo Ulloa Carreón and Héctor Sánchez, Senado de la República, Diario de los debates, No. 10, January 27, 1995, pp. 17–21.

79. Comments of Héctor Sánchez, Senado de la República, Diario de los debates, No. 10, January 27, 1995, p. 20.

80. Interview with Francisco Suárez Dávila, president of the Fiscal Affairs Commission, Chamber of Deputies (1994–1997), Mexico City, December 16, 2005.

81. Graf, "Policy Responses," p. 170.

provisioning to 60 percent, a level that only five banks met in early 1995.[82] For the Mexican authorities—and here I refer particularly to bank regulators at the banking commission (the CNB, which became the CNBV after May 1995)—the most urgent banking problem was how to maintain adequate capitalization levels to avoid bank runs and a general loss of public confidence in the system.

At the center of Mexico's banking-sector rescue operation was the Fund for the Protection of Bank Savings (Fondo Bancario de Protección al Ahorro, or FOBAPROA), a trust fund created by the government in 1981 to administer bank-deposit insurance. FOBAPROA became the primary instrument through which public resources were channeled to the ailing banking system. Under the government's bank rescue plan, FOBAPROA agreed to buy nonperforming loans from troubled financial institutions above their market value under the condition that the shareholders inject new capital: for every two pesos of bad loans purchased by the government, the owners would be expected to contribute one peso. FOBAPROA would buy the loans by issuing zero-coupon "FOBAPROA bonds" with a ten-year maturity.

Once the recapitalization programs were in place, the main problem for bankers was finding sources of fresh capital. Five potential sources existed. One option was to channel profits and dividends into reserve capital. This was a nonstarter, as bank profits fell sharply with the recession.[83] In addition, with US$8.7 billion in certificates of deposit coming due, the banks had to divert profits to service those obligations first.[84] Another option was to issue bonds, but banks receiving support from FOBAPROA's temporary capitalization scheme were not allowed to issue any debt until they had paid back the central bank. Also, Mexican sovereign bonds and corporate paper were downgraded by credit rating agencies,[85] and there were few investors willing and able to absorb large amounts of Mexican bank bonds.

A third possibility was to raise capital from the existing shareholders. Three of the largest banks—Banamex, Bancomer, and Banorte—raised money by selling assets elsewhere in their financial groups, including asset management and insurance companies. Shareholders from two troubled banks, Serfín and Bancrecer, injected genuinely fresh capital, but much of the shareholder money put into other banks was either not new, or it came in the form of poor quality assets. In total, only

---

82. Marcos Chávez, "Previsible aumento en su cartera vencida bruta de 16 mil mdnp; Bancos al borde de la insolvencia," *El Financiero,* February 27, 1995, p. 4.

83. In February 1995, net aggregate profits of the top sixteen banks fell by 62 percent, compared with profit levels a year earlier. Georgina Howard and Marcos Chávez M., "Bajas las utilidades de los bancos," *El Financiero,* February 3, 1995, p. 1.

84. Georgina Howard, "'Entrampados' bancos mexicanos por el vencimiento de 8 mil 700 mdd en Cedes," *El Financiero,* February 6, 1995, p. 7.

85. "Negro panorama, pronostica la agencia británica IBCA," *El Financiero,* February 21, 1995, p. 7.

52 percent of the capital injections were considered by the authorities to be of sufficiently good quality.[86]

A fourth option was to raise capital from Mexican investors not already involved in the banking business. The nonbanking private sector had incurred some US$30 billion of dollar-denominated debt, much of it unhedged.[87] With two exceptions—Grupo Carso and the television group Televisa—sixty-five of the country's most important nonfinancial business groups were caught by surprise when the peso collapsed and saw their debt burdens balloon.[88] As a result, these entrepreneurs had little appetite or capital to purchase weak banks, even at a discount. Meanwhile, Grupo Carso—one of the country's leading *grupos,* headed by Mexico's richest man—already had a financial arm in Banca Inbursa and was not interested in acquiring a troubled bank.[89]

The last option was raising capital from foreign investors. Mexican banks and regulators began to court foreign investors very early in the crisis, starting with banks that already held minority stakes in Mexican institutions. CNBV officials did their best to persuade foreigners to take controlling stakes in the weaker banks and to recapitalize them. In a deal heavily assisted with FOBAPROA funds, Spain's Banco Bilbao Vizcaya (BBV, later BBVA) paid US$350 million to increase its 25 percent stake in troubled bank Probursa to 70 percent.[90]

For the Mexican bank regulators, this sale was important as a signaling device, as a senior bank regulator recalled: "We were very pressed to make the sale [of Probursa]. We needed to send the signal to the markets that there was an appetite for Mexican banks."[91] The deal was also important because it signaled to domestic and foreign investors that the government was committed to reprivatization, not to a "silent takeover" of the banking system by the government.[92] The second transaction was an agreement with the Canadian Scotiabank, which would manage the troubled Inverlat on behalf of the Mexican government, with an option to buy the bank after three years.

---

86. Michael W. Mackey, "Informe sobre la evaluación integral de las operaciones y funciones del Fondo Bancario de Protección al Ahorro, FOBAPROA y la calidad de supervisión de los programas del FOBAPROA de 1995 a 1998," July 1999, p. 133.

87. Rafael Ocampo and Fernando Ortega Pizarro, "Los grandes empresarios se dicen engañados; sólo Azcárraga y Slim renegociaron a pesos, antes de la devaluación, parte de su deuda," *Proceso,* January 2, 1995.

88. Ibid.

89. Paul B. Carroll and Craig Torres, "Two Solid Banks Appear Set to Gain Ground on Weaker Rivals in Mexico," *Wall Street Journal,* March 6, 1995, sec. A, p. 10.

90. BBV would inject US$230 million into Probursa; about US$160 million of this would be Spanish capital. Alicia Salgado, "Exentan de restricciones a filiales extranjeras 'salvadoras'; Retrasar el apoyo a bancos obligará a un ajuste mayor del sistema: CNBV," *El Financiero,* May 31, 1995, p. 4.

91. Interview with Patricia Armendáriz, former vice-president of Banking Supervision, National Banking and Securities Commission, Mexico City, March 31, 2005.

92. Interview with José Sidaoui, Mexico City, April 5, 2005.

Other major sales to foreigners followed, albeit slowly. In 1996, HSBC and the Bank of Montreal acquired minority shares in Serfín and Bancomer, respectively. The following year, BBV acquired two of the weakest banks, Cremi and Oriente, while the BBV's archrival, Banco Santander, made a substantial investment by acquiring a stake in Banco Mexicano. Only in 1998 would a U.S. bank make a significant investment in the Mexican banking system—in this case, Citibank's purchase of the medium-sized Banca Confía. To persuade Citibank to acquire Confía, the Mexican government took on much of the risk.[93]

The bank sales proved very unpopular in Mexico. Leading analyst Luis Rubio captured the essence of the public's criticism: "Instead of saving the banks—which would have been in the public interest—in many cases the government began by saving the bank owners themselves. Eventually this strategy was corrected, but only to fall into an even worse one: the government began to subsidize foreign bankers so that, without putting their capital at risk, they would take over the bankrupt banks."[94]

The Serfín Crisis

Despite these efforts, regulators were confronted in early 1997 with the serious deterioration of Mexico's third-largest bank, Serfín. This bank's condition was described by Moody's, a rating agency, as "perhaps the worst example of a re-privatized Mexican bank that did not have to contend with major fraud."[95] Serfín had had a weak portfolio since before its privatization, as it had been saddled with the financing of several infrastructure megaprojects when it was still in government hands.[96] While the other "Big Three" banks, Banamex and Bancomer, maintained apparently adequate capitalization levels, the situation of the Serfín Financial Group deteriorated steadily, despite capital injections by shareholders and the sale of a large stake in the group's insurance company. FOBAPROA also bought Serfín NPLs and swapped them for N$52 billion worth of bonds—six times the equity value of the bank's shareholders.[97]

Serfín was deemed too big to fail, so saving it became a priority for the banking commission from 1996 onward. In their search for a savior, the banking authorities

---

93. As part of the deal, FOBAPROA would absorb three-quarters of Confía's US$4 billion loan portfolio, and if those loans were sold at a loss, Confía would not be charged with the 25 percent write-off required under FOBAPROA rules.

94. Qtd. in Salinas de Gortari, *México*, p. 1172 (my translation).

95. Qtd. in George Graham, "Serfín Troubles Cut HSBC Price by $126m," *Financial Times*, December 31, 1997.

96. For a detailed account of the road to Serfín's bankruptcy, see Héctor Rogelio Núñez Estrada, "Reforma de la administración pública del sistema bancario y su efecto en la crisis sistémica: 1990–2000 la quiebra de Banca Serfin," paper prepared for the IX CLAD Congress on State Reform and Public Administration, Madrid, November 2–5, 2004.

97. Ibid., p. 9.

sold the British HSBC a 20 percent stake in Serfín in December 1997. As with the Confía sale, the offer included all manner of sweeteners, but the purchase meant that HSBC hit the 20 percent ceiling imposed by the congress in 1995, as Serfín was one of the big institutions to which caps applied.[98]

With the Serfín crisis escalating, the Zedillo administration renewed its efforts to remove the remaining caps on foreign participation. In March 1998, the executive sent to the congress draft legislation that would effectively do this by consolidating banks' A-series and B-series shares into a single class of ordinary, voting shares ("O-series" shares) that could be bought freely by both domestic and foreign investors, as shown in Table 3.2. Combined with the L-series shares, which could make up to 40 percent of total common stock, foreigners could now own all the equity in any Mexican bank. The only restriction left was the ceiling forbidding any individual investor from acquiring more than 20 percent of the common stock of a domestic bank. Foreigners would be able to acquire even the largest Mexican banks, but they would have to do so through a consortium.

The effort to save Serfín was the force behind this initiative. According to a former senior CNBV official, "given the size of Serfín, we realized the bank could not be easily liquidated, so it had to be recapitalized. But it would have been impossible to recapitalize Serfín without foreign capital. It was simply too big."[99] A senior official in the central bank agreed: "Serfín was about to collapse, and there was no bank in Mexico big enough to save Serfín. This is why the ceilings were raised."[100] That the timing of the proposed reform was linked to the Serfín crisis was evident even to outsiders. One analyst wrote, "Among the top three institutions which control nearly 60 percent of market share, leaders Banamex and Bancomer stand to gain little for now: both banks have strong capitalization ratios and neither seems to have foreign investors on its agenda. The reform would seem to be tailor-made for investors in Mexico's third-largest bank, Serfín."[101]

Congressional Breakthrough

President Zedillo's initiative was received by a legislature that had undergone historic recomposition. In July 1997, the PRI failed to win a majority in the Chamber of Deputies for the first time in Mexican history, changing the balance of political

98. HSBC received a substantial discount in its purchase, protection against market losses if the book value of Serfín shares fell below initial purchase levels, protection against future dilution of its share, and a right of first refusal on any future shares issues.

99. Interview with Guillermo Zamarripa, former vice-president of banking supervision, National Banking and Securities Commission, Mexico City, April 8, 2005.

100. Interview with Pascual O'Dogherty Madrazo, director of financial system analysis, Bank of Mexico, Mexico City, April 4, 2005.

101. Michael Tangeman, "Right Place, Right Time," *Latin Finance* (May 1998), 38.

Table 3.2   President Zedillo's 1998 proposal

TYPE OF BANK SHARES	VOTING POWER?	COMPOSITION OF TOTAL BANK STOCK AFTER 1995 REFORM	STATUS QUO AFTER 1995 REFORM	PROPOSED 1998 REFORM
A series	Yes	Up to 51% of paid-in capital	Can be acquired by the government, development banks, and Mexican individuals only	Disappear
B series	Yes	Up to 49% of paid-in capital	Can be acquired those who can acquire A-series shares and by all Mexican and foreign (nongovernmental) entities	Disappear
L series	Limited	Up to 40% of paid-in capital	Can be acquired by Mexicans and foreigners	Can be acquired by Mexicans and foreigners
O series	Yes	Did not exist	Did not exist	Can be acquired by Mexicans and foreigners; can constitute up to 100% of paid-in capital

Source: Author's summary based on draft legislation.

power in the legislature.[102] Having toppled the PRI goliath, the opposition, itching to exercise its newly acquired power, challenged the executive's economic program at every step, and the banking initiative was no exception. The president's proposal was embedded in a controversial bill known as the IPAB Law.[103] The most controversial aspect of the bill was not banking-sector opening but the conversion of FOBAPROA's enormous liabilities into public debt. Left-wing legislators from the PRD denounced the proposal on grounds of economic justice and equity, while PAN legislators supported the conversion but wanted it to take place through annual appropriations authorized by the congress.

Resorting to a divide-and-conquer strategy, the executive negotiated independently with the PAN while the PRD stood in the sidelines, and a PRI-PAN coalition

---

102. The ruling PRI won 48 percent of the seats in the five-hundred-seat chamber. The right-wing PAN won 25 percent, and the left-wing PRD, 24 percent.

103. IPAB, the Institute for the Protection of Bank Savings (Instituto para a Protección al Ahorro Bancario), was FOBAPROA's successor. Among other things, the IPAB law would legally establish and provide resources for the new institute.

forced through the IPAB Law in December 1998.[104] The final version included the president's proposal to lift all ceilings to foreign-bank entry. The lower house approved the package of reforms on December 12 by a wide margin; it was approved by the Senate shortly thereafter. The remaining 20 percent limit on the bank equity ownership by individual institutions would be lifted in 2001 with little controversy.[105]

Scholars have attributed the congressional breakthrough to the fact that the debate over the FOBAPROA liabilities "distracted" the legislators from the banking-sector-opening initiative, but the key factor was a shift in the legislature's composition and beliefs.[106] When the banking commission submitted its conclusions and recommendations to the whole chamber, these reflected attitudes about banking-sector opening that were very different from those that prevailed in 1995. Now they read like a page from a World Bank publication:

> The members of this Commission agree that the participation of foreign capital is a factor that can strengthen and increase the efficiency of the financial system.... The recent experience of foreign investment in our country's banking system by top international financial intermediaries has demonstrated that these institutions have the capacity to contribute additional capital when these institutions face losses. This reduces the risk that the protection mechanisms, and ultimately, the government, will have to devote resources to protect savers' deposits. In addition, foreign banks contribute technology, greater competitiveness, and better supervision.[107]

The legislators also gained some solace from the experiences of their neighbors. They noted that other Latin American countries, including Argentina, Chile, Venezuela, and Brazil, had opened their banking sectors and already exhibited higher levels of foreign participation than Mexico.[108]

---

104. This strategy allowed the Zedillo administration to approve a variety of other economic reforms. See Kenneth C. Shadlen, "Continuity amid Change: Democratization, Party Strategies, and Economic Policy-Making in Mexico," *Government and Opposition* 34:3 (1999), 397–419.

105. The restriction was abolished in April 2001, when the congress approved legislation submitted by the Fox administration amending the Law on Credit Institutions. The amendment allowed any person or corporation, national or foreign, to acquire *all* of an institution's O-series shares, with previous authorization from Hacienda. This allowed foreign investors to acquire Mexican banks more easily, without the need to cobble together a consortium. In addition, the reform stipulated that an individual or corporation could achieve management control over a bank by acquiring 30 percent or more of its voting stock.

106. See Susan Minushkin and Charles Parker III, "Relaciones entre la banca y el gobierno: La nueva estructura financiera en México," *Política y Gobierno* 9 (First Semester 2002), 208, and Thorburn, "Political Economy of Foreign Banks," p. 155.

107. "Dictamen de la Comisión de Hacienda y Crédito Público, con proyecto de decreto por el que se expide la Ley de Protección al Ahorro Bancario, y se reforman, adicionan y derogan diversas disposiciones de las Leyes del Banco de México, de Instituciones de Crédito, del Mercado de Valores y Para Regular las Agrupaciones Financieras, Cámara de Diputados," *Gaceta Parlamentaria* 2:178 (December 12, 1998) (my translation).

108. Ibid.

How do we explain this shift in congressional views? The evidence points to a shift in legislators' causal beliefs. Thanks to changes in the composition of the Fiscal Affairs Commissions of both chambers of congress, some of the staunchest nationalists and most powerful opponents of banking-sector opening in 1995 were replaced by more pragmatic (and comparatively inexperienced) legislators.[109] Indeed, two-thirds of the commissions' 1995 membership changed after the 1997 elections. This changed the tone of the congressional debate. Also, the executive was better prepared this time to make its case. Finance Secretary José Angel Gurría, a charismatic and persuasive figure, was deployed to the congress, where he made a forceful argument for opening the banking sector.[110] Legislators were provided with briefing materials making the case for a liberal banking regime and recounting the experiences of other countries. All of this made the government's case more compelling.

There was also a political consideration. With the press rife with reports about FOBAPROA fund abuse by delinquent bankers,[111] few legislators were prepared to support protection for the big banks, especially since this protection would increasingly come at the expense of the taxpayer, who would directly bear the burden of saving weak banks not acquired by foreign investors. Distancing themselves from the bankers, who had become a political liability, became much easier. Finally, the banking system's desperate need for capital and the imminent collapse of Serfin were factors that were not present in 1995, when the magnitude of the crisis was less clear.

What role did Mexico's embattled banking elite play in the crucial reform of late 1998? The capacity of Mexican bankers to exert pressure declined considerably at this time. With the downturn in its members' fortunes, the bankers' lobbying association, the ABM, was forced to halve its staff and adopt an austerity program.[112] More importantly, positions within the banking community continued to fragment, and the traditional Bancomer-Banamex hegemony in the Bankers' Association began to crack. In 1997—for the first time since the privatization of the banks—a president

109. Interview with Carlos Sales Gutiérrez, president, Senate Fiscal Affairs Commission (1995–1998), Mexico City, December 27, 2005. For example, the president of the Fiscal Affairs Commission of the Chamber of Deputies, Francisco Suárez Dávila, a former undersecretary of finance, veteran financial policy hand, and strong opponent of Zedillo's 1995 initiative, no longer occupied that position in late 1998. In the Senate, another experienced former undersecretary and opponent of the 1995 reform, Carlos Sales Gutiérrez, had left the congress to head Nafin.

110. For a flavor of Gurría's arguments, see his interview with Mario Vázquez Raña, reprinted in Secretaría de Hacienda y Crédito Público, *FOBAPROA: La verdadera historia* (Mexico City: SHCP, 1998), pp. 63–138.

111. Some of these were carefully documented in the "bank reports" by Canadian auditor Michael Mackey. See Mackey, "Informe sobre la evaluación integral."

112. Duncan R. Wood, "Business Association, Regional Integration, and Systemic Shocks: The Case of the ABM in Mexico," in *Organized Business and the New Global Order*, ed. Justin Greenwood and Henry Jacek (Basingstoke, U.K.: Macmillan, 2000), p. 71.

drawn from neither Bancomer nor Banamex was elected to head the ABM, and the following year, the presidency of the association shifted to a foreign-controlled bank for the first time in the seventy-year history of the ABM. Foreign-controlled banks were a growing element in the ABM, and at least some of these institutions were supportive of a liberal banking regime.

Did Trade Negotiations Make a Difference?

Mexico, like the other three cases in this book, was party to the GATS negotiations, which reached their final stage in 1995–1997, just as the country was dealing with its financial crisis and revising its banking regime. Could these negotiations have made a difference to the dynamics of opening? A review of Mexico's five GATS offers on financial services, made between 1994 and 1998, reveals that the commitments the Mexicans made in Geneva either lagged behind or reflected the regulatory status quo at home, meaning that any pressure applied at these negotiations made little difference. Mexico's commitments are listed in Appendix 2.

Mexico's initial GATS offer was made in April 1994, after the NAFTA negotiations were concluded.[113] Under the NAFTA, Canadian and U.S. incorporated banks could purchase up to 30 percent of a domestic bank's equity in the aggregate, but under the GATS, Mexico offered the rest of the world a more restrictive cap of 20 percent in its first offer, matching the NAFTA cap of 30 percent only in mid-1995.[114] However, when the offer was made, the domestic banking regime had already leaped ahead to 100 percent foreign ownership for NAFTA- *and* non-NAFTA-based investors, subject to the 25 percent aggregate cap and the "locks" the congress had imposed on the top three banks. Also, individual foreign investors could own up to 20 percent of domestic banks under the president's 1995 reform, yet Mexico's GATS offer capped equity holdings by individual foreigners at only 2.5 percent.

The GATS commitments put forward by Mexico in February 1998 marked a significant improvement on Mexico's previous offers.[115] Foreigners could now own up to 40 percent of banks' common stock capital and all the "additional" capital made up of nonvoting shares. With special dispensation, individual foreigners could also purchase up to 20 percent of a single institution's equity. In reality, however, this offer only brought Mexico's GATS commitments closer to the regulatory status quo that had been in place since 1995. The 1998 offer gave foreign investors no new participation rights, and to date, the dramatic reforms of December 1998 have not been bound under the GATS.

In sum, Mexico's banking commitments under the WTO consistently lagged behind reforms undertaken unilaterally elsewhere. While the NAFTA negotiations

---

113. GATS/SC/56, April 15, 1994.
114. GATS/SC/56/Suppl. 1, July 28, 1995.
115. GATS/SC/56/Suppl. 3, February 26, 1998.

led to opening that went well beyond the status quo, Mexico's GATS offers were always a diluted version of commitments undertaken under NAFTA or through domestic legislation. Thus, the argument that the GATS negotiations were responsible for the momentous changes in Mexico's banking regime is difficult to maintain. At best, the GATS provided a lock-in mechanism to bind some of Mexico's unilateral opening measures, making reversion to a closed banking regime more difficult.

The Politics of De Facto Opening (1999–2002)

After the Serfín crisis and the regulatory change that followed, Mexico's banking sector was fully open, at least on paper. Bank regulators took advantage of their new maneuvering room to encourage the consolidation of the banking system. Of the top fourteen banks before the crisis, only five would still be in the hands of their original owners by the spring of 2000. Two were absorbed by Bancomer, and seven were bought by large, international banks, with the lion's share going to the Spanish banks Santander and BBVA. Despite HSBC's equity purchase in 1998 and billions of pesos in loan purchases by FOBAPROA, the banking authorities were forced to take over Serfín in 1999. After liquidating HSBC's shares, replacing the management, and cleaning out the bank of NPLs, the authorities sold 100 percent of Serfín's shares to Santander in May 2000 for US$1.56 billion, or 1.6 times the book value. As a senior banking regulator put it, referring to the sale of Serfín to Santander: "The sale was heavily assisted by the government. We put lots of money into it, because the last thing we wanted was to get stuck with the bank."[116]

The other members of the banking triumvirate, Banamex and Bancomer, remained under the control of their original owners, but not because those institutions were in good financial health. Both banks remained undercapitalized, their portfolios bulging with toxic assets. Banamex and Bancomer were kept out of government hands thanks to organized hypocrisy: the bank owners promised the regulators they would find fresh capital, if only the authorities would temporarily postpone the shift to more stringent regulation. At the same time, the regulators applied heavy layers of financial "makeup" to mask the banks' true financial condition, thereby justifying further delays. A key component of this organized hypocrisy was deferred tax credits. Regulators allowed the banks to defer paying taxes and to count deferred taxes as part of their capital.[117] Without these accounting tricks, Bancomer and Banamex would have failed to meet the minimum capitalization

---

116. Armendáriz interview.

117. Deferred tax credits accounted for 32 percent of the total capital of the banks that had not been intervened by the authorities. César Martinez Aznárez, "Maquillaje contable en bancos," *La Jornada*, September 1999.

standard of 8 percent, and the authorities would have been compelled by their own rules to take them over. Mexico's top bankers wanted desperately to retain control over their institutions, and the regulators wanted, equally desperately, to avoid having to take over their banks.

The regulators' reluctance was not the product of direct political pressure by bankers. Instead, Mexican policymakers were strongly averse to takeovers of troubled banks because they worried that renationalization would undermine market confidence in the government's commitment to its flagship policies—privatization and the reduction of the state's role in the economy. They also feared that nationalization would place more of the fiscal burden of recapitalization on the state.[118] In an interview, Finance Secretary Gurría explained what he thought would have happened if the government had taken over the failed banks for an indeterminate period:

> It would have been a lot more expensive; it would have been necessary to inject a lot more public resources, in addition to all the resources that have been injected by the private shareholders throughout all these years. Besides, we must consider that, in this age of globalized markets, in which the role of government in economic life is being reduced in all parts of the world, a nationalization of the banks would have been perceived in a very different way compared to the nationalization of 1982.[119]

Selling the Giants

With the worst of the banking shock behind them, and having injected resources equivalent to some 20 percent of GDP into the troubled banking system, Mexican regulators began to tighten capital requirements, giving banks four years to comply. At the same time, the percentage of deferred tax credits that could be counted as capital would be gradually reduced from 100 to 20 percent. This posed a serious challenge to the remaining bank owners; government estimates put the amount of resources needed to recapitalize the system at US$5 billion, while Standard & Poor's put the figure at a much higher US$15.5 billion.[120] Of the top banks, Bancomer was the most pressed for cash; deferred tax credits accounted for 53 percent of its total equity in October 1999.[121]

In March 2000, the Spanish BBVA proposed a merger with Bancomer, promising to inject US$1.2 billion in a deal that would create the country's largest financial-services conglomerate. Two months later, Mexico's largest bank, Banamex, announced

---

118. Armendáriz interview.

119. Secretaría de Hacienda y Crédito Público, *FOBAPROA*, p. 113 (my translation).

120. "Mexico Regulations: New Rules Pressure Banks to Seek Fresh Capital," *Economist Intelligence Unit,* October 4, 1999.

121. Ibid.

that it would bid for Bancomer, promising a capital injection of US$2.4 billion—double BBVA's offer—through the purchase of 65 percent of Bancomer's shares. In response, BBVA increased its offer to US$1.85 billion.

The prospect of a Bancomer-Banamex merger posed a significant dilemma for Mexican policymakers: should they stabilize the banking system by selling one of its core institutions to a foreign buyer, transferring managing control overseas? Or should they pursue stabilization through a domestic merger, which would have perverse consequences for the sector's level of concentration? Banamex's management and some politicians promoted the merger of the two Mexican banks on nationalist grounds, billing it as an effective way to fight back foreign "*conquistadores*" and applying the "national champion" model followed by the Spanish themselves.[122] Banamex took its case directly to President Zedillo and released an opinion poll purportedly showing that the Mexican public preferred, by a large majority, that Banamex take over Bancomer instead of the Spanish bank.[123] Critics, on the other hand, pointed out that the resulting megabank would severely distort the banking market, stifle competition, and wield so much power in the national financial system that it could eclipse the central bank, the banking commission, and even Hacienda in important policy areas, including monetary policy.[124]

The national-champion dilemma confronted Mexican authorities at a time of growing banking-sector concentration. Five years of bank mergers, acquisitions, and liquidations had reversed the deconcentration pattern of the 1991–1994 period and returned the system to levels of concentration prevalent in the preprivatization years, as shown in Figure 3.1. The authorities were sensitive to transactions that would increase concentration even further. According to participants familiar with the process, President Zedillo was totally opposed to the merger of the two Mexican banks on the grounds that it would have created an unacceptably high level of concentration.[125]

Throughout the process, President Zedillo publicly distanced himself from the debate, arguing that this was a private deal and that the presidency would not intervene; it was up to the competition authorities and to the bank's shareholders to approve or reject the merger. In May 2000, the Federal Competition Commission (CFC) cleared the way for the Bancomer-BBVA merger, declaring that such a

122. Henry Tricks, "BBVA Cast as Conquistador: Unsolicited Bid Stands in Way of Spanish Bank's Latin American Expansion Strategy," *Financial Times,* May 5, 2000, p. 32.

123. "Banamex Poll Finds Mexicans Prefer It to BBV in Merger Battle over Bancomer," *Reforma,* June 8, 2000.

124. The merged entity would have US$60 billion in assets and control 51 percent of the Mexican banking system's capital, 40 percent of all credit, and 42 percent of total deposits. In contrast, the BBVA-Bancomer merger would create an institution with control of 27 percent of total credit and 27 percent of the system's deposits. Alicia Salgado, "Envía Banamex-Accival a Bancomer propuesta no solicitada de fusión," *El Financiero,* May 4, 2000, p. 4.

125. Interviews with Francisco Suárez Dávila, Mexico City, December 16, 2005, and José Sidaoui, Mexico City, April 5, 2005.

FIGURE 3.1. Banking-sector concentration in Mexico, 1980–2002.
Source: Based on data in Haber, "Mexico's Experiments with Bank Privatization and Liberalization, 1991–2002"
(mimeo.), Stanford University, March 23, 2004, Table 4.

combination would not jeopardize competition. The CFC was open to approving the
Banamex-Bancomer deal, but only after imposing very substantial restrictions on
the activities of the merged bank.[126] These restrictions were unacceptable to Banamex, and before a formal CFC ruling was issued, Bancomer accepted BBVA's offer.
Under the deal, BBVA would have total control of the bank by 2004, in exchange for
some US$4.1 billion. Despite President Zedillo's public silence, Hacienda was clearly
relieved by the outcome, observing that the BBVA transaction avoided the creation
of an entity that would have enjoyed an excessive degree of leverage and power.[127]

Cashing Out

With the failure of the Banamex-Bancomer merger, and facing mounting capitalization requirements, the owners of the country's two largest banks chose to cash out

---

126. Alicia Salgado, "Condicionará la CFC la fusión entre Bancomer y Banamex-Accival," *El Financiero,* June 12, 2000, p. 4.
127. Gerardo Flores and Alicia Salgado, "Beneplácito de la SHCP por BBVA-Bancomer," *El Financiero,* June 14, 2000, p. 1.

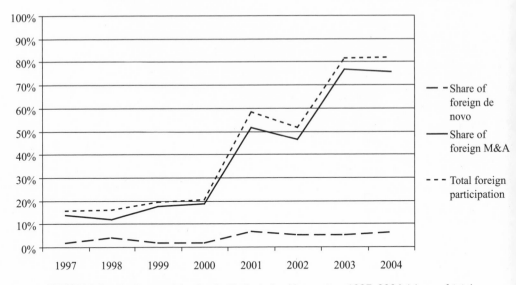

FIGURE 3.2. Foreign participation in Mexico's banking sector, 1997–2004 (share of total system assets, as of Q1 of each year).
Source: Based on data in Haber, "Mexico's Experiments with Bank Privatization and Liberalization, 1991–2002" (mimeo.), Stanford University, March 23, 2004, Table 10.

of the game of Mexican banking. Exit was made possible by the government's willingness to consider and approve foreign acquisitions and by a growing appetite by large international banks for Mexican institutions, which meant that owners could demand attractive prices for their banks. Because the institutions on sale had not been taken over by the CNBV, all the transactions were conducted without government involvement aside from regulatory approval. These were private mergers and acquisitions, and to considerable public outcry, they generated little tax income for the government despite the significant public funds that had been injected into the banks. From the Mexican bank owners' point of view, there were limits on how much of their own money they were willing to inject to keep their banks, particularly in light of the tantalizing deals being offered by foreign investors.[128]

Two major deals followed in short order. In 2001, Citigroup paid US$12.5 billion for 100 percent of Banamex in the largest single FDI transaction in Mexican history. The last case of exit was Bital, the fourth-largest bank, which was acquired by the British bank HSBC in 2002 for US$1.1 billion. HSBC agreed to inject US$600 million immediately to ensure that Bital could meet capitalization requirements. As Figure 3.2 shows, the acquisition of these banks caused foreign participation in the banking system to jump dramatically, reaching 82 percent by 2004.

---

128. On the decision of Bancomer's owners to exit the market, see M. Cilina R. Vansetti et al., "The 'Fall' of Bancomer and the Future of the Indigenous Mega-Banks in Latin America," Moody's Investors Service Special Comment, Global Credit Research, April 2000, pp. 4–5.

This chapter has argued that banking-sector opening in Mexico is best understood as the product of a catalyst and a trigger. The catalyst was an exogenous change in policymakers' causal beliefs, brought about by new presidential leadership, and the trigger took the form of a banking crisis that led to a change of ideas in the legislature, the last bastion of financial protectionism. Before the crisis, there was little opening, even though the Mexican government was under external pressure to open its banking market at the NAFTA and GATS negotiations, as well as at the OECD accession talks. The Salinas administration proved highly adept at defending its vision of a highly protected, domestically owned banking sector with only a small foreign presence. President Zedillo's vision of liberal banking fundamentally changed the policy environment, and when the crisis erupted, the imperatives of rescuing the banking system allowed the administration to overcome powerful congressional opposition to a liberal banking regime and to implement total de jure opening and de facto opening.

Contrary to popular lore, political pressure exerted by the World Bank, the IMF, and the U.S. government, through their policy loans and rescue packages, had no impact on policy (in the case of the World Bank and the IMF) and undermined rather than promoted opening (in the case of the U.S. government) by stoking the fires of nationalism in the legislature. The initiative to open the banking system came from within the Mexican government rather than from Washington.

4

BRAZIL

Pragmatism and the Titration
of Foreign Entry

Brazil's approach to banking-sector opening was different from that adopted by the authorities in Mexico, Indonesia, and South Korea. The Brazilian government implemented opening through a legally opaque method that allowed the government to approve the inflow of foreign capital into the banking system without actually removing a constitutional ban on foreign participation. In Brazil, de facto banking-sector opening took place without de jure opening. As a result, Brazilian policymakers enjoyed more control over the timing and extent of banking-sector opening than did decision makers in other countries. Like chemists regulating the flow of a liquid with the turn of a valve, they were able to titrate the flow of banking-sector FDI and had more freedom set the terms under which foreign capital could enter Brazilian banking.

This chapter explores the forces that pushed Brazilian policymakers to open the banking sector. The emerging narrative points clearly to a banking crisis as the key trigger of reform. In this case, the crisis broke in 1995, and its roots were domestic, not international. There was no sudden change in policymakers' ideas and no major source of external political pressure. Rather, the crisis worked by changing policymakers' priorities of political survival. The shock jeopardized the government's future by threatening its most important political asset—the economic stability brought about by the government's price-stabilization program, the Real Plan. To safeguard the economy and its political future, the Cardoso administration opened the banking sector, but it did so in as limited and discretionary a way as possible, allowing foreign entry only when domestic capital could not be found.

This chapter, like the last one, unfolds in four parts. The first provides a brief overview of the evolution of Brazil's financial structure, banking regime, and relations between the state and the banking elite. The second part examines Brazil's experiment with managed opening and the causal beliefs of key officials in the Cardoso administration. The third section covers the banking shock and its impact on banking-sector opening, and the last one focuses on the politics of de facto opening.

Brazilian Banking: Private Financiers in the Shadow of the State

The evolution of the Brazilian banking system stands in sharp contrast to the Mexican experience. In Brazil, it was the supremacy of public banks that was cemented in the early twentieth century. A robust private-banking sector would eventually emerge, but only in the shadow of enduringly dominant public financial institutions. The early history of banking in independent Brazil was dominated by two forces: the Banco do Brasil (BB) and foreign banks.[1] The Banco do Brasil was above all a deposit-taking commercial bank that functioned as Brazil's de facto central bank until the 1960s, when the Central Bank of Brazil (BACEN) was established. Taking advantage of the liberal entry rules, foreign banks established a presence in the country to finance Brazilian coffee exporters and import companies, with British commercial and merchant banks especially prominent. By 1915, foreign commercial banks accounted for 46 percent of the Brazilian banking sector's assets.[2]

Between 1900 and 1940, the Brazilian authorities took steps to limit and undercut the position of foreigners in the financial system, but these actions did not carry the strong nationalist flavor they did in Mexico and were implemented with a notable lack of zeal. The 1934 Constitution called for "the progressive nationalization of deposit-taking banks,"[3] and the Constitution of 1937 required that all foreign banks be nationalized by April 1941. Yet the deadline for nationalization was postponed until June 1946, and regulatory loopholes were opened for U.S. banks and later for Canadian and British institutions. Then, before the 1946 deadline passed, new legislation was passed allowing Brazilian banks with foreign shareholders to continue operations in the country indefinitely. References to nationalization were quietly dropped in the Constitution of 1946.

1. For informative histories of Brazilian banking, see Raymond W. Goldsmith, *Brasil, 1850–1984: Desenvolvimento financeiro sob um século de inflação* (São Paulo: Harper & Row do Brasil, 1986); Steven Topik, *The Political Economy of the Brazilian State, 1889–1930* (Austin: University of Texas Press, 1987), chap. 2; and Gail D. Triner, *Banking and Economic Development: Brazil, 1889–1930* (New York: Palgrave/United Nations, 2000).

2. Pedro Bodin de Moraes, "Foreign Banks in the Brazilian Economy in the 1980s," Department of Economics, PUC-Rio, August 1990, p. 37.

3. Sidnei Turczyn, *O sistema financeiro nacional e a regulação bancária* (São Paulo: Revista Dos Tribunais, 2005), p. 111.

Starting with the first regime of Getulio Vargas (1930–1945), Brazilian policy-makers adopted increasingly ambitious plans of state-led economic development based on import-substitution industrialization. Partly because of government regulation, Brazilian banks were lending very little: they were channeling less than 3 percent of net national savings into credit, compared with an average of 10–15 percent in the rest of Latin America.[4] In response, the government established a variety of public financial institutions in the 1950s, the biggest of which was the National Economic Development Bank (Banco Nacional de Desenvolvimento Econômico, or BNDE, later BNDES). The Brazilian state soon assumed the status of chief financier in a way the Mexican state never did. By the 1960s, Brazilian public institutions were providing between 70 and 75 percent of all financing to private enterprises and households; the comparable number in Mexico was 15 percent.[5] At the same time, the governments of many of Brazil's states established their own commercial and development banks.

After a coup in 1964, the military came to power and adopted a more discretionary approach to authorizing foreign participation in the banking sector. The new 1964 Banking Law did not explicitly proscribe foreign bank entry, but it stipulated that foreign banks could operate in the country only with approval from the central bank and the president. In practice, permission was granted in only a very few instances and under conditions of reciprocity. The law also placed tight restrictions on the ability of foreign banks already in Brazil to expand and effectively froze their branch numbers. During the late 1970s, approvals of de novo entries increased. In exchange for welcoming the BB into their home markets, eight foreign banks were allowed into Brazil.[6] However, the BACEN soon introduced a series of regulations that set hard ceilings on foreign participation, and in 1986, the authorities effectively banned all foreign holdings in domestic commercial banks.[7]

The height of banking-sector protectionism in Brazil came with the Constitution of 1988. Under Article 52 of its "Temporary Constitutional Provisions" (Disposições Constitucionais Transitórias), the establishment of foreign bank branches or subsidiaries was explicitly forbidden, as was any increase in foreign participation in foreign institutions in the Brazilian banking sector. However, the article contained an additional paragraph allowing the president to override the prohibition in the context of international agreements, under reciprocal arrangements, or when such an exception was deemed to be "in the interest of the Brazilian Government."[8] At the time the

---

4. Wendy J. Barker, "Os bancos, a indústria e o Estado no Brasil," *Revista de Economia Política* 10 (April–June 1990), 135.

5. Sylvia Maxfield, "Bankers' Alliances and Economic Policy Patterns: Evidence from Mexico and Brazil," *Comparative Political Studies* 23 (January 1991), 439.

6. Bodin de Moraes, "Foreign Banks in the Brazilian Economy," p. 40.

7. Fernando Alberto Sampaio Rocha, "Desnacionalização bancária no Brasil, 1997–2000," master's thesis, Institute of Economics, State University of Campinas, February 2002, p. 18.

8. Brazilian Constitution of 1988, Transitional Constitutional Provisions, Article 52, final paragraph.

constitution was promulgated, there were eighteen foreign banks with operations in Brazil and eleven with significant foreign investment in the financial sector.[9]

In the 1980s, the fortunes of Brazil's bankers became closely tied to the country's history of endemic inflation, which averaged 146 percent per year in 1980–1987.[10] Two price-stabilization programs failed to break the inflationary spiral, and in 1993, annual inflation reached 2,700 percent. Brazil's banks adapted very effectively to this environment. Capitalizing on the public's aversion to holding cash, banks raised large amounts of cheap funding by attracting demand deposits, tax receipts, and loan collateral, offering "free" banking services and paying little or no interest on deposits. These liabilities, plus money in transit through the payments system ("the float"), were then invested by the banks in overnight, inflation-indexed securities to generate handsome profits.[11] Over time, the banks perfected this system, and it provided them with a veritable gold mine: inflation-related revenues accounted for no less than 94 percent of the growth of the financial system in the 1980s.[12] Despite their healthy growth and profitability, Brazil's private banking groups could not match in size the country's public commercial banking institutions. By the first half of the 1990s, the two federal commercial banks and all the state-government-owned banks together controlled about half of Brazil's banking system assets, while the private commercial banks had a share of 41 percent. Foreign banks' share of assets was 8 percent.[13] How influential were Brazil's private bankers vis-à-vis the state? Compared with their Mexican counterparts, they faced substantial disadvantages in terms of structural and lobbying power. Brazilian bankers had to share the stage with giant public financial institutions, and the private banks' traditional reluctance to lend long-term in an inflationary environment meant that their contribution to national development was modest, undermining their leverage. That Brazilian private banks were poorly integrated with industrial business groups did not help.[14]

As a lobby group, Brazil's private bankers were also relatively weak. Their business associations were fragmented, with small, foreign, and state banks each forming separate industry groups. Only in 1967 was a national umbrella group established that brought together all the bankers' associations. That peak organization, the Brazilian Federation of Banking Associations (Federação Brasileira de Associações de

9. Rocha, "Desnacionalização bancária no Brasil," p. 23.

10. Based on the figures provided in Werner Baer, *The Brazilian Economy: Growth and Development* (London: Praeger, 2001), pp. 470–471.

11. For details on how this system worked, see Fernando J. Cardim de Carvalho, "Price Stability and Banking Sector Distress in Brazil after 1994," Institute of Economics, Federal University of Rio de Janeiro, Discussion Paper No. 388, March 1996.

12. "Collor Plan and Financial Sector," *Latin American Markets,* April 20, 1990.

13. Luiz Fernando de Paula, "Los determinantes del reciente ingreso de bancos extranjeros a Brasil," *Revista de la CEPAL* 79 (April 2003), 180.

14. On the low level of financial-industrial integration in Brazil, see Carlos Halsenbalg and Clovis Brigagão, "Formação do empresario financeiro no Brasil," *Dados* 8 (1971), and Barker, "Os bancos, a indústria e o Estado no Brasil," p. 135.

Bancos, or FEBRABAN), launched regular "bankers' congresses" to help its members share views and coordinate policy positions.[15] But unlike Mexican bankers, who often acted as a bridge between the government and the rest of the private sector, Brazilian bankers were regarded by the private sector with mistrust and were seen as a political liability.[16]

In addition, the private bankers had to contend with the idiosyncratic characteristics of the Brazilian party system and legislature, which do not facilitate the exercise of policy influence by interest groups.[17] In the 1990s, the private banking community invested considerable resources to cultivate political influence in the federal congress through both legal and illegal campaign contributions.[18] Along with public-works contractors, bankers were the largest contributors to legislative campaigns.[19] Yet weak party discipline, combined with a traditional perception of lobbying as an illegitimate practice in Brazilian politics, meant that FEBRABAN got little bang for its buck. When legislative action was needed on an issue of concern to the financial community, the bankers had trouble mobilizing "their" legislators because party leadership was weak and because the bankers could not lobby legislators in the halls of the congress without risking public opprobrium. "The bank lobby," FEBRABAN's director said in a 1995 interview, "cannot be seen."[20]

In contrast, Brazil's financial bureaucracy was highly centralized and relatively autonomous. Leslie Eliott Armijo observes that between the 1960s and 1980s, "most of the major financial policy innovations came from economists and other technical specialists within the central government bureaucracy. New initiatives usually were not a result of close consultation with leading industrial or financial elites."[21]

---

15. On the creation of FEBRABAN, see Ary Cesar Minella, *Banqueiros: Organização e poder político no Brasil* (Rio de Janeiro: Espaço e Tempo/ANPOCS, 1988).

16. Ben Ross Schneider interview with Paulo Guilherme Monteiro Lobato Ribeiro, president of Banco Real and FEBRABAN director, May 22, 1995.

17. See Ben Ross Schneider, "Organized Business Politics in Democratic Brazil," *Journal of Inter-american Studies and World Affairs* 39 (Winter 1997–1998), 95–127.

18. Reported political contributions amounted to R$3.6 million. Key members of the House of Representatives commission in charge of banking and financial policy issues, including its president and two vice-presidents, received campaign contributions from banks ranging from R$80,000 to R$100,000. Gustavo Patú and Marta Salomon, "Bancos aplicam R$3,6 mi no Congresso," *Folha de São Paulo,* October 8, 1995. Documents leaked in 1995 revealed that forty-two members of the congress received illegal campaign contributions from FEBRABAN for the 1990 congressional elections. The legislators included Antonio Carlos Magalhaes and José Serra, who would serve as minister of planning in President Cardoso's administration. Angus Foster, "Red Faces over a Pink Folder," *Financial Times,* December 9, 1995, p. 3.

19. During the 1994 general elections, FEBRABAN contributed to the campaigns of fifty deputies and candidates it considered worth supporting from parties on both the left and the right. Each FEBRABAN member was allocated five or six candidates and contributed R$70,000 to every candidate, for a total contribution of some R$3.5 million. Schneider interview with Paulo Guilherme Monteiro Lobato Ribeiro.

20. Schneider interview with Paulo Guilherme Monteiro Lobato Ribeiro.

21. Leslie Eliott Armijo, "Brazilian Politics and Patterns of Financial Regulation, 1945–1991," in Haggard et al., *Politics of Finance in Developing Countries,* p. 286.

To be sure, Brazil's return to democracy in 1985 weakened the executive's insulation. Interest groups and the legislature became more active participants in economic policymaking.[22] Nevertheless, both private bankers and legislators remained circumscribed by centralized and relatively insulated executive agencies. Beginning in the 1970s, the ministry of finance used the National Monetary Council, an interministerial body, to tighten its control over the central bank and other economic policymaking agencies.[23] This centralization of power under the hegemony of the finance ministry increased policy cohesiveness and coordination in the executive branch. In addition, the Brazilian executive proved very adept at exploiting constitutional loopholes and provisions that allowed the president to bypass or override the legislature. Indeed, presidential decrees would become the policy instrument of choice for the implementation of macroeconomic stabilization programs, particularly under Presidents Collor and Cardoso.[24]

Experimenting with Managed Opening (1994–1995)

Whereas Mexico's experiment with managed opening was tied to its project to liberalize North American trade, Brazil's was rooted in the need to control inflation and public spending. The banks owned by Brazil's state governments were instruments of money creation that contributed to inflation. In the mid-1990s, Brasilia decided to put an end to this source of inflationary finance by privatizing or closing the state banks, and it introduced limited banking-sector opening in the hope that foreign banks would help by participating in the privatizations. But before delving into the details of Brazil's experiment with managed opening, we must first get a sense of the beliefs and ideas that underpinned the policies of Brazil's policymakers.

Brazilian Pragmatism

From the late 1980s onward, "neoliberal" economic ideas gained currency in Brazil's political circles, particularly during the administrations of Fernando Collor (1990–1992), Itamar Franco (1992–1994), and Fernando Henrique Cardoso (1995–2002). These twelve years of liberal economic policies began with President

---

22. On the role of special interests in the drafting of the 1988 Constitution, see Gary M. Reich, "The 1988 Constitution a Decade Later: Ugly Compromises Reconsidered," *Journal of Interamerican Studies of World Affairs* 40 (Winter 1998), 5–24.

23. Maxfield, *Gatekeepers of Growth*, p. 135.

24. On the use of presidential decrees under Presidents Sarney, Collor, Franco, and Cardoso, see Timothy J. Power, "The Pen Is Mightier than the Congress: Presidential Decree Power in Brazil," in *Executive Decree Authority*, ed. John M. Carey and Matthew Soberg Shugart (Cambridge: Cambridge University Press, 1998), pp. 197–230.

Collor's bold deregulation, privatization, and trade-liberalization initiatives. Collor halved average tariffs in four years and sold off government-owned companies in strategic sectors, including mining, steel, and petrochemicals. These measures continued under the caretaker presidency of Itamar Franco, who took over after Collor's 1992 impeachment.

Cardoso, who had been finance minister under Franco, was elected president in 1994, catapulted to power by the success of the price-stabilization program implemented under his watch and by the wide appeal of his liberal economic platform. This intellectual who famously gave the world *dependencia* theory was elected on a political platform that promised a more limited role of the state in the economy. Cardoso's electoral manifesto pledged that "it will no longer correspond to the state a role as exclusive producer of goods and services, but more as corrector and neutralizer of market distortions, as well as agent to coordinate investment."[25] Cardoso's views were no aberration. By the mid-1990s, a broad swath of Brazil's political elite subscribed to these ideas, including legislators and political parties from the right, center, and even center-left.[26]

Behind Cardoso's economic program was a tightly knit group of mostly U.S.-trained academic economists drawn from the Catholic University of Rio de Janeiro (PUC-Rio).[27] These figures had been active in policymaking since the Sarney administration (1985–1990), but under Cardoso, they reached the top echelon of power. The new president appointed eminent economist and then BACEN president Pedro Malan to head the ministry of finance (the Ministério da Fazenda, or Fazenda), while Pérsio Arida, then president of the BNDES and one of the principal brains behind the Real Plan, was appointed president of the central bank. Two other members of the PUC-Rio group, Gustavo Franco and Chico Lopes, were appointed to the BACEN Board of Directors.

Cardoso and his technocrats were not unquestioning followers of economic orthodoxy. The president did not see the free market and state intervention in the economy as mutually exclusive. For him, privatization was necessary, "but one cannot make the private sector the universal salvation, because it is not," he wrote. "The market does not resolve the problem of extreme poverty. The problem of poverty has to be resolved along the lines of coordinated actions by the state."[28] Another

25. Fernando Henrique Cardoso, *Mãos à Obra, Brasil: Proposta de governo* (Brasilia, 1994), p. 73 (my translation).

26. Timothy J. Power, "Brazilian Politicians and Neoliberalism: Mapping Support for the Cardoso Reforms, 1995–1997," *Journal of Interamerican Studies and World Affairs* 40 (Winter 1998), 51–72. See also Armando Boito Jr., "Neoliberal Hegemony and Unionism in Brazil," *Latin American Perspectives* 25 (January 1998), 31–93.

27. For an informative account of the role of these technocrats in economic policymaking, see Carlos Pio, "A estabilização heterodoxa no Brasil: Idéias e redes políticas," *Revista Brasileira de Ciências Sociais* 16 (June 2001).

28. Qtd. In João Resende-Santos, "Fernando Henrique Cardoso: Social and Institutional Rebuilding in Brazil," in Domínguez, *Technopols*, p. 175.

example was the technocrats' price-stabilization initiative, the Real Plan. The plan sought to stabilize the price level through orthodox means—by controlling the money supply and bringing government accounts into balance—but it also called for a heterodox policy prescription, namely, the creation of a new currency to help coordinate inflationary expectations. Pinheiro, Bonelli, and Schneider characterize the unusual mix of economic orthodoxy and creative statism embraced by Brazilian policymakers as "pragmatic" policymaking.[29] Pragmatic policymaking focuses on the pursuit of relatively specific, measurable goals; it operates on the basis of close, simple connections between means and ends; it calls for flexible implementation to adjust to exogenous shocks or emerging problems; and it privileges gradualism, continuity, and learning from experience over the introduction of wholesale policy shifts.

The causal beliefs of the Cardoso technocrats regarding banking-sector opening were consistent with the notion of pragmatic policymaking. Brazilian policymakers were skeptical that foreign-bank entry would solve the two endemic problems of the banking system: insufficient long-term credit provision and very high interest rates. Also, like Salinas's technocrats in Mexico, the economic team was worried that banking-sector opening would weaken the state's informal control over the financial system. Cardoso's first central bank president, Pérsio Arida, explains:

> Domestic banks accept central bank control easily, but foreign banks do not...During a crisis, you don't want to control banks' lending behavior through regulation. You want to do it informally. In any central bank in the world, telephones matter. For any central bank, the capacity to force the system to behave in a certain way during a crisis is very important. You can deal with banks through regulation in normal times, but during crises you don't have time, you need informal influence. But if the banking system is controlled by foreigners, then this does not work. That was our major concern, and it was a serious concern.[30]

Despite their doubts, Brazilian decision makers were willing to consider banking-sector opening, but within narrowly defined boundaries and for very specific purposes. Unlike Mexico's President Zedillo, who believed that banking-sector opening was worth implementing to improve the long-term efficiency of the banking system apart from any more immediate benefits it might bring, the Cardoso administration was interested in openness only to the degree that it helped the government resolve concrete problems on the basis of close, simple connections between means and ends. In 1995, President Cardoso faced two such problems: controlling inflation and establishing a sustainable fiscal balance.

---

29. Armando Castelar Pinheiro et al., "Pragmatic Policy in Brazil: The Political Economy of Incomplete Market Reform," Discussion Paper No. 1035, IPEA, August 2004.

30. Interview with Pérsio Arida, Oxford, November 9, 2005.

Cardoso's Double Challenge

When the Cardoso administration took office in January 1994, its most pressing challenge was to finalize implementation of the Real Plan and ensure that inflation remained under control. The Real Plan had been a historic feat of macroeconomic policy.[31] Where numerous price-stabilization plans implemented by the Sarney and Collor governments failed, the Real Plan triumphed thanks to the innovative theory of "inertial inflation" developed by the Cardoso economic team, which helped the government diagnose the problem correctly. After nearly a decade of double-digit *monthly* inflation, inflation fell from 50.7 percent in June 1994 to less than 1 percent in September of that year; it oscillated around 3 percent the final two months of 1994.[32]

To make the victory over inflation durable, however, Cardoso's government had to secure a lasting change in inflationary expectations and to rein in government spending, and this meant restoring the public sector's fiscal balance to positive and stable levels. Medium-term public spending patterns had to be altered by reforming government institutions and removing or limiting instruments of fiscal profligacy. A central element of this strategy was the closure or privatization of at least some of the thirty-three banks belonging to Brazil's state governments. State banks had historically been a source of fiscal indiscipline, as governors would use these institutions to finance projects and reward supporters, eventually passing on the financial burden to the central government through regular bailouts.[33] Closing these banks, the technocrats argued, would help enforce fiscal discipline and strengthen the credibility of the government by signaling its commitment to fiscal responsibility.[34] This approach to the privatization of the state banks was consistent with the Cardoso administration's attitude toward privatization in other sectors of the economy, privatization driven not by ideology but by pragmatic problem solving.[35]

However, closing the state banks required overcoming powerful interests. These institutions were backed by powerful governors and local elites, who depended on them to preserve and expand their patronage networks. Attempts by Brasilia to

---

31. There is a large literature on the Real Plan. For background and analysis, see Gustavo Franco, "The Real Plan," remarks delivered at the seminar "Economics and Society in Brazil: New Trends and Perspectives," University of Chicago, November 2–3, 1995, and Werner Baer and Edmund Amann, "The Illusion of Stability: The Brazilian Economy under Cardoso," in Baer, *Brazilian Economy,* pp. 199–219.

32. Baer and Amann, "Illusion of Stability," p. 201.

33. Major bailouts of state governments by the central government took place in 1989, 1993, and 1997. For details, see Alfonso S. Bevilaqua, "State-Government Bailouts in Brazil," Discussion Paper, Department of Economics, PUC-Rio, March 2000.

34. Harry M. Makler, "Bank Transformation and Privatization in Brazil: Financial Federalism and Some Lessons about Bank Privatization," *Quarterly Review of Economics and Finance* 20 (2000), 56.

35. Werner Baer and James T. Bang, "Privatization and Equity in Brazil and Russia," *Kyklos* 55 (2002), 503.

close several state banks between 1987 and 1996 failed, largely because of political obstructionism. Particularly difficult would be closing the banks belonging to the rich state of São Paulo. São Paulo was by far the most indebted state in the country in the 1990s, accounting for over a third of all state government debt. Nearly 40 percent of São Paulo's debt was financed by borrowing from its own state banks, of which Banespa was the largest.

The Cardoso administration used all its political muscle to bring the state banks under federal control. On December 30, 1994, on the last day of the outgoing Paulista governor's term, central bank authorities declared the two largest state banks, Banespa and Banerj, insolvent and assumed administrative control of both. Banerj in Rio de Janeiro had assets of US$2 billion, and the much larger Banespa, in São Paulo, some US$24 billion.[36] Over the next two months, BACEN took over three more state banks. After "federalization," the central government offered to settle state government debts, but in exchange the state governments would have to surrender their banks, paving the way for their privatization, liquidation, or transformation into nonfinancial institutions. For Brasilia, the key objective was to ensure that state banks would behave as commercial entities, not as vehicles for financing governors' pet projects. Here banking-sector opening offered a potentially useful instrument: foreign investors could be enlisted to acquire some of the privatized state banks. Cardoso had already eliminated the legal distinction between companies owned by residents and nonresidents, abolishing the basis for discriminatory regulation against foreign-owned firms.[37] But the banking regime had to be amended as well, as the constitution prohibited any increases in foreign participation.

On March 7, 1995, Finance Minister Malan issued Exposição de Motivos 89 (EM89), a letter to President Cardoso outlining a strategy to privatize the state banks and recommending that foreign banks be allowed to participate in the process.[38] Malan's motivation was clear and specific—to maximize the prices paid for the privatized banks and thus the government's revenue from the sales:

> It is necessary to recognize...that the participation of foreign capital in this sequence is an indispensable condition for the success of the proposed privatization program insofar as it will lead to greater demand for the assets on sale, doubtlessly making possible better bids for the acquisition of shares in each auction, improving the probability that the public sector will recover the resources so far expended for the care of public financial institutions, and contributing, then, to the strengthening of the government's finances.[39]

36. "PROES: Easing State Governments Out of the Banking Industry," *Latin Finance,* September 1997.

37. For details, see David Fleischer, "The Cardoso Government's Reform Agenda: A View from the National Congress, 1995–1998," *Journal of Interamerican Studies and World Affairs* 40 (Winter 1998), 124.

38. "Exposição de Motivos" (EMs) carry no legal force on their own; they merely accompany a draft bill sent to the legislature and explain the executive's rationale for introducing the draft initiative.

39. Pedro Sampaio Malan, Exposição de Motivos No. 89, March 7, 1995 (my translation).

Malan also recommended in the letter a method for sidestepping the constitutional ban on foreign entry into the banking sector. Using a loophole provided
by Article 52 of the constitution's temporary clauses, the president could override
the constitutional ban on foreign bank entry by declaring such entry to be "in the
interest of the Brazilian government" and issuing presidential decrees authorizing
foreign acquisitions on a case-by-case basis. This way, the executive could engage in
de facto banking-sector opening without having to amend the Constitution.

Key participants confirm that the main objective of banking-sector opening at
this stage was to maximize the revenue from state-bank privatization. Paolo Zaghen,
then the BACEN's top official in charge of restructuring the state banking sector,
recalls that the central and state governments were indifferent to the issue of foreign
ownership; the main point of contention was the terms under which the state governments would surrender their banks:

> We [the central bank] had no preference whether the state banks were sold
> to foreigners or to private domestic banks. Our main goal was to increase the
> number of bidders in the process and increase the prices paid for the priva-
> tized banks. The reason there was political opposition [from the states] to
> the privatizations was not because of "foreign-versus-domestic" issues, but
> because of fears over losing control of a source of revenue and fears over lay-
> offs, because jobs would be cut by the new bank owners, whether foreign or
> domestic.[40]

The experiment in managed opening proved a disappointment. Not surprisingly, the major international banks were interested in acquiring only those Brazilian financial institutions with extensive networks, not state banks with mostly
small and regionally concentrated networks. Besides, the balance sheets of many
state banks were weak and would require considerable investment to make them
profitable. In the meantime, the BACEN was forced to inject US$300 million to
support the ailing Banespa—potentially the most attractive of the state banks on
the selling block—after two foreign banks threatened to cut their credit lines to
the embattled institution.[41] Negotiations also began with the World Bank to obtain
financing for the recapitalization of the state banks to make them more appealing
to potential buyers.

While revenue maximization was the overriding objective of managed opening as prescribed by EM89, the letter also made reference to potential efficiency
gains from banking-sector opening: "The proposal made here can be justified not
only by the active interest demonstrated by innumerable foreign groups...but also,
and most importantly, by the operational efficiency and financial capacity of these,

---

40. Interview with Paolo Zaghen, director for the Restructuring of the State Financial System,
BACEN, April 27, 2005, São Paulo.

41. Gustavo Patú, "BC utilizou reservas para socorrer Banespa," *Folha de São Paulo,* May 15, 1995,
Sec. Dinheiro, pp. 2–3.

which, certainly, will introduce more competition into the system, with substantial positive impacts on the price of services and the cost of resources offered to the Brazilian general public."[42]

This generic line was added at the end of EM89, but there is little evidence that the banking authorities believed it. With the exception of Banespa, the banks being privatized were much too small to inject real competition into the national banking system, not to mention reduce interest rates, even if the foreigners had been interested in buying them. If Brazilian policymakers had really believed in the competition-enhancing properties of foreign-bank entry, they would have also opened the private banking sector to foreign participation.

Crisis and Critical Juncture (1995)

Brasilia's experiment with managed opening was short-lived. Only a few months after EM89 was issued, systemically significant private banks began to suffer severe distress. The Cardoso government understood that a full-scale banking crisis would seriously jeopardize the success of the Real Plan and undermine political support for an administration that was elected with a mandate to bring inflation under control. The shock thus triggered a critical juncture, a period in which the government debated reform and decided that more extensive banking-sector opening was in order.

Brazil's Banking Shock

Beginning in mid-1995, Brazil experienced an episode of severe banking-sector distress, triggered by the return to price stability. With the rapid decline of inflation under the Real Plan, the banks' inflation-based profits dried up abruptly, leaving many banks with bloated cost structures. In addition, inflation had helped inefficient or fraudulent banks camouflage irregularities; price stability exposed their weak state. At first, growing demand for credit following price stabilization temporarily compensated banks for the loss of inflationary revenues, but this brief credit boom came to an end when the BACEN, in response to the Mexican financial crisis, tightened monetary policy.[43] The monetary crunch put considerable strain on the banking sector, particularly on banks that had made risky loans in the early 1990s.

---

42. Malan, Exposição de Motivos No. 89 (my translation).
43. The short-term interest rate on government bonds (Selic) was raised 20 percentage points, to 65 percent, in March 1995, and reserve requirements on sight deposits were increased from 48 to 100 percent.

Public banks were the most addicted to inflation-based revenues and were therefore the most severely affected.[44] By mid-1995, the two largest federal banks, the Banco do Brasil and the Caixa Econômica Federal, were reporting heavy losses. The BB reported losses of 143 percent of its net worth in 1994 and 160 percent in 1995—Brazil's largest commercial bank was technically bankrupt.[45] Soon major private banks began to show signs of distress as well. Three were of particular concern to the banking authorities because of their size: Banco Bamerindus, Banco Nacional, and Banco Econômico, which ranked, respectively, as the third, fourth, and sixth largest private banking groups in Brazil.[46]

In mid-1995, the condition of Econômico and Nacional deteriorated sharply. According to the financial press, the former had negative net assets of more than US$1 billion and a reserve shortfall of over US$3 billion by August 1995.[47] Given the size of these institutions, the specter of a financial collapse began to haunt Brazilian policymakers. President Cardoso was in Venezuela when he heard the news of Banco Econômico's deterioration, and thoughts of a looming banking crisis were very much on his mind during his conversations with the president of that country. Cardoso remembers that "in conversations with President Rafael Caldera, his description of the banking crisis experienced by that country the previous year made a big impression on me. The bankruptcy of one bank would unleash a formidable chain reaction."[48] A finance ministry report, looking back at the episode, was more clinical: "In August 1995, with the intervention of the Central Bank in Banco Econômico, it became clear that the adjustments already implemented by financial institutions were not sufficient to adapt the financial system structure to the new conditions of competition and stability brought about by the Real Plan."[49] On August 11, the central bank took over Banco Econômico.

On August 23, less than two weeks later, Finance Minister Malan sent President Cardoso another letter, Exposição de Motivos 311. In the document, Malan observed that the loss of inflationary revenues had undermined the banks' ability to modernize and grow, that foreign capital was already present in the financial system, and that past experience suggested that its presence had not been negative. Rather,

---

44. Inflation-based activities accounted for 67.7 percent of the value added by public-sector banks and for a more modest 19.6 percent in the case of private banks. Rocha, "Desnacionalização bancária no Brasil," p. 77.

45. Carvalho, "Price Stability and Banking Sector Distress," p. 21.

46. The troubles of these three institutions date back to unsound lending practices in the early 1990s. For details, see Carlos Eduardo Carvalho and Guiliano Contento de Oliveira, "Fragilização de grandes bancos no início do Plano Real," *Nova Economia* 12 (January–June 2002), 69–84, and Gentil Corazza, "Crise e reestruturação bancária no Brasil," *Revista Análise,* Porto Alegre, 12:2 (2001), 21–42.

47. Elizabeth McQuerry, "Managed Care for Brazil's Banks," *Federal Reserve Bank of Atlanta Economic Review* (Second Quarter, 2001), 36.

48. Fernando Henrique Cardoso, *A arte da política: A história que vivi* (Rio de Janeiro: Civilização Brasileria, 2006), p. 354 (my translation).

49. Qtd. in Rocha, "Desnacionalização bancária no Brasil," pp. 85–86.

it had helped fill a financial gap in the Brazilian economy.[50] In a paragraph repro-
duced from EM89, Malan also referred to the prospects for increased competition
and lower lending rates. Most importantly, EM311 recommended that President
Cardoso apply the same strategy of presidential decrees first proposed in EM89 to
authorize more financial sector foreign direct investment. This time, however, the
decrees would apply to institutions across the entire banking sector, not just to state
banks waiting for privatization.

Political Survival

How can we explain the decision to issue EM311? The Cardoso government understood the severity of the banking crisis and realized that if it was allowed to spread,
the shock would undermine the administration's most important political asset,
the success of the inflation-control program. "The specter of a financial crisis in
Brazil is today the major preoccupation of the economic team and constitutes a
major challenge for the government," a central bank paper observed. "The effort to
strengthen the financial system is of such importance that it could be said that its
success would also guarantee the success of the Real Plan."[51] Confronted with the
prospect of an escalating crisis, the National Monetary Council quickly came to a
consensus about what to do. BACEN president Arida saw the problem as relatively
straightforward: "We had to avoid a banking crisis, and we didn't have enough capital to absorb all the weak banks. The alternative to opening the sector was to use lots
of central bank resources, expand domestic debt, and increase the concentration of
the sector."[52] Gustavo Loyola, who took over the BACEN presidency in June 1995,
remembered the internal deliberations:

> We perceived a need for the injection of capital into the financial system, but
> we were opposed to greater state participation, and in fact we were pushing the
> process of privatizing the state banks. The alternative—to increase the share
> of public capital in the banking system—was not a real alternative. The only
> way to have new capital without increasing the fiscal costs to the central bank
> was to open the market to foreign banks.... The debate was very short and not
> very heated. We—that is, the central bank and the finance ministry—had a
> problem. We went to the president and presented the problem and suggested
> solutions. The president approved the opening almost immediately without
> any major opposition.[53]

---

50. Pedro Sampaio Malan, Exposição de Motivos No. 311, August 23, 1995.

51. Banco Central do Brasil, "O Banco Central e as novas técnicas de saneamento do sistama financeiro nacional após a estabilização monetária," 1996, qtd. in Rocha, "Desnacionalização bancária no Brasil," pp. 85–86 (my translation).

52. Interview with Pérsio Arida, São Paulo, May 31, 2005.

53. Interview with Gustavo Loyola, former BACEN president (1995–1997), São Paulo, May 5, 2005.

In contrast to the Mexican experience, President Cardoso's move toward total opening did not stumble on the roadblock of domestic politics. By invoking the constitutional loophole of Article 52, the presidency effectively cut the legislature out of the decision-making process.[54] To be sure, the executive could have opened the banking sector by legislative action. After all, the congress had been working for years on detailed financial-system regulations to be incorporated into the 1988 Constitution, including rules that would govern foreign participation into the banking sector. Planalto (as the presidential house is known) even considered going the legislative route during its experiment in managed opening. On taking office, Finance Minister Malan told the press: "We intend...when the recently elected congress meets on 15 February, to introduce some proposals for constitutional revision and these will include changes to Article 192 and the possibilities [of entry] for the foreign banks."[55]

However, Cardoso's economic team eventually rejected the legislative option as too time-consuming and politically risky, especially since the measure would be part of a larger package of financial-system reforms, including one on central-bank autonomy. Given Brazil's cumbersome constitutional amendment process, the change would have to be approved twice by a two-thirds majority in each house of the legislature, and then it would require approval by the Constitutional Court. Legal mechanics aside, the central bank feared that legislators, if given the opportunity, would meddle with the executive's proposal and introduce changes considered undesirable and even dangerous. "The government thought it [going to the congress] would be opening a Pandora's box," BACEN President Arida remembers. "It is better not to start the process if you cannot control it. Lots of very dangerous changes could have been introduced by the legislature if the government had started the process. For example, legislators from the Northeast could have pushed for the creation of a central bank for the Northeast, or demand positions on the central bank board to look after national economic development....So we left it. We were at 'equilibrium.'"[56]

The executive's use of the constitutional loophole had another advantage: it left private bankers unable to fight back. In practice, EM311 did not encounter serious

---

54. The president's reliance on unilateral executive power to authorize foreign-bank entry was not an aberration but part of a larger shift toward the assertion of executive power in economic policymaking. Indeed, Cardoso relied more than his predecessors on presidential decrees, or *medidas provisórias* (MPs), to implement much of the Real Plan, as well as to restructure fiscal relations between the federal and state governments. Between mid-1994 and mid-1995, the president issued every month an average of three times as many MPs as the congress passed laws. See Jorge Vianna Monteiro, *Economia & política: Instituções de estabilização econômica no Brasil* (São Paulo: Fundação Getulio Vargas, 1998), chap. 4, and Power, "Pen Is Mightier than the Congress."

55. "Brazil: A Winner's Bet—Pedro Malan, Brazil's New Finance Minister and the Former President of Banco Central do Brasil (Central Bank), Discusses Reform and the Financial Sector," *Banker* 245:827 (January 1, 1995).

56. Interview with Pérsio Arida, Oxford, November 9, 2005.

opposition from either political parties or private bankers, primarily because the letter itself carried no legal weight. The real political battles would be postponed until the day when the individual presidential decrees were to be issued. According to Loyola, "politicians from various parties, including the PT [Workers' Party], gave speeches against it [banking-sector opening] and argued that the government 'was giving away the market' to foreigners, but there was no major challenge against this particular measure."[57]

Brazil and the World Bank

By the late 1980s, Brazil had become one of the World Bank's most important clients, and therefore the Bank's potential impact on Brazilian banking policy is worth examining. Between 1980 and 1989, the Bank disbursed to Brazil an average of US$900 million annually, rising to US$1.1 billion between 1990 and 2001.[58] Bank lending was heavily concentrated on infrastructure- and agriculture-related projects in the 1980s but became more diversified in the 1990s, with funds channeled into primary education, health, and public-sector management. The Bank was always attentive to financial-sector reform and private-sector development, a category that represented 13 percent of total Bank commitments to Brazil in the 1980s and 9 percent in the 1990s.[59]

Compared with Mexico, where Bank staff had sympathetic interlocutors in government, in Brazil the Bank found the political environment less welcoming. There, the Bank was regarded with suspicion and sometimes outright hostility, not only by elements of civil society but also by powerful groups within the government. The Ministry of Planning, for example, was one of the Bank's most outspoken critics in the late 1980s and actively sought to undermine the Bank's position within the government.[60] At the same time, the Bank's lending in the energy sector led to high-profile clashes with environmental groups and strained relations with Brasilia.[61]

In this environment, the Bank extended a series of financial-sector loans to Brazil, but none of them directly affected the government's thinking on banking-sector opening. In 1989, the Bank offered to make a US$500 million loan to help Brazil restructure its financial system. One of the conditions demanded by the Bank for

---

57. Interview with Gustavo Loyola, São Paulo, May 5, 2005.

58. World Bank, "Brazil: Forging a Strategic Partnership for Results—An OED Evaluation of World Bank Assistance," Operations Evaluation Department, 2004, p. 6.

59. Ibid., p. 7.

60. In 1989, for example, the ministry issued a report concluding that Brazil had been paying the World Bank interest rates that were almost twice as high as prevailing market rates; it estimated Brazil's "loss" at about US$1 billion. "Brazil–World Bank Rift Widens; Ministerial Report Accuses Bank of Usury," *Latin American Weekly Report,* Finance Section, March 23, 1989, p. 7.

61. Ian Guest, "Rambo Factor Brazil: A Major World Bank Project Has Turned into a Salutary Lesson about the Pitfalls of Financing Multilateral Aid for the Environment," *Guardian,* February 2, 1990.

this loan reportedly was greater market access for foreign banks, but the loan was never extended.[62] In 1997, the Bank extended the first of four financial-sector loans to Brazil: two technical assistance loans designed to upgrade the BACEN's regulatory capacity and to strengthen the legal regime and two others to support the privatization of the state banks of Rio de Janeiro (US$250 million) and Minas Gerais (US$170 million).[63] This money would help fund, among other things, the severance packages of workers laid off after privatization. None of the projects dealt with foreign participation in the domestic banking sector, and therefore Bank conditionality was not used as a tool of external pressure.

The Bank's analytical and policy work did not devote attention to banking-sector opening either. Bank studies of the Brazilian financial sector were published in 1990 and 1993.[64] The first raised the issue of excessive banking concentration in Brazil but stopped short of advocating opening the sector to foreigners. The second focused on capital-market development. A 1994 World Bank assessment of the Brazilian private sector got closer to the issue, noting that after macroeconomic stabilization, financial-sector policy should become "a second priority area for reform."[65] Concerns about excessive concentration, extensive directed lending, the crowding out of private investment, and the weakness of the state banks were raised again, but barriers to the entry of foreign capital were not discussed.[66] In sum, the Bank does not appear to have provided the Brazilian government with specific advice on banking-sector opening in the late 1980s and mid-1990s, and it did not use policy conditionality to open banking markets.

Brazil and the IMF

Since the 1982 debt crisis, the Brazilian government's relationship with the IMF was characterized by mutual suspicion and a strong aversion to IMF programs.[67] In the early 1980s, the Figueiredo administration (1979–1985) did its utmost to deal with a balance-of-payments crisis without resorting to the IMF, opting instead to undertake its own austerity program. Even after Mexico's debt moratorium in August 1982, the Brazilian government initially resisted calling the Fund, but in the end, the authorities began an IMF Extended Fund Facility program in December 1982. The program

---

62. Armijo, "Brazilian Politics and Patterns of Financial Regulation," p. 283.

63. See World Bank, "Brazil: Central Bank Modernization Technical Assistance Project," Project Appraisal Document, World Bank Report No. 16867, October 23, 1997, and World Bank, *OED Review of Bank Assistance for Financial Sector Reform,* p. 15.

64. World Bank, "Brazil: Selected Issues of the Financial Sector," Report No. 7725-BR, March 1990, and World Bank, "The Development of Brazilian Capital Markets," Country Operations Division, Report No. 11581-BR, March 1993.

65. World Bank, "Brazil: An Assessment of the Private Sector," Report No. 11775-BR, June 24, 1994, vol. 1, p. 29.

66. Ibid., vol. 2, chap. 5.

67. This paragraph draws on Baer, *Brazilian Economy,* pp. 167–168.

went poorly; targets were missed, and its conditions became highly unpopular. In March 1985, the Brazilian government decided it had had enough and declined further programs. Under pressure from Brazil's Paris Club creditors, the Brazilians promised to "enhance contacts" with the IMF in exchange for rescheduling the country's official debt. There was no more lending, but the Brazilian authorities accepted IMF surveillance missions in mid-1987.

Relations became strained again when the Fund chose not to support the government's Real Plan in 1993–1994. IMF staff believed that the plan was destined to fail because the proposed fiscal adjustment was, in the Fund's view, insufficient.[68] Also, the Fund mistrusted the heterodox elements of the plan and was critical of the deliberate overvaluation of the real.[69] Brasilia ignored the Fund's objections and pressed on with the plan as initially drafted. When the Real Plan proved a resounding success, an IMF monitoring arrangement was launched, largely as a face-saving measure for the Fund. Under the arrangement, IMF staff would visit Brazil twice a year but on an informal basis, and staff reports to the Executive Board would be prepared only after annual Article IV consultation missions.

The environment in which Fund–Brazilian government interactions developed was simply not conducive to the exercise of policy influence by the Fund. Tainted by the Fund's rejection of the Real Plan, IMF-BACEN relations were poor. An IMF evaluation observed that in the mid-1990s there was "a lack of effective dialogue between the IMF and the Brazilian authorities, particularly those at the Central Bank."[70] According to Fund staff, "relations [with the Brazilian authorities] were satisfactory at the working level, but a lack of endorsement from senior levels inhibited the flow of information from the Central Bank, where the staff had limited direct access to sector experts."[71] IMF relations with the finance ministry intensified with the provision of technical assistance, but this would not happen until 1997, well after EM311 had been issued.

Two other factors weakened the Fund's influence in Brazil. At the Brazilian government's request, almost none of the IMF's analytical work on the Brazilian economy and financial system was released to the public, so the Fund could not marshal external support for its policy prescriptions, especially among foreign investors.[72] Second, robust global liquidity meant that Brazil had no trouble raising large amounts of financing in international markets between mid-1995 and late 1997, further weakening IMF leverage. Brazil would return to the Fund's arms in late 1998, when, buffeted

---

68. International Monetary Fund, "The IMF and Recent Capital Account Crises: Indonesia, Korea, Brazil," Independent Evaluation Office, September 12, 2003, p. 120.

69. José Roberto Mendonça de Barros et al. "Brazil and the IMF: Virtues and Limits of the 2002 Agreement," paper prepared for the Asamblea General del Club de Madrid, Madrid, November 1–2, 2003, p. 2.

70. International Monetary Fund, "The IMF and Recent Capital Account Crises," p. 128.

71. Ibid.

72. Ibid.

by Asian and Russian financial crises, the country accepted a US$41.5 billion emergency package from the IMF, the World Bank, and the U.S. government. The package was based on a three-year program with the Fund.

Yet this Fund involvement in 1998 could not have impacted Brazil's policy on banking-sector opening. The initial Letter of Intent included provisions for the banking sector, but the focus was on the privatization or closure of the state banks and the strengthening of the banking system's safety net.[73] Specific banking-sector conditions were subsequently added as structural benchmarks to the Fund program. These included the privatization of Banespa and other state banks, the formulation of a strategy for strengthening the federal public banks, the introduction of a rating system for banks, and the upgrading of financial-institution accounting standards.[74] There was no mention of the removal of barriers to foreign participation in the banking sector, other than an oblique statement that the Brazilian authorities should consider the impact of new institutions on market concentration and competition when approving new bank licenses.[75] Fund influence was further weakened when the Brazilian government, in an effort to signal to markets that fiscal adjustment was well under way, declined to draw all the resources made available to it and repaid a portion of its drawings in advance.[76]

Did Trade Negotiations Make a Difference?

In the mid-1990s, the Brazilian government was involved in two sets of trade-in-services negotiations. Brazil was party to the GATS negotiations and was also involved in regional talks with its Mercosur trade partners.[77] If the trade talks were driving banking-sector opening, we would expect to see the government making commitments at the negotiating table that were more liberal than the status quo prevailing at home.

Brazil's opening position in the GATS negotiations was issued on April 15, 1995, nearly a month after the publication of EM89 and in the middle of Brazil's period of managed opening. Yet, as shown in Appendix 2, there is no mention of foreign participation in the state bank privatization process. Brazil's offer only restated the 1988 constitutional freeze on all foreign participation in banking and declared that foreign banks would face discrimination in minimum paid-in capital and net worth

---

73. "Brazil: Letter of Intent and Memorandum of Economic Policies," November 13, 1998.

74. See Brazil letters of intent for April 20, 2000; November 3, 2000; March 14, 2001; November 30, 2001; and March 4, 2002.

75. "Brazil: Letter of Intent and Memorandum of Economic Policies," March 4, 2002.

76. Under the 1998 LOI, disbursements were scheduled for May and August 2000. However, the Brazilian government did not access them, and in April 2000, it repaid US$6.9 billion to the Fund.

77. For an overview of Brazil's involvement in negotiations on trade in financial services, see Marcos Antonio Macedo Cintra, "Negociações multilaterais e regionais sobre serviços financeiros e seu impacto doméstico," in *Abertura do sistema financeiro no Brasil nos anos 90,* ed. Maria Cristina Penido de Freitas (São Paulo: FUNDAP, 1999), pp. 174–205.

requirements.[78] Brazil's offer caught up with its domestic reality only in July 1995, when Brazil's schedule was revised, giving foreign institutions permission to acquire privatized state banks.

Subsequently, Brazilian negotiators refused to let their negotiating position catch up to existing policy, not to mention making commitments that exceeded the status quo. In October 1995, as the end of the first round of GATS negotiations neared, Brazil did not fundamentally change its July 1995 offer; it only added that any changes to its policy on foreign participation in banking would be incorporated into its GATS commitments within two years after their adoption by the congress.[79] This position was somewhat disingenuous, given that de facto entry in the banking sector, as we have seen, did not (and perhaps never would) require congressional approval, only presidential decrees.

In February 1998, after the collapse of trade-in-services talks in late 1995, the Brazilian government's position finally caught up with the policy in force since August 1995. Brazilian negotiators announced that foreign entry would be allowed, both through de novo entry and through acquisitions, subject to case-by-case authorization by the president. Applying investors would also be required to fulfill "specific conditions."[80] Foreigners buying privatized state banks would be exempt from these restrictions.

Aside from the GATS negotiations, Brazil launched talks in the mid-1980s with three of its neighbors: Argentina, Uruguay, and Paraguay. The talks resulted in the 1991 Treaty of Asunción and the 1994 Treaty of Ouro Preto, which established the foundations for a regional customs union. All these efforts focused on liberalizing trade in goods. Within the framework of the Mercosur, however, trade in services was included through the 1997 Montevideo Protocol. Banking-sector opening thus became part of the negotiations.

Early rounds of talks under the Montevideo Protocol produced very modest results, even when compared with the GATS. The principal obstacle to the opening of banking-services markets was that Brazil had few incentives to open its banking sector to its Mercosur partners, all of which had more open banking regimes. Doing so would have exposed the Brazilians to market penetration by financial institutions from other parts of the world, which could use their Mercosur-based subsidiaries as a springboard to enter the Brazilian market.[81] By 1998, Brazil had made no substantive commitments on financial services at the Mercosur negotiating table. An assessment of the trade talks concluded, "Within Mercosur, where

---

78. GATS/SC/13, April 15, 1994.
79. GATS/SC/13/Suppl. 1, July 28, 1995.
80. GATS/SC/13/Suppl. 3, February 26, 1998.
81. "Mercosur: Breaking Brazil's Banks," *Economist Intelligence Unit*, November 11, 1996.

there is no major money center, one might have expected more progress [on financial services commitments], but virtually none has been made."[82]

In conclusion, there is little evidence to suggest that trade negotiations helped propel Brazil's decision to allow foreign entry into the banking sector. The Brazilian position at the negotiations reflected, rather than shaped, its policy on foreign participation in the banking sector. As in the Mexican case, we can say that the GATS process acted as a lock-in mechanism that helped preserve a modicum of openness, but it did nothing to change the government's discretionary, case-by-case control of banking-sector opening.

The Politics of De Facto Opening (1995–2001)

The central bank's takeover of Banco Nacional and Banco Econômico in 1995 did not put an end to the country's banking troubles, so more aggressive measures were taken. The central bank was given discretionary powers to take over, manage, and liquidate any bank showing signs of distress. In addition, with assistance from the Program of Incentives for Restructuring and Strengthening the National Financial System (PROER), the banks that were taken over by the government were to be recapitalized and sold.[83] PROER credit lines were instrumental for restructuring the banks in preparation for their sale. The program was designed and implemented by the BACEN, which played the central role in resolving the banking crisis.

Because the crisis did not affect seriously the three largest domestic banks at the core of the system, those institutions became the primary source of capital to save undercapitalized banks. Unless a competitive bid from a domestic player could not be found, the government tried to transfer domestic private banks to Brazilian investors in the early phase of de facto opening.[84] The banking authorities came to see the foreign banks as "a second line of defense" from 1995 to early 1997.[85] Favoring Brazilian banks was made easier by the opacity of the sale process: while all privatized state banks were sold in open auctions, the private banks were sold through closed bids presented to the central bank. The BACEN then chose a winner based on its own criteria. This allowed the central bank considerable latitude to choose its preferred buyer.

---

82. Alfonso S. Bevilaqua and Eduardo Loyo, "Openness and Efficiency in Brazilian Banking," Discussion Paper No. 390, PUC-Rio, September 1998, p. 4.

83. For details on PROER's structure and operations, see Geraldo Maia, "Restructuring the Banking System—The Case of Brazil," BIS Policy Paper, September 1999.

84. Interview with Pérsio Arida, São Paulo, April 19, 2005.

85. Interview with Fernando Alberto Sampaio Rocha, BACEN, Brasilia, April 15, 2005.

The BACEN's "domestic-first" approach was on display during the sale of Banco Nacional. After intervention and capital injections from PROER, the central bank began to look for a buyer. Several advanced-economy banks, including Bank of Boston and Citibank, made bids for Nacional. Unibanco, one of the largest domestic private banks, expressed interest in Nacional, and the authorities pressed the bank to match the foreigners' bids. While the government had a clear preference for a national buyer, it was not prepared to accept a much inferior bid. In his memoirs, President Cardoso recalls his thinking during the Banco Nacional episode: "My position was clear: 'Even though I prefer that the buyer be a national bank, in this case, what should prevail is the best offer for the sellers and for the Treasury.'"[86] In November 1995, Banco Nacional was sold to Unibanco, a private Brazilian bank, transforming the merged entity into Brazil's largest private bank. After much searching, the government found another domestic bank, Banco Excel, to take over Banco Econômico, in March 1996. (The central bank first approached two other Brazilian banks, Bamerindus and Bradesco, but they were not interested.) Excel's acquisition had backing from Swiss investors, but management control over Econômico was in the hands of Excel.

This pattern of favoring domestic private capital when bidding prices were roughly similar remained at the center of the government's recapitalization approach for two years. Between 1995 and 1996, six private Brazilian banks were acquired by or merged with other private domestic banks. Meanwhile, the executive approved de novo entry by foreign banks in several instances, but these operations were marginal and did not significantly affect ownership patterns.[87] In short, the availability of domestic capital to recapitalize the banking system gave the government room to regulate the timing and magnitude of foreign entry into the sector. In 1997, domestic capital became less cooperative, and foreign capital came to play a more prominent role.

Selling Bamerindus

The sale of Banco Bamerindus marked a turning point in the implementation of banking-sector opening in Brazil, as this was the first time that a major Brazilian bank was sold to foreign investors. Bamerindus was one of the five largest private banks in the country, with total assets of over US$10 billion and a network of 1,200 branches. Weak after a boom of unsound lending in the early 1990s, the bank was dealt a major blow by the return to price stability and the monetary contraction that followed. Bamerindus began showing signs of severe distress in 1997, when its net worth turned negative.

---

86. Cardoso, *A arte da política,* p. 364 (my translation).

87. For a list of new foreign entrants in 1995–1998, see Maria Cristina Penido de Freitas, ed., *Abertura do sistema financeiro no Brasil nos anos 90* (São Paulo: Fundap, Fapesp, 1999), p. 116.

The owners of Banco Bamerindus—the Andrade Vieira family—were politically well connected, and the family used all its political capital to retain control of the bank. The bank's largest shareholder, Senator José Andrade Vieira from the state of Paraná, lobbied President Cardoso to save Bamerindus.[88] However, the BACEN rejected Andrade Vieira's restructuring proposal, and in March 1997, the regulators took over the bank. Having persuaded HSBC to buy a 6 percent stake in Bamerindus back in 1995, the Brazilian authorities then brokered a complex deal whereby the British bank would acquire control of Bamerindus and R$7 billion of the bank's assets.[89] Although the bank was technically bankrupt and had a negative net worth, the central bank demanded—and HSBC reportedly paid—R$380 million to acquire the "goodwill" of the Bamerindus brand, although the BACEN also provided HSBC with significant guarantees to seal the acquisition.[90]

Consistent with their "first line of defense" approach, the Brazilian authorities initially turned to Brazil's largest domestic banks, in the hope that they would acquire Bamerindus. However, they were not interested, most likely because the bank's rehabilitation was seen as too expensive and risky. Indeed, it appears that the major Brazilian bankers hoped that Bamerindus, an important rival, would "disappear."[91] The government then approached HSBC, which already had a minority stake and had been pondering acquisition. For the British bank, acquiring management control was crucial, and its executives made this clear to the Brazilian authorities.[92] According to the ministry of finance, HSBC was ultimately permitted to acquire Bamerindus "because there simply was no other institution capable of doing so."[93]

The Bamerindus acquisition caused consternation in Brazil's financial circles and the legislature, but there were no serious attempts to block the transaction. Bamerindus's president, Mauricio Schulman, was the director of the bankers' federation, FEBRABAN. When his bank was seized by the authorities and Schulman's assets were frozen, the director was forced to resign, throwing the association into a temporary leadership crisis. More importantly, the centralized, discretionary system for authorizing foreign-bank entry established by EM311 left the bankers with

---

88. "Bamerindus Solution Lies in the Hands of Malan," *Gazeta Mercantil Online,* March 6, 1997.

89. "HSBC Acquired R$7 Billion in Bamerindus Assets, Says Loyola," *Gazeta Mercantil Invest News,* June 26, 1997.

90. HSBC committed to recapitalizing the bank by making a direct investment of nearly US$930 million. As part of the transaction, HSBC received R$2.5 billion from the federal deposit insurance fund. The bank's nonperforming real estate portfolio was bought by the Caixa Econômica Federal (CEF), the Brazilian federal savings bank, with a R$2 billion credit from the PROER fund. "Bamerindus: From Liability to Asset," *Emerging Markets Debt Report,* April 7, 1997. In total, PROER injected R$5.8 billion into Bamerindus. Arthur Pereira Filho, "HSBC Bamerindus marca a nova fase," *Folha de São Paulo,* September 28, 1997. For details on the Bamerindus deal, see also Carlos A. Vidotto, "Crise, PROER e desnacionalização Bancária sob o Plano Real" (mimeo.), 2006.

91. Celso Pinto, "Mais bancos estrangeiros," *Folha de São Paulo,* August 26, 1997.

92. Richard Burns, "'We've Been Trying to Get into Brazil for a Very Long Time,'" *Latin Finance,* June 1997, p. 28.

93. Bevilaqua and Loyo, "Openness and Efficiency in Brazilian Banking," p. 8.

no access point to influence the policy process. The congress had been similarly sidelined, and from this point onward, its role would be limited to forming investigative commissions and summoning BACEN and ministry of finance officials to testify before them. However, little came of these hearings.

Growing Foreign Demand

Like the Probursa and Inverlat sales in Mexico, the Bamerindus transaction helped trigger a wave of foreign interest in Brazilian banks. As foreign appetite grew, so did the prices foreign investors were willing to pay, and the BACEN began to favor foreign acquisitions over domestic ones. HSBC's purchase of Bamerindus was followed by a rapid inflow of Iberian capital, primarily from Santander, which aggressively expanded its presence in Brazil. Santander was allowed to acquire two medium-sized banks in 1997 and then the larger, family-owned bank Bozano, Simonsen the following year. Reacting to its arch-rival's acquisitions, the Spanish BBVA bought the recently merged Excel-Econômico in 1998, and the Portuguese banks Caixa Geral de Depósitos and Banco Espírito Santo also made acquisitions that year. Indeed, so eager did foreign players become to buy into the Brazilian market that the BACEN had to issue a statement reminding everyone that the central bank had to be consulted first before deals could be closed or acquisitions announced to the public.[94] In addition, the BACEN issued a communiqué outlining the application and authorization procedures for foreign acquisitions in an effort to bring some order and transparency to what had been a largely improvised and opaque process.[95]

The increased inflow of foreign capital was partly the consequence of foreign investors' growing appetite for Brazilian assets more generally, an appetite that surged starting in the late 1990s. Between 1991 and 1995, the sale of Brazilian state assets had been slow; the total value of companies sold was US$9.3 billion, with practically none of them going to foreign investors.[96] However, sales picked up quickly in the second half of the 1990s, and the government began to demand payment in cash. In 1998 alone, the government sold US$31.9 billion worth of assets, with foreigners playing an important role in the privatization of Telebrás.[97] By 2001, the Brazilian government had collected about US$100 billion in revenue from the sales, and Brazil was being called "privatization's poster child."[98]

Growing interest in Brazilian assets strengthened the leverage of the banking authorities vis-à-vis foreign entrants when setting the terms of each acquisition.

---

94. See BACEN Communiqué No. 5,796, September 9, 1997.

95. BACEN Communiqué No. 5,798.

96. "Brazil: Privatization," *Cambridge International Forecasts Country Report,* March 1999.

97. John Barham, "Privatisation Is Succeeding Despite Awkward Episodes: Brazil," *Financial Times,* October 8, 1999, p. 9.

98. Tony Smith, "Flush from Sell-Offs, Brazil Is Privatization's Poster Child," BC cycle, Associated Press, January 16, 2001.

BACEN president Gustavo Franco, who replaced Loyola as head of the central bank in August 1997, believed strongly in maximizing the price paid by foreigners for entry into the Brazilian market. Franco introduced the practice of charging foreign entrants a *pedágio,* or "toll," for entry into the domestic banking sector. Criteria for setting the *pedágio* were theoretically based on a table approved by the central bank's directors, but in practice the amount was set informally in negotiations between BACEN and the interested foreign party. The central bank collected over R$200 million from the bank sales through the *pedágio.*[99] These mandatory "contributions" were meant to help the BACEN recover resources expended in the bank rescue, though in practice these payments did not come close to covering the total PROER resources disbursed.

In addition, BACEN officials began requiring informally that foreign banks interested in acquiring private banks also bid for state banks still waiting to be privatized. For example, the authorities demanded that BBVA, which was interested in purchasing BCN, a large private bank, also make a minimum bid for Banco Meridional, a state bank on the selling block. Similarly, ABN Amro was required to purchase Bandepe, formerly the bank of the state of Pernambuco, as a condition for its purchase of Banco Real, a large private institution.

Selling Banco Real

The next watershed in Brazil's de facto opening was the sale of Banco Real, the seventh largest private bank in Brazil, to the Dutch banking giant ABN Amro. Since 1995, banking-sector opening had been justified by the government and understood by the private sector as a necessary step to help resolve the crisis. However, Banco Real was no troubled institution: profits in 1997 reached 12.3 percent of net worth.[100]

Admittedly, the circumstances surrounding the sale were idiosyncratic. With no heirs to take over the family business and ready to retire at age 78, Banco Real's owner decided to sell his bank. The BACEN quickly stepped in to manage the sale in a closed bidding process. The Dutch bank ABN Amro and three Brazilian banks expressed interest and submitted bids. BACEN officials declared the Dutch bank the winner in a process later criticized for its lack of transparency.[101] According to the central bank, the best domestic offer did not amount to even half the foreign bank's bid.[102] ABN Amro paid around US$3 billion for Banco Real, including the

99. Gustavo H. B. Franco, "Bancos estrangeiros, bancos estaduais e o pedágio," *Boletim da Tendências,* February 16, 2000.

100. Rocha, "Desnacionalização bancária no Brasil," p. 124.

101. It should be noted that whereas all the privatized state banks were sold in open, public auctions, all Brazil's private banks were sold in rounds of secret bids coordinated by BACEN.

102. Franco, "Bancos estrangeiros."

highest single *pedágio* ever paid—R$200 million.[103] At the government's request, the Dutch bank also agreed to buy Bandepe, one of the privatized state banks, for R$183 million.

In public, the government declared that Banco Real had simply gone to the highest bidder. In private, however, BACEN officials admitted that levels of banking-sector concentration had also been a consideration. Since the beginning of the restructuring process, consolidation had led to a rapid increase in the concentration of the private banking sector. By mid-1997, when PROER ended, management control of 72 of the country's 271 banks had been transferred to another institution as a result of intervention, liquidation, merger, or acquisition.[104] As a result, the concentration index (HHI) for private-sector deposits almost doubled between the first semester of 1994 and the last semester of 1998, while the index for assets and credit operations increased by some 75 and 60 percent, respectively, during the same period, as shown in Figure 4.1.[105]

The restructuring of the banking system not only concentrated the system in the aggregate; it also led to significant expansion in the size and market shares of the three largest private institutions, Bradesco, Itaú, and Unibanco. Between 1995 and 1998, those three financial groups absorbed, directly or indirectly, many of the system's weakest institutions, often with heavy assistance from the government. In light of this trend toward high concentration, Brazilian policymakers looked favorably on a foreign entrant. According to BACEN president Loyola, "the risk of increasing the concentration of the banking system was a factor we considered. We did not want to end up in a situation where the banking system was controlled by three or four banks."[106]

The Legislature: A Reluctant Veto Player

During the period of de facto opening, the Brazilian executive retained virtually complete autonomy from the congress. Legislators made no attempt to close the Article 52 loophole that underpinned Cardoso's strategy of banking-sector opening by amending the national charter. Why was the legislature so passive? Part of the answer is that closing the loophole entailed very high political and administrative costs. The law stipulated that Article 192 of the constitution, which deals with

---

103. José Fucs, "O que significa a venda do Real," *Exame*, July 29, 1998, p. 50.

104. "Proer: A Soft Landing for Wayward Private Banks," *Latin Finance*, September 1997.

105. Concentration is generally measured by a concentration ratio, which is typically defined as the percentage of sales in the industry accounted for by the largest *n* firms. In banking, concentration is often measured by the percentage of assets, deposits, or loans accounted for by the largest *n* banks, where *n* is a small number, generally four, five, or at most ten. Concentration is also frequently measured by a Herfindahl Hirschman Index (HHI), which provides a more accurate picture of competition in a market than a simple concentration ratio. The HHI is calculated as the sum of the squares of the market shares (in percentages) of the firms in the industry.

106. Interview with Gustavo Loyola, São Paulo, May 5, 2005.

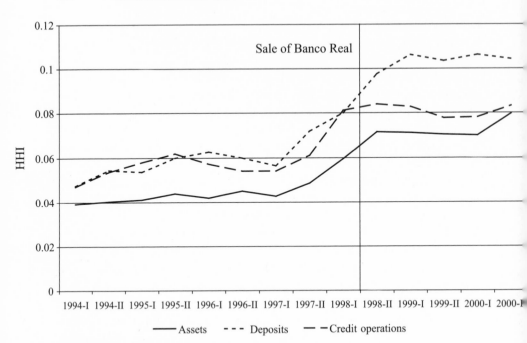

FIGURE 4.1. Banking-sector concentration in Brazil: HHI of total private banking groups in the private banking industry.
Source: Based on data in Rocha, "Evolution of Banking Concentration in Brazil (1994–2000)," Annex I.

the financial sector, could not be enacted piecemeal; the mass of complex measures had to be approved as a single package, through the same Complementary Law. This requirement imposed onerous costs on the legislators and created massive delays, as no single aspect of the financial system could be reformed until the entire constitutional article was complete. A second reason is that most key legislators with influence over financial policy favored giving the executive discretion over banking policy. Perhaps fearful of interfering with the implementation of an inflation-control plan that seemed to be working, the legislators were loath to cause financial problems for which they might later be blamed and be made to pay politically. Thus, the congress consistently deferred to the BACEN and Fazenda on financial matters.

This attitude is clearly reflected in the proposals that came out of the Brazilian congress. Legislators prepared three draft texts of regulations dealing with foreign participation in the banking sector.[107] All three granted the executive branch the exclusive power to authorize and regulate the entry of foreign banks. Two of the

---

107. For details on these drafts, see Júlio Sérgio Gomes de Almeida and Maria Cristina Penido de Freitas, "A regulamentação do sistema financeiro," IE/UNICAMP, Campinas, Discussion Paper No. 63, March 1998, pp. 36–37.

drafts set no limits on foreign participation, while a third proposed a cap of 50 percent of total system capital. None of the proposals tried to close the loophole mentioned in EM311. Of the three drafts, only one was actually put before the legislature in 1996. This proposal essentially formalized the status quo: it left intact the executive's discretionary powers over foreign-bank entry and imposed no caps on foreign participation. As of this writing, the draft had yet to make its way into the 1988 Constitution. In sum, the legislature proved both unwilling and unable to play a role as a veto player in Brazil's banking-sector opening, blunting the influence of the domestic banking community and allowing the executive to guide the process with little outside interference.

The Private Sector: Sidelined and Fragmented

Throughout the process of de facto opening from 1997 onward, Brazil's private bankers remained internally divided and unable to muster a unified position on how to deal with the opening of the banking sector. In the first half of the 1990s, FEBRABAN's members debated the matter, but no common position emerged.[108] As late as December 1997, FEBRABAN president Roberto Setúbal admitted that despite his own personal opposition to further opening, there was no consensus among FEBRABAN members. Ironically, Banco Real's director emerged as a strong advocate for limits on foreign participation, while the owners of Excel-Econômico supported unrestricted foreign-bank entry.[109] After much discussion, a majority of private bankers agreed to a proposal that looked very much like the government's position before 1988. Foreign banks should be allowed to enter the national market and enjoy the same freedom to operate as domestic banks, subject to prior permission from the president and the BACEN. Approval would be conditional on reciprocal treatment of Brazilian banks by foreign governments.

The sale of Banco Real was met with vociferous opposition from some bankers. FEBRABAN members saw the transaction as the beginning of an uncertain and potentially dangerous period in which the banking authorities seemed poised to authorize foreign entry into the sector indiscriminately. The sale's chief critic was FEBRABAN President (and CEO of Banco Itaú) Setúbal. In a high-profile public clash, Setúbal attacked the government's policy on banking-sector opening as opaque and undemocratic.[110] He also called for a public debate on the issue and warned that "excessive" opening would reduce the government's ability to control credit allocation and to induce private banks to hold government bonds. The

---

108. Schneider interview with Paulo Guilherme Monteiro Lobato Ribeiro.
109. Celso Pinto, "O risco dos bancos externos," *Folha de São Paulo,* December 21, 1997.
110. Vanessa Adachi and Ricardo Grinbaum, "Política monetaria causa temor," *Folha de São Paulo,* July 9, 1998.

president of another leading bank, Bradesco, made similar statements.[111] BACEN president Franco countered these arguments and defended the sale.[112] Aside from the public sparring, the bankers had little ability to challenge the Cardoso administration's policy. With the legislature sidelined, the domestic banking community divided, and the executive firmly holding the reins, de facto banking-sector opening continued.

Closing the Spigot

The last significant sale to date of a Brazilian bank to foreign investors involved the sale of Banespa—the public bank of the state of São Paulo—to Spain's Banco Santander. Banespa was by far the largest of the state banks. In 1995, it was the third largest banking institution in the country; with assets of US$24 billion, it was larger than any private bank.[113] After its takeover by the BACEN in December 1994, Banespa was managed by the federal government, which rehabilitated its finances and prepared it for privatization.

In its efforts to privatize Banespa, the Cardoso administration found aligned against it a powerful coalition. Representing Banespa's almost 34,000 employees, the São Paulo bank workers' union threatened to go on strike to block the privatization and to protect the jobs of its members. Paulista deputies in both the state legislature and the lower house of the federal congress were also opposed to the privatization. And naturally, São Paulo governor Mario Covas would not give up his state's bank without a fight. Covas was given three choices by the BACEN: pay off state debts and regain control of Banespa, allow the bank to be privatized, or face the outright liquidation of the state bank. Covas chose to fight for control of the bank, at one point offering a debt package that included privatizing railways and other assets to pay off state debts. Yet the Cardoso government prevailed through a mix of guile and fiscal concessions.[114] In the end, the government agreed to absorb state debt under preferential terms if the state authorities would surrender control of Banespa and agree to its privatization. The São Paulo government accepted, although the privatization of Banespa would be delayed for almost five years because of judicial challenges and complications. In 1999, President Cardoso issued a decree permitting foreign investors to bid for Banespa, and the sale was completed the following year. Spain's

---

111. Vanessa Adachi, "Brandão critica falta de transparência," *Folha de São Paulo*, July 10, 1998, Sec. Dinheiro, pp. 2–5.

112. "Franco rebate as declarações de Setúbal," *Folha de São Paulo*, July 10, 1998, Sec. Dinheiro, pp. 2–5.

113. "PROES: Easing State Governments Out of the Banking Industry."

114. For details on the political maneuvers behind the privatization of Banespa, see Christopher Garman et al., "Impactos das relações banco central x bancos estaduais no arranjo federativo pós-1994: Análise à luz do caso Banespa," *Revista de Economia Política* 1 (January–March 2001), 40–61.

Santander outbid local and foreign competitors, paying US$3.6 billion—almost three times the minimum allowable bid.[115]

To be sure, the political struggle over Banespa's privatization was chiefly about federal-state relations and public versus private ownership, rather than about foreign versus national control. Nevertheless, the sale was a significant episode in Brazil's banking-sector opening, for two reasons. First, it changed the ownership patterns at the apex of the Brazilian banking system by allowing a foreign bank to acquire and control one of the country's largest financial institutions, though one with regionally concentrated operations. As shown in Figure 4.2, the Banespa acquisition brought the total level of foreign participation in the banking system to almost 30 percent of total system assets and 25 percent of deposits.

Second, as of 2008 the sale of Banespa marked the last time a major Brazilian bank was authorized for acquisition by foreign investors, which leads one to wonder whether Brazil's highly idiosyncratic banking regime has now closed for the foreseeable future. The federal government retains a major presence in the banking sector through the Banco do Brasil and the Caixa Econômica Federal and shows no intention to privatize these institutions.[116] Interestingly, between 2000 and 2003, the level of foreign participation in the Brazilian banking system declined somewhat, as foreign banks had trouble holding their own in the market. In the period from 1995 to 2001, foreign banks were less profitable than domestic banks.[117] Some foreign banks, including BBVA, reduced their presence and sold their operations to private Brazilian bankers.

In contrast to Mexico, there was no radical change in the causal beliefs of Brazilian policymakers. Throughout the period examined here, the Cardoso administration displayed a consistent preference for a banking sector owned and controlled primarily by Brazilian nationals and for a "pragmatic" style of policymaking: banking-sector opening was used opportunistically to solve narrowly defined policy problems, namely, privatizing state banks, recapitalizing weak institutions in which Brazilian banks were unwilling to invest, raising revenue for the government, and reducing the concentration of the private banking sector. There is no evidence that external pressure was a significant factor. No IMF program was in place and there was no relevant World Bank lending or policy advice, Brazil's relations with the IMF were poor, and neither the GATS nor the Mercosur negotiations resulted in concessions that opened the sector beyond the status quo.

A change in the domestic balance of power among actors is also difficult to identify. Thanks to the structure of Brazilian political institutions, private bankers

---

115. Rocha, "Desnacionalização bancária no Brasil," p. 139.

116. According to BACEN president Arminio Fraga (1992–2003), at no time during his tenure was the privatization of the federal banks considered. Interview with Arminio Fraga, Rio de Janeiro, May 3, 2005.

117. Pedro Guimarães, "How Does Foreign Entry Affect the Domestic Banking Market? The Brazilian Case," *Latin American Business Review* 3:2 (2002).

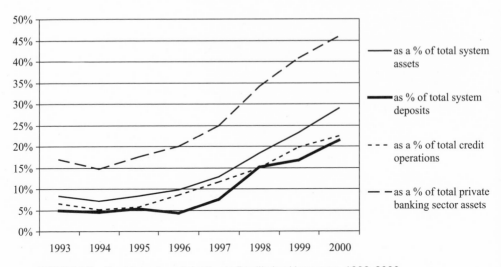

FIGURE 4.2.   Foreign-bank participation in Brazil's banking sector, 1993–2000.
Source: Fernando Alberto Sampaio Rocha, "Desnacionalização bancária no Brasil, 1997–2000," master's thesis, Institute of Economics, State University of Campinas, Brazil, 2002, p. 142.

had trouble influencing government policy before, during, and after the opening, despite their best efforts to lobby the authorities. Thanks to the government's use of the constitutional loophole and to the legislature's unwillingness to challenge executive prerogatives, the opening process was closely controlled by a finance ministry and a central bank that sought limited and discretionary de facto opening, so the process can hardly be characterized as a struggle between protectionist and liberalizing forces. There was no real de jure opening, only de facto liberalization.

In Brazil, banking-sector opening is best explained as a product of a banking crisis, this time an internally induced one. The banking shock was the trigger, and in this case, it operated by changing the government's priorities of political survival. Fearful that if left unchecked the banking crisis would destroy the achievements of the Real Plan and undermine the economic gains on which the Cardoso government had staked its political future, the government turned to banking-sector opening as a safety valve to rescue the banking sector and protect its political fortunes. In the end, the gamble paid off. The banking system was stabilized, the gains of the Real Plan survived, and Cardoso was reelected in 1998 by a margin of 22 percent over his opponent, labor leader Luíz Inácio Lula da Silva.

5

INDONESIA

External Pressure and Ethnic Politics

At first glance, the many similarities between Indonesia and Mexico would suggest that the drivers and process of banking-sector opening were similar in both countries. In the early 1990s, both countries had stable, corporatist, "soft authoritarian" regimes. A single party had a monopoly on power, political repression was rare but targeted, and a degree of consent from the electorate was purchased with robust, if uneven, economic growth. In both countries, economic and financial policy was in the hands of U.S.-educated technocrats with strong orthodox leanings, a deep faith in integration with the global economy, and robust relationships with the Bretton Woods institutions. For different reasons, both countries had politically weak cadres of private bankers. And in the 1990s, both suffered severe capital account and banking crises, resorted to large IMF assistance packages, and opened their banking sectors fully after the crisis. In both countries, the legislature played an active role.

This chapter shows that a banking crisis was the key trigger of banking-sector opening in Indonesia. But while external pressure undercut the opening process in Mexico, in Indonesia it was crucial for keeping the reform moving forward, especially after the champions of opening within the government were sidelined. Also, the chapter argues that the crisis changed the president's priorities of political survival, leading him to embrace banking-sector opening despite—not because of—his ideas and beliefs.

Mirroring the previous chapters, this one begins by surveying the history of banking-sector protectionism in Indonesia, as well as the nature of the relationship between bankers and the state. The second section describes Indonesia's experiment in managed opening, which lasted from 1988 to the eve of the Asian financial crisis, in 1996. Then, from 1997 to 1999, the country suffered a severe banking shock, triggering a critical juncture during which the rules of entry into the banking sector were revised. These events are covered in the third section. Finally, the last segment covers the period from 1999 to 2005, during which the politically charged process of implementing the new banking rules unfolded.

Indonesian Banking: State Supremacy and Ethnic Politics

The Indonesian state has historically played a dominant role as chief banker, but unlike its Brazilian counterpart, it did little to promote the development of private banks until very late in the twentieth century. Therefore, for most of Indonesia's post-independence history, no robust class of private bankers emerged; there was no marriage of finance and industry, and no alliance between financiers and bureaucrats. The result was a highly asymmetric structure with large public institutions on one hand and fast-growing but politically weak private banks on the other. This was the defining characteristic of the Indonesian banking system until the 1990s.

Indonesia inherited from the Dutch colonial government a financial system dominated by foreign institutions and designed primarily to support international trade and colonial exploitation.[1] On securing its independence from the Netherlands in 1949, the government of General Sukarno (1949–1966) set about transforming the colonial financial system into one more suitable to the needs of the new republic. In 1951, the Dutch-owned Bank of Java was nationalized, renamed Bank Indonesia (BI), and designated the country's central bank.[2] Several public commercial and development banks were also created to provide credit to specific sectors. Together the state banks and the seven foreign banks still operating in Indonesia dominated the formal financial system throughout the 1950s. In 1958, all Dutch assets and companies, including the three remaining Dutch banks, were nationalized.[3]

---

1. For informative histories of the Indonesian banking system from independence to the late 1950s, see Harold K. Charlesworth, *The Banking System in Transition* (Jakarta: New Nusantara Publishing Co., 1959); Douglas S. Paauw, *Financing Economic Development* (Glencoe, Ill.: Free Press, 1960); Michael T. Skully, "Commercial Banking in Indonesia: An Examination of Its Development and Present Structure," *Asian Survey* 22 (September 1982), 874–893; and Benjamin H. Higgins and William C. Hollinger, "Central Banking in Indonesia," in *Central Banking in South and East Asia*, ed. S. G. Davies (Hong Kong: Hong Kong University Press, 1960).

2. For a historical account of Bank Indonesia, see Ali Wardhana, "The Indonesian Banking System: The Central Bank," in *The Economy of Indonesia: Selected Readings*, ed. Bruce Glassburner (Ithaca: Cornell University Press, 1971), pp. 338–358.

3. For details on the nationalization, see Richard Robison, *Indonesia: The Rise of Capital* (Sydney: Allen & Unwin, 1986), p. 72.

After nationalization, the Sukarno government decided to keep the banks under state control because the indigenous entrepreneurial class was seen by the military regime as too weak to undertake the strategic role of financial intermediation. Also, the government was not keen on turning over the banks to members of Indonesia's ethnic Chinese minority. This minority—which numbered some 2.5 million people in the late 1960s, 30 percent of whom held Indonesian citizenship—has long been seen with suspicion by the *pribumi*, or "indigenous Indonesian" majority. The main source of tension, resentment, and occasional violence between the groups was (and remains) the ethnic Chinese minority's disproportionately large role in Indonesian industry, trade, and finance.[4] Under Sukarno, businesses owned by the ethnic Chinese minority were allowed to flourish, within bounds, for the sake of national development. In the 1950s, new domestic private banks, established mostly by these Chinese-Indonesian business groups, proliferated rapidly, though most of them were very small and did not engage in significant banking activity.[5]

In 1966, amid economic chaos, President Sukarno was toppled in a military coup that inaugurated the thirty-two-year rule of General Suharto (1966–1998), a period commonly known as the New Order. Suharto's government moved quickly to control inflation, secured new arrangements with Indonesia's creditors, and restored macroeconomic stability. To build a banking system that could support state-led industrial development, Suharto's economic team, led by a team of U.S.-trained technocrats, restructured the financial system.[6] Credit allocation remained firmly in government hands, and public banks continued to be the preferred financial pipeline. Private domestic banks and foreign financial institutions were denied access to central bank resources, stunting their development. The result of these policies was the extraordinary growth of the public banking sector in both absolute and relative terms.[7]

To promote competition, Indonesia allowed foreign banks to enter the country in the late 1960s, but they were subject to onerous restrictions. Established foreign banks could expand through new branches, and new foreign entrants could establish operations through joint ventures. However, foreign banks could not offer savings deposits, open more than two branches, or lend outside Jakarta. After an outbreak of violence with a strong antiforeign flavor in early 1974, the Suharto government

---

4. See, for example, Yuan-li Wu and Chun-hsi Wu, *Economic Development in Southeast Asia: The Chinese Dimension* (Stanford, Calif.: Hoover Institution Press, 1980), and Leo Suryadinata, *Pribumi Indonesians, the Chinese Minority and China* (Singapore: Heinemann Asia, 1992).

5. Heinz Arndt, "Banking in Hyperinflation," *Bulletin of Indonesian Economic Studies* 5 (October 1966), 47.

6. For details on the reform, see J. Panglaykim and D. H. Penny, "The New Banking Laws," *Bulletin of Indonesian Economic Studies* (February 1968), 75–77.

7. Andrew Rosser, *The Politics of Economic Liberalization in Indonesia* (Richmond, U.K.: Curzon Press, 2002), p. 55.

retreated from its liberal position, imposing controls on foreign investment.[8] All foreign investment projects, including those in banking, had to be in the form of joint
ventures with indigenous Indonesian partners, and the foreign party had to transfer
majority control to the Indonesian partner within ten years. In banking, the ownership provision was a moot point, because even before the riots, the government
had simply stopped issuing licenses for joint-venture banks and new foreign-bank
branches.[9]

The end of the oil boom triggered two fiscal crises in Indonesia, one in 1983 and
another in 1986. To mobilize domestic sources of finance, the Suharto government
began dismantling the "repressed" financial system in two waves of reform, one
in 1983 and another in 1988–1989.[10] The October 1988 financial reform package,
known as the PAKTO, was designed to increase competition by reducing barriers to
entry—both foreign and domestic—in the banking system. By the end of the reform
period, Indonesia had one of the most deregulated banking systems in the developing world, although barriers to foreign participation remained high. The reforms
led to the explosive growth in banking system assets, which expanded by 26 percent
per year from 1988 to 1990.[11] By the early 1990s, the total assets of private banks
equaled those of public banks for the first time in the country's post-independence
history.[12]

In the emerging financial structure, private commercial banks were embedded within a structure of large, diversified conglomerates, similar in some respects
to Mexico's *grupos*. Indonesian business groups consisted of closely held (usually
family-owned) holding companies under which were grouped dozens, sometimes
hundreds, of related companies, including major banks. Most of the conglomerates
were owned and controlled by ethnic Chinese Indonesians; the few leading *pribumi*
conglomerates were usually linked to members of the first family or the president's
closest associates. Most of the top conglomerates had their own banks, and many

---

8. Robison, *Indonesia*, p. 167.

9. Clyde Mitchell, "The New Indonesian Bill," *New York Law Journal*, March 25, 1992, p. 3.

10. A large literature exists on the deregulation of Indonesia's banking system in the 1980s. For details
on the substance and motivations of the 1983 and 1988 reforms, see Ali Wardhana, "Financial Reform:
Achievements, Problems, and Prospects," in Ross McLeod, *Indonesia Assessment 1994: Finance as a Key
Sector in Indonesia's Development* (Singapore: ISEAS, 1994), pp. 79–93; David C. Cole and Betty F. Slade,
Building a Modern Financial System (Cambridge: Cambridge University Press, 1996), chap. 5; Binhadi,
Financial Sector Deregulation, Banking Development, and Monetary Policy (Jakarta: Institut Bankir Indo-
nesia, 1995); and Radius Prawiro, *Pergulatan Indonesia Membangun Ekonomi: Pragmatisme Dalam Aksi*
(Jakarta: PT Elex Media Komputindo, 1998), chap. 8.

11. John Bresnan, *Managing Indonesia: The Modern Political Economy* (New York: Columbia University Press, 1993), p. 265.

12. Government-owned bank deposits fell from 75 percent of total system deposits in the early 1980s
to less than 50 percent in 1990, while domestic private banks increased their share of deposits from less
than 10 percent in 1972 to close to 50 percent in 1990. Hal Hill, *The Indonesian Economy* (Cambridge:
Cambridge University Press, 2000), p. 192.

had more than one bank.[13] By the 1990s, conglomerate-controlled banks represented the largest segment of the banking system.

Politically, private bankers in Indonesia were a feeble group, especially when compared with their counterparts in Mexico and Brazil. Indonesian private banks did not control a sufficiently large portion of credit flows to exercise significant structural power, and when they finally came to hold a majority of system's assets in the 1990s, their dominant position did not last long. In addition, the banking community was fragmented, with domestic private banks, government-owned banks, and foreign banks each having separate business associations. Third, and most importantly, Indonesia's biggest bank owners were constrained by ethnic sensitivities. Perceptions that Chinese-Indonesian bankers collectively were lobbying the government would have been greeted with an explosive, anti-Chinese backlash, a situation both bankers and politicians were careful to avoid. Instead, lobbying was conducted privately, discreetly, on a one-on-one basis. If in Brasilia the bankers' lobby could not be seen, in Jakarta it could be neither seen nor heard.

Yet Indonesian bank owners, *as individuals,* could exercise significant influence. After all, the owners of Indonesia's largest private banks also headed large, diversified conglomerates, many of which had flourished with the support of—and often in partnership with—the first family or President Suharto himself. They enjoyed access to the upper echelons of government through their personal relationships with the president and members of his inner circle. This kind of lobbying was very effective at securing narrowly customized benefits, such as special treatment (or nontreatment) from bank regulators or preferential credit from state banks.[14] But by its very nature, this system effectively precluded bankers from organizing politically around their collective interests; they could secure special favors but not demand broad changes in economic or financial policy. Thus, when it came to "architectural" financial-sector reforms and monetary policy, Suharto's technocrats enjoyed a high level of autonomy from business interests, including bankers.[15] In short, the Indonesian state in the last two decades of Suharto's rule displayed the paradoxical combination of technocratic insulation in high-level policy formulation but permeability to particularistic business interests in policy implementation.

---

13. Of the top thirty-five business groups, twenty-eight of them had one or more banks. Yuri Sato, "Post-Crisis Economic Reform in Indonesia: Policy for Intervening in Ownership in Historical Perspective," IDE Research Paper No. 4, Institute for Developing Economies (IDE-JETRO), September 2003, p. 42.

14. For an assessment of the Indonesian central bank's autonomy, see Natasha Hamilton-Hart, *Asian States, Asian Bankers: Central Banking in Southeast Asia* (Ithaca: Cornell University Press, 2002), chap. 3. Examples of regulatory forbearance by bank regulators have been well documented. See, for example, Richard Robison and Vedi R. Hadiz, *Reorganising Power in Indonesia: The Politics of Oligarchy in an Age of Markets* (London: Routledge-Curzon, 2005), and Adam Schwarz, *A Nation in Waiting: Indonesia's Search for Stability* (Boulder, Colo.: Westview Press, 2000).

15. Andrew J. MacIntyre, "The Politics of Finance in Indonesia: Command, Confusion, and Competition," in Haggard et al., *Politics of Finance in Developing Countries,* p. 148.

Experimenting with Managed Opening (1988–1996)

Indonesia's experiment in managed opening began in 1988 with the PAKTO reforms. Under the PAKTO, foreign banks could participate in the Indonesian banking market, but only in partnership with Indonesian investors.[16] Joint ventures were designed to make banking-sector opening more politically palatable to the public and to nationalist groups, as well as to facilitate the transfer of knowledge, skills, and technology to the local partners.[17] Although joint-venture banks faced a variety of restrictions and regulatory requirements, foreign investors reacted enthusiastically.[18] By 1992, eighteen new joint-venture banks had been established.[19] That year, the government took a decisive step by reforming the Banking Act, permitting foreigners to own minority stakes in domestic banks—both public *and* private—that were listed in the Jakarta Stock Exchange, subject to certain caps.[20] The 1992 law also expanded the number of cities in which joint-venture banks could open branches outside Jakarta from six to eight. Why did Indonesian policymakers decide to crack open the doors into the commercial banking sector?

The Dynamics of Technocratic Influence

The politics of economic policy in pre-1998 Indonesia are best understood as a struggle among three groups fighting to influence President Suharto.[21] The first group was composed of academic economists-turned-policymakers, the "technocrats,"

---

16. The foreign partner could own up to 85 percent of the joint venture's shares, while the local partner had to control at least 15 percent.

17. Interview with Adrianus Mooy, governor, Bank Indonesia (1988–1993), Jakarta, April 5, 2006.

18. Minimum paid-up capital for joint-venture banks was set at Rp50 billion, but at only Rp10 billion for domestic commercial banks. Joint-venture banks were authorized to open branches only in six cities and Jakarta, and after a year in operation, they had to be lending at least half of their total portfolio as working capital and investment credits to export-oriented companies. After 1989, joint venture banks, along with foreign and domestic private banks, also had to allocate a minimum of 80 percent of their credit in foreign currency to borrowers in non-oil-export industries. For details, see Binhadi, *Financial Sector Deregulation*, pp. 70–71.

19. Mitchell, "New Indonesian Bill."

20. Act of the Republic of Indonesia No. 7 of 1992 Concerning Banking. On the details of the legislation, see Ross H. McLeod, "Indonesia's New Banking Law," *Bulletin of Indonesian Economic Studies* 28 (December 1992), 107–122. In 1992, listed banks included ten private institutions, all among the largest: Panin Bank, Bank Surya, Bank Niaga, Bank Internasional Indonesia, Lippo Bank, Bank Danamon, Bank Bali, Tamara Bank, Bank Dagang Negara Indonesia, and Bank Duta. In late 1992, bank shares listed in the Jakarta Stock Exchange comprised some 11 percent of total market capitalization. Suhaini Aznam, "Banks for All Buyers: Indonesia Opens Up Important Stock Sector," *Far Eastern Economic Review* 155 (November 19, 1992), 74.

21. For descriptions of the policymaking process under Suharto, see Bresnan, *Managing Indonesia;* Robison, *Indonesia;* Schwarz, *Nation in Waiting;* Andrew J. MacIntyre, "Politics and the Reorientation of Economic Policy in Indonesia," in *The Dynamics of Economic Policy Reform in South-East Asia and the South-West Pacific,* ed. Andrew J. MacIntyre and Kanishka Jayasuriya (Oxford: Oxford University Press,

who favored a liberal, market-oriented economy.[22] Like their counterparts in Mexico and Brazil, these were academic economists educated primarily in the United States and associated with a prestigious national university, in this case, the University of Indonesia (UI). Plucked from academia by Suharto in the mid-1960s to help control inflation, these professors sat atop the key economic ministries for most of his thirty-two-year rule and were the government's primary interface with the international financial institutions.

The second and more heterogeneous group usually falls under the rubric of "nationalists" or "technologists." Including cabinet members from key spending ministries and some senior military officers, this group generally favored an activist role for the state in protecting industry and allocating capital, usually to support indigenous (*pribumi*) entrepreneurs. The third group, which became especially prominent in the 1990s, was composed of "cronies." Unlike the other two categories, cronies generally had no government positions. They were large business entrepreneurs with close ties to the president and to members of Suharto's family and associates. The members of this group sought government favors to strengthen and expand their business empires, and they were willing to let cooperative officials share in the profits.

Although formally in charge of economic policymaking and ensconced in the top echelons of government, the technocrats' influence depended on the vicissitudes of the economy. The technocrats were few and had no political base of support inside or outside government. Apart from their highly trained brains, their only source of political power was their relationship with the international financial institutions and their purported ability to speak to "the markets" on the government's behalf. The president valued the technocrats primarily as expert crisis managers and economic fixers, which meant that their clout peaked during times of economic turmoil.

But during times of relative stability and prosperity, nationalist and crony interests tended to dominate policy, and all the technocrats could do was to try to curb some of these groups' worst excesses. Acutely conscious of their fluctuating influence, the technocrats became keenly attuned to crisis-induced windows of opportunity, and they worked hard to capitalize on these politically auspicious moments.[23]

1992); and Jeffrey A. Winters, *Power in Motion: Capital Mobility and the Indonesian State* (Ithaca: Cornell University Press, 1996).

22. For a clear exposition of the technocrats' economic philosophy, see Ali Wardhana, "Structural Adjustment in Indonesia: Export and the 'High Cost' Economy," keynote address at the 24th Conference of Southeast Asian Central Bank Governors, Bangkok, January 25, 1989; reprinted in *Indonesian Quarterly* 17 (3rd quarter, 1989), 207–217. On the role of the technocrats, see Takashi Shiraishi, "Technocracy in Indonesia: A Preliminary Analysis," RIETI Discussion Paper Series 05-E-008, March 2006.

23. Winters, for example, has argued that the technocrats were sophisticated political operators whose status was so dependent on crisis conditions that they may even have deliberately promoted or exacerbated crises to enhance their own power. See Jeffrey A. Winters, "The Politics of Created Crisis: Indonesian Banking Reform in the 1980s" (mimeo.), Northwestern University, June 10, 1996.

Fortunately for the technocrats, Suharto was a pragmatic man, a leader not wedded to ideology and open to policy experimentation.

Suharto's technocrats had long favored deregulation and liberalization as a way of checking nationalist and crony excesses and reducing distortions in what they referred to as "the high-cost economy." The clearest exposition of the technocrats' world view comes from Ali Wardhana, longtime finance minister and chief architect of Indonesia's banking reforms. According to him, Indonesia could not rely on oil for all of its foreign exchange because of its price volatility; non-oil exports therefore had to be promoted. Export promotion, in turn, required liberalization, deregulation, and greater reliance on competitive markets.[24]

The technocrats' beliefs about the banking system were a natural extension of this line of thinking. For them, the state's monopoly on banking had generated large distortions, creating inefficiency and slowing economic development. Leading technocrats therefore began to call for deregulation and an end to government-directed credit very early in the Suharto era. First-generation technocrat Mohammad Sadli recommended in 1967 that "banks should be able to attract large savings deposits from the public...and implement active and selective credit policies. [The practice of] making available large amounts of credit because of political considerations should be reduced, or, better still, eliminated completely."[25]

Privatization by Other Means

The technocrats' drive to reduce—and ultimately eliminate—the state's monopoly on banking was based on more than abstract economic theory; it was also a response to pressing concerns about the impact of the public banks on government accounts. In 1978, the government-owned Bank Bumi Daya reported that one-third of its loans (US$948 million at the time) were either overdue or uncollectible, even though it had already written off nearly US$200 million in bad debts.[26] Another public bank, Bank Rakyat Indonesia, reported in 1980 that because of government lending requirements, it was facing massive credit backlogs.[27] All these losses had to be covered by the state.

The technocrats wanted to reduce the government's role as chief banker, but they understood that privatization of state banks was politically unfeasible.[28] An

24. Wardhana, "Structural Adjustment in Indonesia," p. 208.

25. Mohammad Sadli, "Commemorating the Economic Policies of 3 October 1966," in *The Politics of Economic Development in Indonesia: Contending Perspectives,* ed. Ian Chalmers and Vedi R. Hadiz (London: Routledge, 1997), p. 53. See also Radius Prawiro, "Back to the Wisdom of the Market Economy," in Chalmers and Hadiz, *Politics of Economic Development,* p. 148.

26. Robison, *Indonesia,* p. 225.

27. Ibid.

28. When the technocrats recommended to President Suharto in the early 1980s that the state banks be privatized by "going public" through an initial offering in the stock market, he reportedly replied: "What

alternative path was to "privatize" the banking system indirectly, by promoting the growth of private banks and letting them compete away the government-owned banks' market share. Banking-sector opening became a promising instrument in this task: "The goal of the PAKTO was to contain the growth and size of the state banks by getting the domestic private banks to grow," remembers the IMF's resident representative in Indonesia in late 1980s. "We called it the '*de facto* privatization' of the banking sector."[29] Ali Wardhana himself corroborates this view:

> The problem is that there were only two private banks of any importance, and there was a very nationalistic attitude that state banks were better than private banks. In fact, the idea of private banks was taboo....With the 1992 reform, we hoped to see more foreign investment in the private banks, not so much in the state banks. Those, we preferred to merge. The idea was to make the private banks stronger....I just wanted to get rid of the state banks.[30]

Unlike Mexico's technocrats, who had very clear ideas about how far they wanted to open the sector during the NAFTA negotiations, Indonesian policymakers had no preconceived views, favoring instead a flexible approach. Indeed, the initial draft of the 1992 Banking Act sent by the government to the legislature would have given the government full discretion to determine the permitted level of equity ownership by foreigners, and it said nothing specific about ownership ceilings in state banks. The technocrats were aiming for open-ended liberalization, but the legislature soon imposed caps on banking-sector opening. The new banking law had to be approved by the House of Representatives (DPR), starting with the chamber's sixty-five-member Commission VIII for Finance, State Budget, and Science and Technology. When the draft legislation came to DPR in June 1991, the issue of foreign owner-ship immediately became controversial, with legislators insisting on hard ceilings on foreign equity ownership. A compromise was eventually reached whereby foreigners could own up to 49 percent of the shares of a domestic private bank and up to 24.5 percent of a state bank.

The Role of Foreign Advisers

Like their Mexican counterparts, whose ideas about managed opening were influ-enced by Canadian and British thinking, the Indonesian technocrats also drew on foreign expertise. Two groups of experts were actively advising the Indonesian government on banking reform. The World Bank's advice focused most heavily on reducing the state's presence and intervention in the banking sector. In a 1981 report

do you mean 'go public'? These banks are already public!" Interview with Adrianus Mooy (BI governor, 1988–1993), Jakarta, April 5, 2006.

29. Interview with Lloyd Kenward, IMF resident representative in Indonesia (1987–1989) and senior economist, World Bank Indonesia office (1994–1998), Jakarta, March 22, 2006.

30. Interview with Ali Wardhana, Jakarta, April 11, 2006.

on Indonesia, the Bank called for the removal of fixed ceilings and preferences in credit policy and an end to preferential credit for *pribumi* investors.[31] The technocrats also had their own foreign advisers, drawn mostly from the Harvard Institute for International Development (HIID). These were intimately involved in the preparation of all the major banking reforms, including the PAKTO and the 1992 measures.[32]

Like Mexican and Brazilian finance officials during their own periods of managed opening, the Indonesians did not blindly follow the advice of the Bretton Woods institutions. Rather than guide the Indonesians on policy design, IMF and World Bank staff in Jakarta served as "intellectual sparring partners" for the technocrats, allowing the Indonesian officials to test and refine their own policy ideas.[33] The Indonesian officials thus developed their own thinking on financial policy, set their own agenda, and implemented it at their own pace. They ignored IMF advice not to open the capital account before liberalizing trade and engaged in more extensive banking-sector deregulation than the Fund had recommended.[34] In addition, the technocrats relied more heavily on their HIID consultants, who sat in the finance ministry and were paid directly out of the ministry's budget, than on the World Bank's staff. Looking back on that period, a member of the World Bank's staff in Indonesia working on banking-sector reform said that "the Bank did not have nearly as much leverage as it thought it did, or as much commitment from the regulator [Bank Indonesia] as it imagined. They had commitment from the ministry of finance, but not from the regulator or from the top leadership."[35]

Though it marked an important shift in policy, Indonesia's experiment with managed opening produced only small changes in the structure of the banking sector. The foreign and joint-venture banks focused their lending on a narrow segment of Indonesian top-tier corporations and foreign multinationals, resulting in intense competition within this part of the market. Meanwhile, domestic banks, rather than compete directly against the foreign entrants, moved to the "middle market" of second-tier corporations, small and medium-sized enterprises, and individuals. They also began to focus more on retail banking. But despite increased competition, net-interest and operating margins did not show a clear declining trend.[36]

---

31. World Bank Report on Indonesia, 1981, qtd. in Robison, *Indonesia*, p. 380.

32. For a historical context of HIID's advisory role in Indonesia, see Joseph J. Stern, "Indonesia–Harvard University: Lessons from a Long-Term Technical Assistance Project," *Bulletin of Indonesian Economic Studies* 36 (December 2000), 113–125.

33. Interview with Ali Wardhana, Jakarta, April 11, 2006.

34. Cole and Slade, *Building a Modern Financial System*, p. 101.

35. Interview with Lloyd Kenward, Jakarta, March 22, 2006.

36. Mari Pangetsu, "The Indonesian Bank Crisis and Restructuring: Lessons and Implications for Other Developing Countries," G24 Discussion Paper No. 23, UNCTAD, November 2003, p. 7.

Crisis and Critical Juncture (1997–1999)

This period of managed opening came to an end with the Asian financial crisis. The twin crisis was particularly traumatic for Indonesia, which suffered the largest economic contraction and the most severe currency depreciation in the region. The economic collapse then sparked social violence, led to President Suharto's resignation, and ushered in a new and uncertain period in Indonesian politics. At the center of the conflagration was a banking crisis, one whose resolution would prove to be among the costliest in history.[37] As in Mexico and Brazil, the banking crisis created a critical juncture that led to a rapid de jure opening of the banking sector on an unprecedented scale.

Indonesia's Banking Shock

The causes and consequences of the Asian financial crisis in Indonesia are the subject of a large literature.[38] Here I highlight only the aspects of the crisis that are most relevant to the collapse and restructuring of the banking system. Indonesia's banking sector suffered from three kinds of vulnerabilities.[39] The banks and especially their corporate clients held large amounts of unhedged, foreign-currency-denominated liabilities, exposing them to sudden shifts in the exchange rate. In addition, because many of Indonesia's largest private banks were owned by industrial conglomerates, the banks lent extensively to related parties (usually firms within their own group), often in violation of legal lending limits and without adequate risk evaluation. This exposed the financial institutions to massive credit risk.[40] Finally, Bank Indonesia's

---

37. Even after the sale of bank assets taken over by the government as part of the rescue program, the Indonesian government lost an estimated Rp520trillion, or US$60 billion, in the program. This amounts to over 40 percent of GDP in 1999. Ross H. McLeod, "Lessons from Crisis Management," *Jakarta Post,* March 18, 2004.

38. On the crisis in Indonesia, see J. Soedradjad Djiwandono, *Bank Indonesia and the Crisis* (Singapore: ISEAS, 2005); Lloyd R. Kenward, *From the Trenches: The First Year of Indonesia's Financial Crisis of 1997/98 as Seen from the World Bank's Office in Jakarta* (Jakarta: Center for Strategic and International Studies, 2002); Jeffrey A. Winters, "The Determinants of Crisis in Southeast Asia," in *The Politics of the Asian Economic Crisis,* ed. T. J. Pempel (Ithaca: Cornell University Press, 1999); and Jonathan Pincus and Rizal Ramli, "Indonesia: From Showcase to Basket Case," *Cambridge Journal of Economics* 22 (1998), 723–734.

39. For useful analyses of Indonesia's banking crisis, see Charles Enoch et al., "Indonesia: Anatomy of a Banking Crisis: Two Years of Living Dangerously, 1997–99," IMF Working Paper WP/01/52, May 2001; Charles Enoch et al., "Indonesia's Banking Crisis: What Happened and What Did We Learn?" *Bulletin of Indonesian Economic Studies* 39 (April 2003), 75–92; and Ross H. McLeod, "Dealing with Bank System Failure: Indonesia, 1997–2003," *Bulletin of Indonesian Economic Studies* 40 (April 2004), 95–116. For participants' accounts, see I Putu Gede Ary Suta and Soebowo Musa, *Membedah Krisis Perbankan* (Jakarta: Yayasan Sad Satria Bhakti, 2003), and Kenward, *From the Trenches.*

40. In 1995, Bank Indonesia reported that out of a total of 240 banks in the system, 70 banks had violated legal lending limits, 21 were not in compliance with the established capital-asset ratios, and 18 did not meet the established loan-deposit ratio. John Montgomery, "The Indonesian Financial System: Its Contribution to Economic Performance, and Key Policy Issues," IMF Working Paper WP/97/45, p. 15.

capacity to supervise and regulate the banking system—which had experienced explosive growth in the preceding five years—was weak and prone to political interference.[41]

In August 1997, this vulnerable structure was subjected to stress from two sources. To protect the value of the currency when Indonesia's pegged exchange rate came under attack, Bank Indonesia severely tightened the money supply, causing banks' balance sheets to deteriorate. Then, when the authorities allowed the value of the rupiah to float freely on August 14, the currency depreciated rapidly, losing 34 percent of its value between July and October 1997. The depreciation led to large foreign exchange losses for the banks, forced them to scramble for liquidity in a prohibitively expensive interbank market, and put enormous pressure on the banks' borrowers, who were suddenly faced with ballooning foreign-currency-denominated debts and (declining) local-currency-denominated revenues.[42] Bank Indonesia began providing troubled banks with emergency liquidity, what would become known as BLBI (Bantuan Likuiditas Bank Indonesia, or Bank Indonesia Liquidity Assistance). The volume of emergency liquidity disbursed by Bank Indonesia grew at an alarming rate, from 2 percent of GDP at the end of October to 9.5 percent by mid-January 1998.[43] In October 1997, regulators identified at least fifty "problem banks," of which thirty-four were deemed to be insolvent, including two state-owned banks and twenty-six private banks.[44]

With the banking system undercapitalized and facing a crisis of confidence, the Indonesian banking authorities took more aggressive action in early January 1998. They extended a blanket guarantee on all deposits in the system and set up the Indonesian Bank Restructuring Agency (IBRA), which, at least on paper, was a powerful government agency in charge of administering the deposit guarantee, restructuring and privatizing the weakest banks, managing and disposing of the toxic assets of closed banks, and recovering from bank owners as much of the central bank's liquidity support as possible.

IBRA moved quickly to take over the system's weakest banks. After taking over fifty-four banks in February 1998, the agency brought another fourteen banks under its control two months later. Together the seven largest institutions received almost three-quarters of total BI liquidity support disbursed up to that point.[45] Indonesia's

---

41. For details, see Burhanuddin Abdullah and Wimboh Santoso, "The Indonesian Banking Industry: Competition, Consolidation and Systemic Stability," in "The Banking Industry in the Emerging Market Economies: Competition, Consolidation, and Systemic Stability," BIS Working Paper No. 4, August 2001, pp. 82–83.

42. The World Bank, whose projections were on the conservative side, estimated that the external debt of Indonesia's private sector amounted to some US$72 billion in 1998 (US$62 billion owed by nonfinancial corporations and US$8 billion by private banks). World Bank, "Indonesia in Crisis: A Macroeconomic Update," Washington, D.C., July 16, 1998, pp. 2–3.

43. Djiwandono, *Bank Indonesia*, p. 124.

44. Enoch et al., "Indonesia: Anatomy of a Banking Crisis," p. 28.

45. Ibid., p. 34.

largest private bank, Bank Central Asia (BCA), suffered a run, and on May 29, IBRA took over the bank, suspended the owners' rights, and replaced the management.

In the first few months of 1998, the full extent of the banking shock began to dawn on Indonesian policymakers. Audits of the seven banks IBRA had taken over in April 1998 revealed a nonperforming loan rate of at least 55 percent in each one.[46] In addition, all seven state banks were insolvent and would have qualified for closure under the same criteria applied to private banks. In response, the government merged four state banks into one giant state-owned bank, Bank Mandiri, which became the largest commercial bank in the system with about a quarter of all banking-system assets. Recognizing that the state banks were too big to fail, the authorities began the costly process of recapitalizing them. By late 1998, the Indonesian government realized that it would need all the help it could get to inject resources into the banking system.

The decision to open the Indonesian banking sector to foreign capital was taken in the first half of 1998, and draft legislation was sent to the legislature amending the Banking Law by August of that year.[47] Under the proposed legislation, joint-venture and state banks would cease to be designated distinct categories under the Banking Act, ending regulatory discrimination against foreign institutions. Foreign entry without a local partner was still forbidden, but now any foreign legal entity—not just banks—could form joint ventures. This change opened the door to investment from private equity firms and hedge funds. More importantly, foreign citizens or legal entities were allowed to purchase shares of *any* Indonesian private or public commercial bank, not only through the stock exchange but also directly from the owner. No ceilings were set on foreign participation; at least on paper, the authorities could authorize up to 100 percent foreign ownership of any commercial bank. Through subsequent regulations, Bank Indonesia set the foreign-participation ceiling at 99 percent for listed banks, and after the issue of an additional decree, foreigners could purchase up to 99 percent of unlisted banks' equity as well.[48] In short, these amendments amounted to total de jure banking-sector opening.

The Role of the Bretton Woods Institutions

Indonesia's modern relations with the IMF date back to 1967, when Indonesia rejoined the Fund. (The country withdrew its membership during Sukarno's government.) President Suharto's incoming economic team proved adept at controlling inflation and restoring fiscal balance in the early 1970s, and thereafter the technocrats

---

46. Ibid., p. 36.

47. Act of the Republic of Indonesia, No. 10 of 1998 Concerning the Amendment to Act No. 7 of 1992 Concerning Banking.

48. This was authorized by BI Decree on the Purchase of Shares in Commercial Banks and a related regulation on May 7, 1999.

adopted a staunchly independent attitude vis-à-vis the Fund. Indonesia took its last IMF standby loan in 1970, and until the 1990s, it made use of the Fund's Compensatory Financing Facility only in years of falling commodity prices. The Indonesian authorities chose to deal with fiscal shocks in 1983 and 1986–1987 through home-made rather than IMF-designed stabilization plans, and they became, in the words of a prominent technocrat, "allergic to IMF standbys."[49] Other than that, Indonesia's interaction with the Fund was limited to annual Article IV consultations and technical assistance on monetary issues.

Like the IMF, the World Bank reengaged Indonesia after Sukarno's fall and largely served as a pipeline for U.S.-sponsored assistance to a country that had become a bulwark against communism in Southeast Asia. In the succeeding two decades, the archipelago became one of the Bank's most important borrowers. The Bank's most ambitious precrisis financial-sector project in Indonesia was built on a US$300 million loan launched in 1992 to support state bank recapitalization and rehabilitation. However, the project was a complete failure, in large measure because overzealous Bank staff members alienated Indonesian officials.[50] Returning to the drawing board, Bank staff prepared a new financial-sector development strategy in 1996.[51] The document did not explicitly call for opening the banking sector to foreign investment but recommended that "state banks should go public, preferably with a tranche to be marketed abroad, to maximize disclosure," and argued that "in the long term, the only real solution [to the problem of weak state banks] is full privatization, which may require amendment of the Banking Act."[52]

The severity of the 1997–1998 crisis left Jakarta highly dependent on external resources to stabilize the economy. Putting aside its tradition of self-reliance, the Suharto government turned to the IMF for assistance in early October 1997.[53] On October 31, the authorities signed the first of many Letters of Intent (LOIs) with the Fund in exchange for up to US$18 billion in loans.

For the Indonesian economic team and the Bretton Woods institutions, the crisis opened a window of opportunity to implement structural reforms which they had

---

49. Kenward, *From the Trenches*, p. 42.

50. Interview with Dennis de Tray, Washington, D.C., October 4, 2006. See also World Bank, "Indonesia Country Assistance Note," Report No. 19100, Operations Evaluation Department, March 29, 1999, p. 20.

51. World Bank, "Indonesia's Financial Sector: A Strategy for Development," Report No. 15735-IND, June 14, 1996.

52. Ibid., pp. iv–v.

53. On the role of the IMF in Indonesia, see Cyrillus Harinowo, *IMF: Penanganan Krisis dan Indonesia Pasca-IMF* (Jakarta: PT Gramedia Pustaka Utama, 2004), chaps. 27–29; J. Soedradjad Djiwandono, "Role of the IMF in Indonesia's Financial Crisis," in *Governance in Indonesia: Challenges Facing the Megawati Presidency*, ed. Hadi Soesastro, Anthony L. Smith, and Han Mui Ling (Singapore: ISEAS, 2002), pp. 196–228; Paul Blustein, *The Chastening: Inside the Crisis that Rocked the Global Financial System and Humbled the IMF* (New York: Public Affairs, 2001); and Leonardo Martinez-Diaz, "Pathways through Financial Crisis: Indonesia," *Global Governance* 12 (October–December 2006).

long considered necessary but which had foundered in the face of political resistance from powerful groups. Between October 1997 and January 1998, the Fund, the
Bank, and the Indonesian technocrats worked together to incorporate their favored
reforms into the LOIs. The Fund team described the situation this way: "IMF management…viewed the program as an opportunity to assist the reformist team in
pushing desirable reforms and the team viewed the program as providing leverage to do so."[54] An internal World Bank evaluation was more direct: "Ironically, the
crisis provided an opportunity for the Bank to get action on many of the necessary
structural changes. By January 1998, Bank staff had managed to incorporate into the
IMF programs most of the reforms it wanted."[55] World Bank staff took the lead role
on banking-sector reform.

Banking-sector opening was part of IMF conditionality from the very beginning.
In its first agreement with the IMF, signed on October 31, 1997, the Indonesian
government committed to opening the banking sector to foreign investment. In its
Memorandum of Economic and Financial Policies, the government pledged: "Regulations concerning foreign ownership of financial institutions will be modified to
facilitate entry of international banks and investors into the Indonesian banking
system."[56] In subsequent documents, the commitment became more precise and
time-bound. In the Memorandum attached to the Letter of Intent signed on January 15, 1998, the authorities observed, "As part of its WTO negotiations for liberalizing trade in financial services, the government has decided to: lift restrictions on
branching of foreign banks by February 1998; in addition, it will submit to Parliament a draft law to eliminate restrictions on foreign investment in listed banks by
June 1998."[57] This commitment was reaffirmed in the memoranda submitted by the
government in April and again in June 1998, and it was incorporated into the matrix
that breaks down reforms into concrete tasks to be completed by specified dates.[58]
Amendments to the Banking Act of 1992 were submitted by the government to the
DPR in August, and in October the legislature approved the changes.

To be sure, the technocrats did not need to be pressed much to include these
provisions in Indonesia's commitments with the IMF. The spirit of the commitments was consistent with the technocrats' thinking on banking-sector reform. Bank
Indonesia Governor Djiwandono, in particular, was intimately familiar with the
frustrations and dangers of trying to regulate bankers, both public and private, who
routinely used their political connections to circumvent prudential regulations.[59] Any

54. International Monetary Fund, "The IMF and Recent Capital Account Crises," Annex I, p. 76.
55. World Bank, "Indonesia Country Assistance Note," p. 9.
56. Indonesia—Memorandum of Economic and Financial Policies, October 31, 1997.
57. Indonesia—Memorandum of Economic and Financial Policies, January 15, 1998.
58. Indonesia—Supplementary Memorandum of Economic and Financial Policies, April 10, 1998,
Appendix II, and Indonesia—Second Supplementary Memorandum of Economic and Financial Policies,
June 24, 1998.
59. See Djiwandono, *Bank Indonesia*.

measure which helped break these incestuous links between finance and politics, and which promised to improve governance in the banking sector, was welcome.

In addition, the economic team understood that, given the high costs of recapitalizing the banking system, foreign capital could help reduce the financial burden on the government. According to Governor Djiwandono—who along with Finance Minister Mar'ie Muhammad led the Indonesian team that negotiated with the IMF in October 1997—the decision to open up the banking sector was largely influenced by the need to address the problem of undercapitalized banks.[60] Cyrillus Harinowo, then a senior official at Bank Indonesia and alternate executive director at the IMF after April 1998, confirms this: "BI realized that it could not do it [recapitalize the banks] alone, and that foreign help was needed."[61]

The progressive hardening of commitments in IMF documents appears to have been the product of pressure from some of the Fund's largest members, including the United States. According to a study by the Fund's Independent Evaluation Office, the October 31 LOI included only general commitments so that the technocrats could have discretion "to push when and where they felt they could achieve results."[62] However, when the program failed to stabilize the economy, Fund staff came under pressure from Washington, both from IMF headquarters and from the U.S. Treasury, to increase the pressure on the Indonesians. This is clear even in the cautious language of the Evaluation Office: "At the time of the Executive Board meeting on November 5, 1997, several Executive Directors had expressed their unhappiness with what they regarded as the vague and general nature of the structural conditionality, arguing that no progress would be likely in needed reforms without specificity and a clear timetable.... This led to a much more specific and time-bound approach to structural conditionality in the January 1998 program."[63]

That the Fund's influence was critical in shepherding the banking-sector-opening initiative all the way to its enactment is even clearer if we consider that the technocrats' influence within the government declined precipitously in early 1998. At this time, President Suharto realized that the reforms his economic team supported were undermining the economic interests of his family and closest associates while failing to halt the decline of the rupiah or to stabilize the economy. Consequently, the technocrats were abruptly shut out of the policy process. The president removed Finance Minister Muhammad as his chief negotiator with the IMF, opting instead to participate directly in the negotiations. He also replaced four of Bank Indonesia's seven managing directors without consulting the central bank governor. In February, Governor Djiwandono himself was dismissed, and in March, Finance Minister

60. Correspondence with Soedradjad Djiwandono, May 5, 2006.

61. Interview with Cyrillus Harinowo, head, Capital Markets Division, Bank Indonesia (1994–1998), and alternate executive director, IMF (1998–2000), Jakarta, April 5, 2006.

62. International Monetary Fund, "The IMF and Recent Capital Account Crises," Annex I, p. 76.

63. Ibid.

Muhammad and Coordinating Minister of the Economy Saleh Affif were replaced by decidedly nontechnocratic members of the president's inner circle.[64] After the technocrats' demise, the banking-sector-opening reforms lost their internal champions, and their movement through Indonesian politics came to depend exclusively on a combination of IMF pressure and the fiscal imperatives imposed by the ever-worsening condition of Indonesia's banks.

Political Survival and Domestic Politics

As the IMF program was being negotiated, Indonesia experienced a turbulent political transition.[65] In the first months of 1998, Indonesia's financial crisis unleashed a wave of violence—much of it with a distinctly anti-Chinese bent—that left over a thousand people dead. With the political elite and the military no longer behind him, President Suharto resigned on May 21. Vice-president and longtime Suharto minister B. J. Habibie took over the government and promised to hold elections in October 1999.[66] Suharto's thirty-two years of authoritarian rule came to an end, and a gradual transition to democracy—or at least to a real competition for political power—began.

President Habibie took office in an environment rife with urban violence, economic chaos, and political uncertainty, and his political survival was a priority. His unelected presidency was condemned as illegitimate by the mass-based, pro-democracy Reformasi movement, and he faced challengers within his own party. The president's priorities during his sixteen-month tenure were therefore to legitimize his rule, to fight off political rivals, and to secure reelection in 1999. This meant stabilizing the economy first, and Habibie, a key leader of the statist, nationalist wing of Suharto's government, was ready to use the IMF plan to do it. Habibie's finance minister remembers:

> I believe that President Habibie clearly recognised his strategic options. He knew that fixing the economy was likely to earn him the greatest advantage of all the avenues open to him at that time. This also offered the greatest chance for his re-election. Moreover, the blueprint for fixing the economy was readily at hand. It was spelled out in detail in the revised program agreed with the Fund on 24 June 1998. Thus his best bet was to throw his full weight behind the program.[67]

---

64. Coordinating Minister Saleh Affif had to step down because of health reasons.

65. For informative accounts of this period, see Kevin O'Rourke, *Reformasi: The Struggle for Power in Post-Suharto Indonesia* (Sydney: Allen & Unwin, 2002), and Theodore Friend, *Indonesian Destinies* (London: Belknap Press, 2003).

66. On the politics of the Habibie presidency, see Robison and Hadiz, *Reorganising Power in Indonesia,* chap. 7.

67. Boediono, "The International Monetary Fund Support Program in Indonesia: Comparing Implementation under Three Presidents," *Bulletin of Indonesian Economic Studies* 38:3 (2002), 387.

Banking-sector opening was an explicit condition of IMF assistance, so Habibie's embrace of the IMF program meant accepting total de jure opening. Once the Habibie administration promised the IMF to prepare legislation opening the banking sector, the political battle shifted to the legislature.

Indonesia's bicameral legislature, and its lower house in particular (the House of Representatives, or DPR), has traditionally been a weak political actor. Under the constitution, the DPR had the right to initiate legislation and to approve or veto legislation. But in practice, the parliament was a passive actor during the New Order, as it was thoroughly dominated by Suharto's corporatist party, Golkar (Golongan Karya in Indonesian, or "Functional Groups").[68] After Suharto's fall, the DPR suddenly became an active participant in economic policymaking, and its Commission VIII for Finance, State Budget, and Science and Technology became a key player in decisions concerning the banking sector.

As it had promised to the IMF, the executive submitted a draft law to the DPR on August 24, 1998, allowing foreigners to purchase shares in Indonesian banks directly as well as through the stock market, lifting existing ceilings on foreign participation in both state and private banks, and leaving the issue of any new ceilings up to the executive. The executive's message to the legislature and the media was simple: "We're now in a crisis, and don't think that we're healthy," a BI director told the media, referring to the Indonesian banking system. "If foreign investors... are being restricted, they won't come in."[69] But even though the president's party enjoyed a majority in the legislature, the proposal met with strong opposition both from within Golkar and from the Muslim-based United Development faction. Most of the legislators supported banking-sector opening in principle, but they favored limits to foreign participation, claiming (rather ironically given the recent history of Indonesian banking) that a banking sector with a large foreign participation would not be sufficiently sensitive to national development. To the executive's frustration, the legislators proposed a ceiling on foreign participation of 75 to 85 percent.[70]

Indonesia's private bankers made their own contribution to the debate. Before Suharto's resignation in May 1998, the bankers never lobbied the executive to ask for protection, either as a group—through their business association, Perbanas—or as individual banks. The Bank Indonesia's governor recalls that before the crisis, "there were no strong feelings raised against the opening up of the banking sector to foreign investors, as I recall.... In general, there were no concerted efforts by

68. Between 1973 and 1990, legislation produced by the House of Representatives amounted to a mere 8 percent of the major legal acts introduced at the central government level. See Andrew MacIntyre, "Political Parties, Accountability, and Economic Governance in Indonesia," in *Democracy, Governance, and Economic Performance: East and Southeast Asia in the 1990s,* ed. Jean Blondel et al. (Tokyo: United Nations University Press), 1999.

69. "100% foreign holdings OK'd in RI banks," *Jakarta Post,* October 17, 1998.

70. "House against Proposal to Give IBRA Special Power," *Jakarta Post,* September 15, 1998.

the national banks to lobby for protection from foreign participation....I guess in general, the private sector took the government's policy for granted, a combination of their trust in the 'technocrats' and more subdued acceptance of Suharto's (authoritarian) rule."[71]

But in the post-Suharto era, as the 1998 amendments to open the banking sector were being debated in the DPR, the private bankers' association began to push, through the media and in congressional committees, for limiting the amount of equity any single investor could own in a private or state bank to 20–25 percent.[72] The proposal was justified (somewhat cynically) as a way to curb abuses by majority shareholders and improve the governance of banks. Although the bankers' proposal was not explicitly antiforeign, the initiative would effectively protect Indonesian banks from foreign takeovers.

In the end, the executive was able to secure the liberal legislation it wanted. Golkar's parliamentary leadership apparently put heavy pressure on party members to fall into line on this and other reforms. Two days before the DPR was scheduled to vote on the banking amendments, three members of the Golkar parliamentary faction—including a finance commission member who was one of the most outspoken advocates of limits on foreign participation in banking—were dismissed suddenly by the party's leadership, along with sixty-seven members of the legislature's less powerful upper house.[73] The dismissals, the party chairman said, were because the members were no longer loyal to the party. It is not clear whether the dismissals were directly related to the banking initiative, but the move must have had a chilling effect on dissent among Golkar legislators.

Did Trade Negotiations Make a Difference?

Just before the crisis, the Indonesian government was engaged in two sets of trade-in-services negotiations: the GATS negotiations and regional talks with its ASEAN partners. During the second half of 1997, Indonesia was subject to intense international pressure, especially from the U.S. government, to expand its commitments at the GATS negotiating table. These efforts bore richer fruits in Indonesia than in Brazil. As the negotiations progressed, the Indonesian authorities made important concessions and agreed to bind the level of openness they had achieved by 1992 through the Financial Services Agreement. However, the really crucial changes in Indonesia's banking regime—the lifting of restrictions on the foreign ownership of domestic state and private banks—was neither triggered by trade-related international pressures nor locked into place by the GATS because the Indonesians declined

---

71. Correspondence with Soedradjad Djiwandono, May 5, 2006.
72. "Call for Limiting Share Ownership in Indonesian Banks," *Asia Pulse,* June 16, 1998, and "Stakes in Banks 'Should Be Limited' to 20 Percent," *Jakarta Post,* June 16, 1998.
73. "Sacked Golkar Legislators Protest Their Dismissal," *Jakarta Post,* October 16, 1998.

to bind this crucial policy change. Appendix 2 shows how Indonesia's GATS offers evolved.

Indonesia's initial offer at the financial-services negotiations was identical to its de jure position in 1992: branching by foreign banks was restricted, discriminatory paid-up capital requirements were in place, joint ventures were authorized on the basis of reciprocity, and foreigners could own stakes of no more than 49 percent in listed banks.[74] The 1992 changes liberalizing ownership rules had been enacted long before Indonesia's GATS opening position was presented in 1994, and as we have seen, the 1992 reforms were driven by the technocrats' long-planned scheme to liberalize the banking system. Indeed, there is no reference to the GATS or to any other trade-in-services negotiations or agreements in the 1992 Banking Act or in the policy writings and speeches of the technocrats.

As the final December 1997 deadline for the negotiations approached, and under considerable pressure to make significant concessions, Jakarta promised national treatment for foreign banks by 2020, if other countries reciprocated.[75] This offer was of little practical significance, given that the concessions would not come into effect until twenty-five years later, assuming reciprocity by other countries. The Indonesians also included in their offer the right of foreign and joint-venture banks to open additional branches in eight designated cities. After that offer was made, the U.S. government launched its inauspicious "diplomatic offensive," deploying senior Treasury officials to Jakarta in August. However, Indonesia offered no new concessions by the time the Financial Services Agreement was finalized in December 1997.

Then, in February 1998, Jakarta submitted a revised offer that made some real concessions.[76] Discriminatory paid-up capital requirements would be scrapped. Restrictions on foreign staffing would be relaxed, and restrictions on branching by both foreign and joint-venture banks would be lifted. Transfers of ownership within joint-venture banks would have to be approved by both the domestic and the foreign partner, protecting the foreign partner from government efforts to "indigenize" a joint-venture bank by forcing the foreign partner to sell its shares. However, these concessions were the product of IMF pressure, not of pressure exerted in the multilateral trade arena. Indeed, Indonesia's commitment to lift branching restrictions on foreign banks through the GATS was explicitly articulated in the January 1998 Letter of Intent. Crucially, the most important opening measure—the right of foreign investors to own up to 100 percent of the equity of domestic banks—was not included in Indonesia's GATS commitments in 1998 or even in 2003, even though 100 percent foreign ownership of *nonbank* companies was included in Indonesia's WTO commitments.[77]

---

74. GATS/SC/43, April 15, 1994.

75. GATS/SC/43/Suppl. 1, July 28, 1995.

76. GATS/SC/43/Suppl. 3, February 26, 1998.

77. Full foreign ownership of insurance companies was allowed under Indonesia's 1998 GATS offer.

Indonesian trade negotiators were also involved in a second round of multilateral talks on financial services. The ASEAN Framework Agreement on Services (AFAS) was launched at the end of 1995 to eliminate intraregional trade restrictions among Southeast Asian nations and expand the scope of services liberalization beyond those already undertaken through the GATS.[78] Under the AFAS, initial negotiations focused on a variety of service industries, including financial services. An initial package of commitments was endorsed on October 16, 1997, a few weeks before the conclusion of the Financial Services Agreement. A second package was concluded on October 7, 1998 (days before the Indonesian legislature approved total de jure opening of the banking sector), and a third in October 2001.

The most notable concession made by member countries under the AFAS was a commitment to national treatment in banking services by 2010, ten years before national treatment under the GATS. Indonesia added a minor concession to its regional trade partners; under the AFAS, foreign and joint-venture banks based in the region could open offices in eleven cities, rather than in the eight cities specified in national legislation and in Indonesia's GATS schedule. Unlike the GATS, the AFAS was not used by the IMF to lock in reforms, and the timing and very modest scope of the AFAS commitments suggest that these negotiations did not drive banking-sector opening in Indonesia.

The Politics of De Facto Opening (1999–2005)

In the process of rescuing the banking sector, the Indonesian authorities took over much of the banking system, and in the aftermath of the crisis, they began the delicate task of selling the banks and their assets back to the private sector. With de jure banking-sector opening already in place, those institutions and assets could also be sold to foreigners. Thus began a heated competition among the executive, the legislature, and foreign and domestic business interests for control of Indonesia's largest financial institutions. The politics of reprivatization and the politics of de facto banking-sector opening thus became different faces of the same struggle.

With the political crisis as a backdrop, Bank Indonesia and the Indonesian Bank Restructuring Agency struggled to contain the banking shock. This required recapitalizing the weakest institutions through a combination of public resources and injections from the bank owners and restructuring the sector through the reorganization, merger, and sale of the banks taken over by IBRA. A clear picture of the volume of resources needed to recapitalize the system began to emerge in March 1999.

---

78. For background on the AFAS, see Ramikishen S. Rajan and Rahul Sen, "Liberalization of Financial Services in Southeast Asia under the ASEAN Framework Agreement on Services (AFAS)," Centre for International Economic Studies Discussion Paper No. 0226, Adelaide University, October 2002.

Audits revealed that seventy-four banks enjoyed "adequate" capital-asset ratios of 4 percent.[79] Nine banks, all with negative capital-asset ratios, qualified for "joint recapitalization"—the government would inject 80 percent of the required fresh capital and shareholders the remaining 20 percent.[80] This category comprised several large institutions, accounting for 10 percent of system assets. Seven other banks failed to qualify for joint recapitalization and were taken over by IBRA.[81] The remaining thirty-eight banks, comprising 5 percent of the system's total assets, were deemed beyond salvation and were scheduled for liquidation. Once the state banks were included, the government's estimated cost of recapitalizing the banking system ballooned to Rp351 trillion (some 32 percent of 1999 GDP), with the state banks accounting for nearly two-thirds of the total, as shown in Table 5.1.[82]

Unfortunately, the joint recapitalization was largely a failure. The two largest banks to be jointly recapitalized—Niaga and Bali—failed to raise the requisite 20 percent of fresh capital and had to be taken over by IBRA. In addition, the widespread abuse of emergency-liquidity funds greatly increased the cost to the government and, ultimately, to the Indonesian public. The government projections cited above underestimated the final cost of bank recapitalization by a considerable margin—by the end of 2000, the government had issued Rp644 trillion in recapitalization bonds, some 58 percent of 1999 GDP.[83] Meanwhile, largely as a result of the bank-rescue operation, Indonesia's debt-to-GDP ratio in 1999 quadrupled from its 1996 level.[84]

In the Eye of the Storm

The Indonesian Bank Restructuring Agency soon found itself at the center of decision making over the future of the country's banking sector. Through its takeover of some of the country's largest banks, IBRA effectively became a large government-owned banking conglomerate and asset-management company. It also became the country's largest holder of both financial- and real-sector assets. By late 1999, IBRA

---

79. Audit results are from Sukarela Batunanggar, "Indonesia's Banking Crisis Resolution: Lessons and the Way Forward," paper prepared for the financial stability research project at the Centre for Central Banking Studies, Bank of England, December 2, 2002, p. 38. The authorities' first inclination was to set the minimum CAR at the international standard of 8 percent, but they soon realized this would have left most of the private banks in the system in the "undercapitalized" category, so they halved the figure.

80. These banks were Bukopin, Bank Bali, Bank Arta Media, Bank Patriot, Bank Universal, Bank Lippo, Bank Internasional Indonesia, Bank Prima Express, and Bank Niaga.

81. These banks were Bank Duta, Bank Nusa Nasional, Bank Pos Nusantara, Bank Jaya, Bank Tamara, Bank Rama, and Bank Risyad Salim Internasional.

82. Raden Pardede, "Survey of Recent Developments," *Bulletin of Indonesian Economic Studies* 35 (August 1999), 26.

83. George Fane and Ross H. McLeod, "Banking Collapse and Restructuring in Indonesia, 1997–2001," *Cato Journal* 22 (Fall 2002), 287.

84. O'Rourke, *Reformasi*, p. 324.

Table 5.1 Government contributions needed to recapitalize banks to 4 percent capital-asset ratios, government projections, 1999

	NO. OF BANKS	RP TRILLION
Cost of meeting deposit guarantee for closed banks	58	53.8
Phase 1 Immediate capital injections to:		
Private banks nationalized in 1998	4	80.5
Other private banks being jointly recapitalized	7	22.1
Regional development banks	12	1.2
Total phase 1	23	103.8
Phase 2 Later capital injections to:		
State banks	7	233.3
Private banks nationalized in 1999	4	12.1
Other private banks being jointly recapitalized	1	2.5
Total phase 2	12	247.9
Total	93	405.5

Source: Raden Pardede, "Survey of Recent Developments," *Bulletin of Indonesian Economic Studies* 35 (August 1999), 27.

had assumed control of assets with a face value of Rp441 trillion, about 36 percent of GDP.[85] Given IBRA's role as chief arbiter in what would be a massive redistribution of corporate assets, the agency became the focus of enormous political pressures.

From the beginning, the agency suffered from inadequate human resources, equivocal support from the government, and hostility from the legislature.[86] IBRA's operations and leadership quickly became politicized; seven different chairmen passed through IBRA in its first four years of existence, each with different political loyalties and ideas about how the agency should do its job. After 2001, under President Megawati, IBRA would come under close control of the Ministry of State-Owned Enterprises. Most of the sales of Indonesian banks to foreign investors would take place during the tenure of IBRA's most dynamic and longest-serving chairman, Syafruddin Temenggung.

Regardless of who occupied the presidential palace or IBRA's chair, the agency's mission to sell off the banks it had taken over was never in question. IBRA's leadership made its thinking on this matter clear:

> The divestment of bank shares, held by the Indonesian government, serves two key purposes. First, it provides the Government with a convenient exit strategy to recover funds utilized in its bank restructuring program. Second, and perhaps more importantly, it provides a method to set the national banking sector

---

85. Enoch et al., "Indonesia: Anatomy of a Banking Crisis," p. 39.
86. "House against Proposal to Give IBRA Special Power."

in motion by returning the bank ownership to the private sector, as it should be. Certainly, it would be difficult for Indonesia to develop a competitive and thriving banking sector if virtually all of its banking system was held by the government as the single majority shareholder.[87]

The government needed to raise cash urgently, and the IMF, using all the leverage its program-based conditionality afforded it, applied constant pressure to keep bank reprivatization on track. In addition, fifteen years after the technocrats had started to deregulate the banking system, few Indonesians in government advocated a return to a mostly state-owned banking system.

The Bankers' Early Exit

What role did Indonesia's private bankers play in the process of banking-sector opening? Their role was very limited because they exited the political stage early and quickly. They had powerful incentives to do so. As we have seen, banks linked to industrial conglomerates had lent heavily to the nonfinancial firms in the conglomerates. Once these firms began to suffer losses, they had no incentive to repay their banks, especially after the government signaled its willingness to rescue many of them. Conglomerate owners rushed to save their equity in the more valuable nonfinancial corporations and to pass on the corporate losses to their banks and eventually to the government. Instead of injecting fresh capital into the troubled banks, conglomerate owners were busy shielding their assets by moving them abroad, passing off overvalued assets to IBRA, and trying to repurchase through intermediaries assets the government had seized. The legal system was rarely of assistance to IBRA in bringing delinquent bank owners to justice.

Not surprisingly, bank owners were both unwilling and unable to oppose banking-sector opening. They were unwilling to do so because foreign capital could help the government recapitalize the banks they had no intention of recapitalizing themselves. But in addition, the bankers lost all political voice and influence, both as a group and as individuals, for two reasons. First, nine of the top ten private banks in 1996 were taken over by the government, merged, or closed down between 1997 and 1999, as shown in Table 5.2. This amounted to an effective nationalization of the private banking sector, and therefore bankers lost whatever structural and lobbying power they might have held. Second, bank and conglomerate owners—especially those of ethnic Chinese origin—became very unpopular in Indonesian public and elite opinion. Lobbying the government openly or even privately for continued protection from foreign competition had become unthinkable.

Meanwhile, the private bankers' association, Perbanas—never the forum of choice of Indonesia's big bank owners anyway—became a lobby group for the surviving

---

87. Annual Report, Indonesian Bank Restructuring Agency, 2000, p. 11.

Table 5.2   Fate of Indonesia's top ten private banks during the crisis

BANK	GOVERNMENT ACTION	SHARE OF EQUITY CONTROLLED BY IBRA IN 2000 (PERCENT)
BCA	Taken over by IBRA	70.3
Danamon	Taken over by IBRA; absorbed eight smaller banks	99.3
BII	Recapitalized under IBRA	56.8
BDNI	Closed	—
Lippo	Recapitalized under IBRA	59.3
Bali	Taken over by IBRA; later merged with Bank Permata	98.2
Niaga	Taken over by IBRA	97.1
BUN	Closed	—
Panin	No government action	—
Duta	Taken over by IBRA; merged with Danamon	—

Source: Equity shares from IBRA Annual Report, 2000, p. 13.

private banks, which were mainly small and medium-sized institutions. In 1998 and 1999, the Perbanas leadership focused, mostly unsuccessfully, on lobbying the government to make crisis-management regulations less onerous on small banks.

The Politics of Divestment

Reprivatizing the banks in IBRA's portfolio was a slow and politically charged process, pushed forward by firm IMF pressure and by the fiscal needs of the state. Once the banks had been audited by the government, IMF staff pressed for the immediate reprivatization of the largest banks. In its July 1999 Letter of Intent with the IMF, the government promised to accelerate the privatization timetable for four formerly private banks, including two of the largest, Danamon and BCA; the latter was supposed to be sold by March 2000.[88] However, parliamentary approval would be necessary for each of these sales, and this allowed the legislature to have a say in the matter.

The burning question surrounding the sales was about who should own the country's most important commercial banks, control the flow of credit, and profit from the interest to be paid on the billions of dollars of recapitalization bonds that swelled the banks' portfolios. Two contentious issues shaped the debate. The first was whether former bank owners should be allowed to participate in the reprivatization. From a purely financial standpoint, the former owners were the obvious

---

88. Letters of Intent of the Government of Indonesia, July 22, 1999, and January 20, 2000.

first choice. All of them had incurred considerable losses during the crisis, but they also shielded important parts of their corporate empires and used BLBI funds to stash liquid assets offshore. These entrepreneurs were naturally interested in buying back their own banks after they had been purged of bad loans by the government, and no one doubted that they could raise sufficient funds to do so. In the spring of 2000, IBRA's chairman outlined his own strategy for selling the agency's assets: sell first to ethnic Chinese Indonesian investors (many of them former bank owners), then to foreign hedge funds and other short-term investors, and finally to foreign long-term strategic investors, whom he expected would feel more confident once the ethnic Chinese had returned.[89]

However, this option was a political dead end, as former bank owners had become politically radioactive. In mid-2001, auditors reported that 96 percent of central bank emergency-liquidity funds, amounting to some Rp138 trillion, were subject to some form of abuse, ranging from minor infractions to outright embezzlement.[90] While forty-eight banks received BLBI funds, just four of them accounted for between two-thirds and three-quarters of the total (BCA, Danamon, BDNI, and Bank Umum Nasional). All four were owned by entrepreneurs close to President Suharto. Former bank owners—and those four, in particular—were widely seen as bearing heavy responsibility for Indonesia's crisis, for mismanaging their banks, and for plundering public funds. The government therefore barred former owners from bidding on their own assets, and IBRA was required by law to cancel any transaction if evidence emerged that previous owners were behind a winning bid.[91]

The second issue that shaped the ownership debate was the redistribution of assets across ethnic lines. Former bank/conglomerate owners were resented not only for their mismanagement and corruption but also because of their ethnicity. Those resentments had flared into anti-Chinese violence.[92] At the same time, a group of legislators saw the bank privatizations as an opportunity to redistribute assets formerly belonging to ethnic Chinese Indonesian banks to indigenous Indonesian entrepreneurs. This wealth-redistribution agenda was endorsed by the People's Consultative Assembly (MPR), the seven-hundred-member body that is Indonesia's highest constitutional authority. In November 1998, the body issued a decree stipulating that "the implementation of economic democracy shall seek to avoid

---

89. Hugh Patrick, "Corporate Governance and the Indonesian Financial System: A Comparative Perspective," Discussion Paper No. 16, APEC Study Center, Columbia Business School, August 2001, pp. 38–39.

90. O'Rourke, *Reformasi*, p. 61.

91. Shoeb Kagda, "Reflections on a Clean-Up Campaign," *Business Times Singapore*, March 13, 2004.

92. In May 1998, violence was directed at the largest of the ethnic Chinese banks, particularly at Salim's Bank Central Asia, known among some segments of the public as "Bank of Chinese Ancestry." One hundred and twenty-two BCA offices were damaged and several set on fire. Dozens of the bank's ATMs were also vandalized. The riots led to a massive run on deposits at BCA. At least some of the violence may have been actively promoted by military figures seeking to undermine Suharto's rule and to take political advantage of the situation. For details, see O'Rourke, *Reformasi*, chap. 7.

the concentration of economic assets and forces in the hands of a small number of people and companies....Banks and financial institutions shall give top priority to cooperatives and SMEs while continuing to work within the principles of sound business management."[93] Although the word *pribumi* was dropped from the decree after some debate, the mention of "economic democracy," SMEs, and cooperatives was a thinly veiled reference to indigenous-owned businesses. The decree strengthened the hand of those pushing for a redistribution of wealth across ethnic lines. President Habibie, however, was careful not to endorse this policy overtly.

Individual bank sales soon became enmeshed in ethnic politics. President Habibie himself was accused of reneging on his pledge to help *pribumi* businesses make inroads into the ethnic Chinese–dominated economy after the government closed down eleven indigenous-owned banks in March 1999.[94] Legislators demanded that the government give priority to local investors in the purchase of BCA shares in September 2001, and a consortium of indigenous entrepreneurs, loosely allied with nationalist members of the legislature, prepared a plan to buy a controlling stake in BCA.[95] *Pribumi* attempts at taking control of the banks at the expense of foreign and ethnic Chinese investors ultimately failed, but they left a lasting impression on the method through which de facto opening was undertaken.

Selling BCA

The sale of Bank Central Asia was a crucial episode in the process of de facto opening. BCA had been the largest private bank in the country, and even after the merger of the state banks in 1998, it was the second-largest commercial bank in the system. It had a base of some seven million depositors and a network of 2,075 ATMs and 795 branches nationwide.[96] After a massive injection of liquidity from the central bank and the transfer of its bad loans to IBRA, BCA was in good condition, and its new owners stood to profit handsomely from the long stream of interest payments on the bank's hefty stock of recapitalization bonds. In the words of one prominent banker, BCA was "a one-billion-dollar company with seven or eight billion dollars worth of [recapitalization] bonds."[97]

IBRA and Bank Indonesia wanted to sell a majority stake in BCA through a single transaction, correctly assuming that foreign investors would be more interested (and willing to pay more) if they could be immediately ensured full ownership and

93. Decree No. XVI/MPR/1998 on Political Economy with Economic Democracy, cited in Lisa Cameron, "Survey of Recent Developments," *Bulletin of Indonesian Economic Studies* 35 (April 1999), 30.

94. Praginanto, "Indonesia Moves to Trim Its Bloated Banking Sector," *Nikkei Weekly,* March 22, 1999.

95. Nugroho Dewanto, Agus S. Riuyanto, and Endah W. S., "The Death of SMEs' Dream Child," *Tempo* 5 (October 9–15, 2001).

96. Vincent Lingga, "BCA: Major Deal of the Year," *Jakarta Post,* September 3, 2001.

97. Confidential interview with senior BCA official, Jakarta, April 3, 2006.

management control of the bank. On the other hand, legislators in the DPR's finance commission advocated a privatization method with two characteristics: (1) phased sales, meaning that the bank shares would be sold one minority stake at a time, and (2) "double-tracked" sales, meaning that each bank would be sold through a combination of private placement (selling shares to a specific investor) and secondary-market placement (selling shares to the public).

The legislators justified this scheme on the grounds that it would increase transparency and make it more difficult for former bank owners to buy back their own banks. However, it would also facilitate the purchase of IBRA assets by *pribumi* investors, whose more limited capacity to raise funds meant buying minority stakes first and slowly increasing their share over time by purchasing shares in the secondary market. In short, the legislature's proposal was a way to help indigenous entrepreneurs compete with foreign investors in the purchase of IBRA assets.

The government's retort was that foreign investors, especially international banks, would find the purchase of a minority stake too risky if they could not be ensured majority control in a single transaction. This fear was not unfounded. In August 2001, a 25.5 percent stake in the government-owned Semen Gresik, Indonesia's largest cement company, was sold to Cemex, a Mexican cement maker, using a formula similar to the one proposed for the sale of BCA. But when the foreign investor tried to exercise a call option to buy the remaining 25.5 percent at a later date, it was opposed by a powerful alliance of DPR members, provincial and local governments, and organized labor. The transaction was paralyzed, and five years later, the investor would sell its minority stake and leave Indonesia in defeat.[98] Even in 2001, the risk was clear: phased sales opened gaps between transactions that could be exploited by domestic actors to delay or derail majority control by foreign investors.

The legislature prevailed, and the phased, double-track method was used to sell BCA. An initial public offering in May 2000 resulted in the sale of 22.5 percent of BCA's shares to the public, and in 2001, the legislature approved the sale of an additional 51 percent in two stages: 30 percent would be sold first, and the remaining 21 percent would be sold as a call option, giving the buyer of the 30 percent stake the right of first refusal. Bank Indonesia and the finance ministry were resigned to this outcome, and the IMF could not challenge it because the government's Letters of Intent promised only that BCA would be sold but did not specify how.

IBRA hoped to find a strategic investor, one with a long-term mindset and the resources and expertise to transform the institution. Ideally, it would be a large international bank such as the ones that purchased recapitalized banks in Mexico and Brazil.[99] But the authorities found it difficult to attract large international banks,

---

98. For details on the Semen Gresik story, see "The Privatization of Semen Gresik," *Van Zorge Report on Indonesia* 3 (November 2001); Jose Manuel Tesoro, "How Vested Interests Tried to Derail Gresik Privatization," *Asiaweek*, January 22, 1999; and "Cemex Calls It a Day," *Jakarta Post*, May 10, 2006.

99. Interview with Cyrillus Harinowo, Jakarta, April 5, 2006.

partly because these global players were busy exploring options in South Korea and Thailand, partly because they were uncertain about the quality of BI's bank supervision, and—most importantly—because after the crisis, few Western banks had a desire for more exposure to Indonesian risk.[100]

Standard Chartered, a British bank with extensive experience in Asia and Africa, was the only major international bank keen on purchasing Indonesian banks, but it fared badly in the bidding wars.[101] To increase the pool of bidders, IBRA modified its criteria to allow hedge funds and private-equity firms to bid for BCA. In March 2002, IBRA sold 51 percent of BCA to Farindo, a consortium composed of a U.S.-based hedge fund (Farallon Capital Management) and Indonesian cigarette-maker Djarum for US$568 million, beating Standard Chartered and seven other foreign and domestic bidders.[102] (The consortium initially bought 30 percent and was able to exercise its option to buy another 21 percent shortly thereafter.) Djarum, owned by the Chinese-Indonesian Hartono family, put up most of the cash for the purchase, and in 2006, the Farallon transferred most of its shares to the cigarette maker, leaving Djarum with a stake of 92 percent. Naturally, Djarum was extremely discreet during the original sale about the extent of its role in the consortium, and publicly, Farindo was billed as a "Farallon-led consortium." It proved to be a smart deal—by 2006, Djarum had assumed control of the financial group, and Farindo had reaped a sevenfold return on its investment.

Extending the Model

As in Mexico and Brazil, the sale of BCA and the gradual stabilization of Indonesia's economic and political life acted as a positive signal to foreign buyers. IBRA sold the majority of its remaining banks at a relatively brisk pace between 2001 and 2004, when the agency was disbanded. The divestments were undertaken using dual-track sales, combining private and secondary-market placements. They were also phased, but unlike the BCA sale, some transactions began by putting a 51 percent stake on the block from the start.

The details of each deal varied, but a clear pattern emerged: although the privatization method was intended to improve the chances of acquisitions by domestic investors, the controlling shares in all of IBRA's important banks were sold either to foreign entities or to consortia in which foreign entities were the dominant partners, at least at the time the purchases were made. Despite their best efforts, *pribumi*

---

100. Interview with Richard McHowat, chief executive officer, HSBC Indonesia, Jakarta, April 6, 2006.

101. Standard Chartered narrowly lost out in the bidding for BCA. It then bid for Bank Bali and was close to acquiring the bank when labor opposition and a scandal involving millions of dollars of diverted Bank Bali funds led the company to drop its bid. In 2004, Standard Chartered finally purchased Bank Permata, which was formed by the merger of several banks, including Bank Bali.

102. For a list and information on the other bidders, see Nugroho Dewanto and Endah W. S., "Who Will Acquire BCA?" *Tempo* 13 (December 4–10, 2001).

entrepreneurs failed to acquire majority control of any of Indonesia's big banks. It was not for lack of interest. Several consortia of Indonesian investors—groups headed by the owners of domestic banks Mega and Panin, for example—bid for IBRA's banks, but they were outbid by foreign players or lost out to competitors based on nonfinancial criteria. Despite political pressure to give priority to domestic investors, IBRA successfully defended its autonomy and consistently awarded winning bids to foreign-led consortia. By 2005, foreigners owned some 40 percent of the country's bank assets, including foreign acquisitions of and portfolio investment in Indonesian banks.

On occasion, the workers of individual banks organized against foreign takeovers, and in one instance they temporarily derailed a foreign acquisition.[103] But the labor movement invariably failed to stop the transactions because the sales were a top priority for the government, which used all its political weight to complete them.[104] Also, Bank employees did not have a strong union, given the fragmentation of the banking system; they could organize only one bank at a time. In addition, foreign buyers provided assurances that they would not fire workers for a predetermined period following the acquisition, taking some pressure off the government.

Despite Indonesian authorities' best efforts to attract major global banks, much of the private banking system came to be controlled by foreign, nonbank financial entities, most prominently, Farallon Capital (a hedge fund), Temasek Holdings (a large investment company owned by the Singaporean government), and two Malaysian investment and asset-management companies (Khazanah and Commerce Asset Holdings Berhad). Together these nonbank entities bought majority stakes in all of Indonesia's top private banks. The main reason was probably appetite for risk: short-term investors were willing to face uncertainties about Indonesian banks that advanced-economy banks were not prepared to stomach. Also, Singaporean and Malaysian investors probably felt they had a better understanding of the local market than banks based in the United States or Europe.

The privatization method fractured ownership patterns, forcing foreigners to share ownership and control of their acquired banks with the local investors and the government. Even though the majority shareholders tried to consolidate their position by buying up as many of the outstanding shares as possible, the ownership structure of the Indonesian banking system, as well as the composition of the banks' boards of directors, remains a patchwork of foreign, government, and private domestic owners. Since the privatizations, the government has gradually sold off its minority stakes in some of the private banks. In August 2005, for example, the government sold off its stake in Bank Danamon to the public through the stock market,

---

103. The reference here is to the attempted acquisition of Bank Bali by Standard Chartered Bank.

104. After thousands of BCA workers staged mass protests in various cities across the country in March 2002, the government stood firm, citing its obligations to the IMF. See "BCA Sale to Go on Despite Protest," *Jakarta Post,* March 12, 2002.

and the following year, it sold its remaining 26 percent stake in Bank Permata to the majority owners.[105] This suggests that the government does not intend to keep a foothold in all the privatized banks, though there is little interest in divesting majority shares in the large public banks.[106]

This chapter has argued that banking-sector opening in Indonesia was triggered by the banking crisis that started in 1997–1998, and that the shock led to reform through two channels. First, it magnified external political pressure by compelling the government to undertake a major IMF program, one that explicitly included banking-sector opening in its conditionality. In contrast to Mexico, where external pressure undermined the opening by exacerbating nationalist opposition, external pressure in Indonesia was essential to keep the opening on track, particularly after the technocrats were marginalized and banking-sector opening lost its internal champion. Second, the crisis changed the government's priorities of political survival. President Habibie, leading a nation in crisis, facing serious questions about the legitimacy of his government, and beset by political rivals on all sides, saw the IMF program and its banking-sector provisions as the only way to stabilize the economy, save his government, and maximize his chances of reelection.

This was not a story of shifting ideas and causal beliefs: Habibie was one of Suharto's staunchest economic nationalists and champions of protectionism, and the major liberalization reforms were approved and implemented after the technocrats had been pushed from the scene. While it was true that the domestic bankers were decimated by the crisis and walked away from their banks, the weakness of the bankers' lobby facilitated but did not drive the opening process, in either its de jure or its de facto stages. After all, Indonesia's private bankers—never politically influential as a group and as individuals effective only at securing individualized special treatment—had not been an obstacle to the government's opening initiatives in 1988 and 1992. The real roadblock to total opening was the legislature's reluctance to allow foreign control of Indonesian banks, and that obstacle was decisively overcome only by external pressure and by arm-twisting in the legislature by the leadership of the ruling party.

---

105. "Indonesia's Banks: Grip of the Dead Hand," *Economist,* September 16, 2006, p. 86.

106. In sharp contrast to Mexico and Brazil, banking-sector concentration was never a significant factor in policymakers' decisions to sell IBRA's banks to foreign investors. The problem in Indonesia was not too much concentration but rather too little. Despite the crisis, Indonesian banking authorities still believe that there are too many banks in the system and have been trying to reduce their number. Interview with Rusli Simanjuntak, director, Directorate of Bank Supervision 2, Bank Indonesia, Jakarta, April 4, 2006.

6

SOUTH KOREA

Rescuing Gradualism from the Imperatives
of Crisis

Of the four case studies, South Korea stands out as the country in which the state
exercised the most extensive and prolonged control over the commercial banking system. Mexico's banking system was controlled by the private sector. In Brazil
and Indonesia, a class of private bankers took root and eventually flourished in the
shadow of large state-owned banks, but in Korea, no discrete, politically independent class of bankers emerged at all. Korean commercial banks were owned and
controlled by the government throughout the 1960s and 1970s, and even after they
were privatized in the 1980s, government influence remained strong. For this reason, in Korea banking-sector opening was staunchly resisted not by private-sector
incumbents but by government bureaucrats and politicians. Yet by the late 1990s,
Korea's banking system was wide open, and by the end of the 2000s, it had one of
the highest levels of foreign participation in the emerging world.

This chapter argues that Korea's twin financial crisis was the critical trigger
behind its rapid and extensive banking-sector opening. In contrast to Mexico, however, no radical shift took place in policymakers' ideas about the benefits of total
liberalization of the banking regime. Political survival was not a major motivation
in Korea either, as was the case in Brazil and Indonesia. In Korea, the key channel for
liberalization was external political pressure. The banking crisis forced the authorities to reconsider their banking regime, while capital account crises magnified the
leverage that external actors, particularly the IMF and the U.S. government, could
bring to bear. Together, the twin crisis pushed Seoul into embracing total de jure
opening and a good measure of de facto opening.

The chapter unfolds in four parts. After providing a brief historical overview of
the relationship between bankers and the state, the chapter describes Korea's careful

experiment with managed opening in the mid-1990s. Korea's negotiations to join the OECD were a central part of this exercise. The third section describes how the twin crisis that started in 1997 compelled Korean policymakers to engage in rapid de jure liberalization, and the chapter finally examines the politics of implementation.

South Korean Banking: Serving the Developmental State

Korea's modern financial system came into existence during the country's thirty-five years of Japanese colonial occupation (1910–1945).[1] During this period, all banks in Korea were owned and controlled by the Japanese; their activities were aimed at promoting Japanese industrial and commercial expansion and, in the last years of occupation, at financing the war effort. After Japan's defeat in 1945, all Korean financial institutions were taken over by the U.S. Military Government, which in turn transferred them to the fledgling Korean government in 1948. The new government then moved to reorient the financial system toward reconstruction and development. The Bank of Chosun became the Bank of Korea in 1950 and was designated the liberated country's central bank. After the Korean War, the government created the Korea Development Bank (KDB), which, like Brazil's BNDES, was to provide medium- and long-term loans to industry. A second institution, the Korea Agriculture Bank, was established to finance farmers' associations.

Control of the country's commercial banks became an object of contention over the next two decades. At the urging of U.S. experts brought in to advise the government, the Korean authorities sold four nationwide commercial banks to private investors by 1957. The banks were bought by a small group of businessmen who had made windfall profits thanks to government-granted import licenses. These men were also major contributors to the party of President Syngman Rhee (1948–1961), and they would later become the heads of some of Korea's giant industrial groups, the *chaebol*.[2]

This age of private commercial banking proved to be only a brief interlude. After a coup in 1961, the military government of Park Chung Hee (1961–1979) repossessed the privatized banks, and for the next twenty years, Korea's commercial banks were owned and controlled by the government. The finance ministry set their annual

1. For useful histories of the Korean banking system, see David C. Cole and Yung C. Park, *Financial Development in Korea, 1945–1978* (Cambridge, Mass.: Harvard University Press, 1983), and Leroy Jones and Il Sakong, *Government, Business, and Entrepreneurship in Economic Development: The Korean Case* (Cambridge, Mass.: Harvard University Press, 1980).

2. Samsung, Korea's largest *chaebol* at the time, bought controlling equity stakes in two of the four privatized banks. For details, see Wonhyuk Lim, "The Emergence of the *Chaebol* and the Origins of the *Chaebol* Problem," in *Economic Crisis and Corporate Restructuring in Korea: Reforming the Chaebol,* ed. Stephan Haggard et al. (Cambridge, Mass.: Harvard University Press, 2003), pp. 35–52.

budgets and handpicked the top management, while their lending portfolios were managed by government bureaucrats. The central bank, too, was brought under the firm control of the ministry of finance at this time.

Seeking to promote much-needed capital inflows to help finance industrial development, the Park government invited foreign banks into Korea in 1967. The original entrants were major U.S. and Japanese institutions, including Chase Manhattan, Citibank, Bank of America, the Bank of Tokyo, and Mitsubishi Bank. Conditions for entry were restrictive: no subsidiaries were allowed, only branches; no foreign bank could open more than one branch (though in exceptional cases, permission was given for two); new entrants had to demonstrate that their entry would make positive contributions to the Korean economy; and the mix of foreign banks' home countries had to be relatively balanced to prevent banks from any single country from becoming preponderant. Under these circumstances, foreign entry for the rest of the decade was slow. By 1976, only thirteen foreign bank branches had been established.[3]

Meanwhile, the Korean banking system became a central element of what scholars have called the developmental state, a capitalist system that combines private ownership with state guidance.[4] Mexico, Brazil, and Indonesia all possessed elements of the developmental state, but it was in Korea (and Japan before it) that this economic model took its most sophisticated form. In Korea, the paradigm resulted in highly institutionalized forms of communication and collaboration between businessmen and bureaucrats, and this symbiosis contributed to what is arguably one of the most successful economic experiments of the twentieth century. Under this paradigm, the state-controlled banking system served, in the words of one scholar, as "the fundamental tool with which Korean policymakers induced business cooperation and compliance in their efforts to promote exports and economic growth."[5] The banking system became a key instrument to channel resources to preferred sectors and to elicit cooperation from the *chaebol*, whose highly leveraged financial structures rendered them heavily dependent on

3. Yoon-Dae Euh and James C. Barker, *The Korean Banking System and Foreign Influence* (London: Routledge, 1990), p. 20.

4. For the seminal work on the developmental state, see Chalmers A. Johnson, *MITI and the Japanese Miracle: The Growth of Industrial Policy, 1925–1975* (Stanford, Calif.: Stanford University Press, 1982). See also Meredith Woo-Cumings, ed., *The Developmental State* (Ithaca: Cornell University Press, 1999). Other scholars characterize the Korean paradigm as a "quasi-internal organization" in which the state, financial system, and private sector essentially operate as a single corporate entity and the flow of finance and information is coordinated by bureaucrats, not markets. See Joon-Kyung Kim and Chung H. Lee, "The Political Economy of Government, Financial System, and the *Chaebols* before and after the 1997 Financial Crisis in Korea," CCAS Working Paper No. 11, Center for Contemporary Asian Studies, Doshisha University, April 2008.

5. Byung-Sun Choi, "Financial Policy and Big Business in Korea: The Perils of Financial Regulation," in *The Politics of Finance in Developing Countries,* ed. Stephan Haggard et al. (Ithaca: Cornell University Press, 1993), p. 23.

government bank loans. Through the commercial banks, Korean policymakers could exert influence across the whole economy, reorganizing industries and restructuring individual firms.

State control over the banking system continued throughout the 1980s and early 1990s, even after the government's decision to reprivatize the nationwide commercial banks and to deregulate interest rates.[6] To prevent the *chaebol* from buying up the banks as had happened in the 1950s, the government imposed an 8 percent cap on the amount of bank shares a single individual or corporation could own. Ceilings were also placed on the loans and loan guarantees banks could extend to the *chaebol.* Credit allocation remained subject to government guidance, and the selection of bank heads informally remained a government prerogative. As one study observed, "the privatization of commercial banks was nothing but a superficial change in legal ownership with no effect on the way the banks are governed or managed."[7] Compared with Indonesia, Korea had relatively few nationwide commercial banks, though its nonbank sector expanded rapidly.

In the 1980s, Korean policymakers eased somewhat the restrictions on the entry of foreign capital into the banking system. To promote competition and stimulate capital inflows, the government authorized the creation of two joint-venture banks, partnering local and foreign investors.[8] (The foreign partner was limited to a maximum equity share of 49 percent of the joint venture.) In addition, foreign bank branches were allowed to use the central bank's rediscount facilities, to engage in the export financing and trust business, and to join the National Banks Association and Clearing House. The number of foreign banks grew sharply as a result; by 1987, there were fifty-seven foreign bank branches, accounting for over 10 percent of total banking-sector assets and for 63 percent of all foreign exchange loans by deposit banks.[9]

How can we characterize the political influence of bankers in Korea? Because for most of its history Korea's banking sector was under government control, it makes little sense to speak of bankers as a discrete political grouping with preferences and interests. Korean banking is better understood through its role in the evolving relationship between the state and the *chaebol.*[10] Beginning in the 1960s, the Korean government came to see the banking system as an instrument to guide, constrain, and at times coerce the industrial private sector.[11] Over time, the balance of power

6. Interest rates were deregulated in three phases, implemented in 1991, 1993, and 1995.

7. Kim and Lee, "Political Economy," p. 21.

8. The two banks were Shinhan Bank, capitalized by Korean residents in Japan, and KorAm, which was a joint venture between Korean companies and Bank of America.

9. Kim and Lee, "Political Economy," p. 22.

10. On the relationship between the government, the financial system, and the *chaebol,* see Haggard et al., eds., *Economic Crisis and Corporate Restructuring in Korea,* and Chung H. Lee, "The Government, Financial System, and Large Private Enterprises in the Economic Development of South Korea," *World Development* 20 (1992), 187–197.

11. On this point, see Woo, *Race to the Swift.*

between the state and the *chaebol* shifted in favor of the corporate sector, but the government's influence over the banking system did not diminish until after the 1997 crisis.

The government's control over the Korean banking system was based on several elements. Until the early 1980s, the government held controlling stakes in the commercial banks, which gave it management control. After privatization, the government maintained strong influence over the banks because the 8 percent cap kept private ownership fragmented, and the banks' corporate governance practices kept the private-sector shareholders weak. For example, non-executive directors had no clearly defined roles, and they had little access to the information needed to monitor the enterprise. Bank presidents were rotated quickly, and their appointment always began with a recommendation of a finance ministry committee.

In addition, the government controlled banking activity through regulation and legislation, and because these powers were highly centralized in the finance ministry, bankers could not play one government agency against another. Since the days of President Park, the Bank of Korea was legally and effectively subservient to the Ministry of Finance (MOF).[12] The strength of the MOF increased further in 1994, when it was merged with the Economic Planning Board, a senior ministry responsible for the coordination of economic policy. The new entity—the Ministry of Finance and Economy (MOFE)—was extremely powerful, combining budget management, taxing powers, financial and monetary policy setting, and coordination of domestic and international economic policy. In the face of such highly centralized policymaking power, there was little private bankers could have done to challenge the government.

In any event, private Korean bankers were not interested in challenging government policy. In contrast to their Indonesian or Mexican counterparts, they were not part of large industrial conglomerates. Under the law, no commercial bank could own more than a 10 percent stake in any other corporation. (The *chaebol* would eventually come to own large portions of the financial system, but only through nonbank financial institutions such as securities insurance companies, credit unions, and merchant banks.) In addition, the heads of Korean banks, appointed with the acquiescence of the government and always under the vigilant eye of the MOF/MOFE, had few incentives to cause political trouble.

Finally, Korean bank owners had a much less developed sense of collective identity than their equivalents in other countries. In Korea, an association of bankers had existed since the 1920s, when it was a vehicle for communication and cooperation among the Japanese-controlled financial institutions. It was renamed the Seoul Bankers' Club in 1948 and the Korean Bankers' Association in 1975, when it became a truly national organization. However, for most of its history this entity was a

---

12. See Maxfield, *Gatekeepers of Growth*, pp. 107–120.

committee of government bureaucrats rather than a true business association. After privatization in the 1980s, what emerged was a group of passive, minority investors in government-managed commercial banks, rather than a politically self-aware class of private owner-managers whose livelihood depended on the business of banking.

Experimenting with Managed Opening (1995–1997)

Korean policymakers began experimenting with the managed opening of the banking sector in the mid-1990s, during the presidency of Kim Young Sam (1993–1998). This experiment was in large measure propelled by Korea's intention to join the Organization for Economic Cooperation and Development (OECD). The liberalization measures adopted by Korea under the OECD's terms of entry were significant. Foreign banks and securities firms from OECD countries would be allowed to establish subsidiaries as of December 1998. Also by that date, foreign investors from member countries would be permitted to establish and hold 100 percent ownership in any type of de novo financial institution, meaning that the 49 percent cap on joint ventures would be lifted, allowing the foreign partner to own a majority of the equity in a joint venture. In short, the doors of the Korean banking sector were poised to open, with the important exception that both foreigners and the *chaebol* were forbidden from owning controlling shares in domestic commercial banks. How can we account for Korea's decision to engage in the managed opening of the banking sector?

Globalizing, within Reason

In February 1993, Kim Young Sam became Korea's first civilian president in thirty-three years. The constitution had been revised only five years earlier following massive protests, marking Korea's transition to democratic rule and opening long-closed political space for civil society.[13] Arriving at such a critical juncture, Kim—who himself had been banned from politics by the military government—came under intense pressure to break with Korea's authoritarian past. Almost immediately, the new president launched an anticorruption campaign, requiring government and military officers to disclose their financial records. In a dramatic move, Kim had both of his predecessors arrested on charges of corruption and treason, winning convictions against both.[14] The new president also granted amnesty to thousands of

---

13. Among other things, the 1988 Constitution restored the direct election of the president, who was limited to a single, five-year term.

14. Former president Chun Doo Hwan was sentenced to death and former president Roh Tae Woo was sentenced to twenty-two years in jail. An appellate court later spared Chun's life and reduced Roh's sentence substantially.

political prisoners and put former military leaders and five *chaebol* heads on trial for corruption.

On economic matters, Kim sought to break with the past by adopting a strong anti-*chaebol* stance and embracing liberal reforms. Kim's cocktail of economic liberalism and opposition to big business was not novel. Presidents Chun Doo Hwan (1979–1987) and Roh Tae Woo (1987–1992) had also mounted campaigns against the conglomerates to curry favor with the middle class, forcing the *chaebol* to sell off assets and restricting their tentacular expansion into multiple sectors. Advised by a cadre of U.S.-educated technocrats, both presidents embraced liberal reforms, cutting tariffs and deregulating the nonbank financial sector.[15] But in both cases, the anti-*chaebol* strategy failed or backfired, as the conglomerates were able to circumvent government restrictions and in some cases drew strength from liberalized markets.[16]

Like his predecessors, Kim was eventually forced to seek accommodation with the *chaebol*. A sharp economic downturn in 1993—exacerbated by a "strike by capital" in which the conglomerates withheld needed investment—demonstrated the structural power of big business and the need for the government to secure *chaebol* cooperation if growth was to be restored and unemployment avoided. The Kim government therefore shifted its focus to policies emphasizing the role of big business in export promotion and in fostering rapid economic growth. "Deregulation" and "globalization" (*segyewah*) became the organizing principles of economic policy, and competitiveness became a mantra.[17] President Kim warned his countrymen in December 1993: "Globalization and openness have become irrevocable trends. Without drastic changes in our thinking, we will be relegated to a second or third rate nation. Korea's main goal should be reinforcing our national competitiveness....In the era of globalization, national competitiveness should be centered around companies and regions. The central government needs to act as their supporter."[18]

Accordingly, the economic bureaucracy was reorganized. The finance ministry became the MOFE, and a new policy planning staff position was created at the Office of the President (the "Blue House") to assist with the globalization policy. Also, a Globalization Promotion Committee composed of eminent experts was created under the Office of the Prime Minister to advise the government on administrative reform, education policy, and science and technology.

---

15. On the role of the technocrats, see Meredith Woo-Cumings, "Slouching toward the Market: The Politics of Financial Liberalization in South Korea," in Loriaux et. al, *Capital Ungoverned*, pp. 57–91.

16. Chung-in Moon, "Patterns of Business-Government Relations in South Korea," in *Business and Government in Industrializing Asia*, ed. Andrew MacIntyre (Ithaca: Cornell University Press, 1994), pp. 142–166.

17. For details on the globalization policy, see Barry K. Gills and Dongsook S. Gills, "Globalization and Strategic Choice in South Korea: Economic Reform and Labor," in *Korea's Globalization*, ed. Samuel S. Kim (Cambridge: Cambridge University Press, 2000), pp. 29–51.

18. Kim Young Sam, "Reforms for Stronger Competitiveness," address at the National Policy Review Conference at Chong Wa Dae, December 27, 1993.

Despite the discourse of deregulation and globalization, the leading technocrats in the Kim government remained convinced that financial globalization should have limits. They were intensely worried about the potential consequences of opening the banking sector in an economy that was dominated by concentrated industrial conglomerates. If the barriers to entry were removed, they reasoned, the business groups would gain control of the commercial banks and use them as private coffers for financing their own operations.[19] If the *chaebol* ever got into trouble, their banks would be forced to provide financing on any terms to keep their business groups afloat, with disastrous consequences for the banks' financial health. The government would eventually have to bail them out to protect depositors, and the costs would ultimately fall on the taxpaying public. As we have seen, this is precisely what happened in Indonesia.

From this perspective, banking-sector opening was no solution to the "concentration problem." Indeed, foreign entry could make things worse by facilitating capital outflows. Yung Chul Park, an influential adviser to the Blue House on financial matters, made the point clearly:

> Relaxation of the barriers to entry into the banking industry is not an answer to the concentration problem.…Entry into the banking industry cannot be completely liberated. Even when entry requirements are relaxed, the business groups could exercise market power to block the establishment of or control new entrants. Opening the bank intermediation market to foreign competition will not help mitigate the problem. Foreign bank branches could in fact add to the instability as their actions are freer to move in and out of the market, as they are dictated solely by profit earnings, and they could also serve as a conduit for capital flight.[20]

In this frame of mind, Korean policymakers approached the next important step of the president's *segyewah* policy: gaining accession into the exclusive club of the world's richest countries, the Organization for Economic Cooperation and Development (OECD).

Joining the Club

International kudos in the aftermath of the 1988 Olympic Games in Seoul first convinced the administration of President Roh Tae Woo that the country was ready

---

19. Interview with Lee Kyu Sung, minister of finance and economy (1988–1990 and 1998–1999), Seoul, June 9, 2008.

20. Yung Chul Park, "Financial Repression, Liberalization, and Development in Developing Countries," Working Paper, Korean Development Institute, 1987, p. 49. Park was president of the Korea Institute of Finance (1992–1998), an influential think tank. He also served on the Globalization Promotion Committee under the Office of the Prime Minister (1995–1998) and on the Presidential Commission on Financial Reform (1997–1998).

to join the world's industrial powers in the OECD. Mexico's entry into the orga-nization in May 1994 must have created peer pressure to join as well. Some mem-bers of the administration saw OECD membership as a way to force the *chaebol* to restructure and embrace international practices and standards.[21] There was another advantage to making OECD commitments. "The commitments helped us increase transparency," recalls Korea's lead negotiator for OECD accession. "The government could announce its policy intentions ahead of time, so it could manage expectations about where things were going. This is part of the 'Korean style' of economic policy, based on five-year plans.'"[22]

Korean negotiators fought tooth and nail to clear the OECD's membership bar with the least possible constraints on financial policy. The Koreans' opening posi-tion was that if many OECD members had taken twenty to thirty years to complete their financial liberalization process, they should not be expected to take less.[23] This position was not well received by the OECD Committee on Capital Movements and Invisible Transactions, and it led to slow and difficult negotiations. Abdelal contrasts Korea's recalcitrance with the attitude of other applicants for accession: "The discus-sions with Prague were hardly negotiations; they were practically instructions. The Czech authorities were eager to please other OECD members, and to learn the con-stitutive norms of membership in the developed country club. The negotiations with South Korea, by contrast, were difficult, even occasionally tense as the authorities in Seoul sought to maintain as much autonomy from Paris as possible and to do the minimum required to enter the club."[24]

While Korean diplomats were negotiating with the OECD in Paris, Seoul also came under pressure from the IMF to speed up capital account liberalization and financial-sector reform. In its 1996 Article IV consultation reviewing the Korean economy, Fund staff argued that Korea's financial sector and capital account trans-actions remained overregulated and that a more explicit liberalization timetable was required.[25] Now-declassified minutes of the Executive Board's discussion of the report provide a glimpse of the arguments the G7 governments were invoking to pressure the Korean authorities into accelerating capital account liberalization and

21. Stephen L. Harris, "South Korea and the Asian Crisis: The Impact of the Democratic Deficit on OECD Accession," in *International Financial Governance under Stress,* ed. Geoffrey R. D. Underhill and Xiaoke Zhang (Cambridge: Cambridge University Press, 2003), p. 144.

22. Interview with Duck-Koo Chung, former chief negotiator on OECD accession (1996), former vice-minister of finance (1998–99), and former minister of commerce, industry, and energy (1999–2000), Seoul, June 10, 2008.

23. Jan Schuijer, "OECD Members' Experience with Capital Account Liberalization and Its Relevance to Other Countries," comments at the Global Forum on International Investment, Shanghai, Decem-ber 5–6, 2002.

24. Abdelal, *Capital Rules,* p. 109.

25. SM/96/262, Korea—Staff Report for the 1996 Article IV Consultation, October 22, 1996, IMF Archives, p. 18.

banking-sector opening. The French director, for example, attacked Korea's managed opening approach:

> On the pace of liberalization, like the staff, I am not convinced by any gradual approach to liberalization in the case of Korea.... I would advocate a fast track program of reform concerning capital account liberalization, domestic financial sector, and monetary policy modernization.... Concerning the financial sector, the present vulnerability might be best addressed by introducing a higher degree of competition than by maintaining a strongly regulated environment. In any case, external opening of the financial sector would not be, in my view, a major factor of macroeconomic destabilization for Korea.[26]

The Japanese executive director, while more circumspect in tone, was in agreement, calling for an end to gradualism and for accelerating the pace of reform.[27] The U.S. representative also strongly urged speedier financial liberalization, arguing that with Korea's imminent OECD accession, barriers to the flow of capital had become anachronistic:

> Korea's prospective membership in the OECD and the commitments made to capital account and financial liberalization confirm the authorities' recognition of the linkage between efficient capital markets and future growth. The question is not over the direction of policies, it is over the pace of change.... We believe that the balance of benefits is clearly tilted toward the side of faster liberalization. To use [U.S. Executive Director] Ms. Lissakers' metaphor, the schoolboy has clearly outgrown his uniform.[28]

In October 1996, South Korea won approval to become the OECD's twenty-ninth member.[29] In the end, Korea accepted about 65 percent of the OECD codes on financial liberalization, compared with an average acceptance rate of 89 percent for the rest of the membership.[30] However, the Koreans made some significant concessions, the most important of which was a promise to allow OECD-based foreign banks to enter the country through subsidiaries (and not only through branches) as of December 1998. This restriction had been identified by the Office of the United States Trade Representative as "among the most problematic constraints" faced by U.S. banks in Korea.[31]

---

26. EBM/96/103, Minutes of Executive Board Meeting 96/103 (November 15, 1996), IMF Archives, pp. 50–51.

27. Ibid., p. 50.

28. Ibid., pp. 55–56.

29. For details on the terms of accession, see "Statement by the Government of the Republic of Korea Concerning the Acceptance by the Republic of Korea of the Obligations of Membership in the Organization for Economic Co-Operation and Development," October 9, 1996.

30. Dobson and Jacquet, *Financial Services Liberalization*, p. 238.

31. Office of the United States Trade Representative, *National Trade Estimate—Korea*, 1997, p. 246. Under Korean regulations, credit limits, limits on foreign exchange trading, and capital adequacy and liquidity requirements were calculated for foreign-bank branches on the basis of local capital, not on the

Foreign bankers in the advanced economies were naturally pleased with the outcome, but given the code's voluntary nature and weak enforcement mechanisms, there was significant skepticism about the Korean government's willingness to implement the reform. Also, it was not clear what regulatory constraints might be imposed on subsidiaries, as those important details would not be known until detailed regulations were formulated. "The crux of this issue is not whether (foreign) banks can open branches in Korea," an analyst said about the government's pledge at the OECD. "It is how much money they can bring onshore to lend, and that is still being debated."[32]

Finally, the Korean government did not budge on the issue of local ownership of Korean banks, which remained tightly capped for foreigners and residents alike. The government had been gradually lowering the ceilings on the amount of shares in a Korean firm that foreigners, in the aggregate, could own. Under the accession agreement, investors from OECD countries would be allowed to purchase up to 100 percent of a Korean firm's listed shares (in virtually all sectors) after the year 2000. However, this was of little consequence for banking-sector opening, since individual foreign ownership in domestic banks was capped for foreigners and residents alike at 8 percent, and after 1994, at 4 percent. Numerous foreign entities could, in theory, acquire all the shares of a Korean bank, but none would have management control. Having secured entry into the prestigious club of wealthy nations, the Kim government turned to rethink financial policy at home.

A Blueprint for Financial Reform

To prepare for the next step in the process of financial liberalization, President Kim launched a Presidential Commission for Financial Reform in January 1997. Composed of thirty-one academics, civil servants, and business leaders, the group prepared and delivered over the course of 1997 a comprehensive blueprint for reforming Korea's financial system.

The commission's diagnosis of the country's financial system was consistent with President Kim's vision of an ever-globalizing world in which Korea had to strive to remain competitive lest it be overrun by its economic rivals. In its report, the commission concluded that years of government protection had "derailed" the management of Korean banks and undermined the soundness of financial institutions. "Korean banks are years behind their western counterparts in product and service innovation, information processing capability, and risk management," the report observed. "With the advent of the WTO and Korea's entry into the OECD, open

---

parent bank's global capital base. This was not true for subsidiaries. This unusual feature of Korean regulation meant that foreign banks were more interested in entering the Korean market through subsidiaries than through branches—the opposite of the situation in other countries.

32. Anne Lowell and Ed Paisley, "Proud Seoul," *Institutional Investor* 31 (December 1997), 73–75.

competition may result in the dominance of foreign firms in the domestic market if the Korean financial industry fails to raise its competitiveness to global standards."[33] In language familiar to policymakers accustomed to the workings of the developmental state, the commission called on the government to transform the country's financial industry into a "strategic industry" through "unfettered competition and structural reorganization."[34] Among the group's key recommendations were consolidating financial supervision in a single watchdog agency, authorizing the establishment of financial holding companies, and allowing financial institutions to expand their business lines and move toward universal banking.

On barriers to entry and foreign participation, however, the commission was conservative. The cap on individual shareholding in nationwide commercial banks should be raised from 4 to 10 percent, but the percentage of *voting* shares should remain capped at 4 percent. Permission to increase ownership to 10 percent would require a rigorous screening of the entrant, including management capabilities, capital base, and any adverse effects on competition. Joint-venture banks and foreign banks should not be subject to ownership limitations if their parent companies were widely held. The commission was strangely silent on the issue of foreign subsidiaries. In short, the group's recommendations on ownership, while allowing for greater foreign and *chaebol* investment in banks, would not significantly change the patterns of ownership and control in the Korean banking sector.

Soon after the commission issued the second installment of its report, President Kim ordered the finance ministry to draft legislation based on its recommendations. The proposed legislative package was announced in June 1997. The government's proposals mirrored the commission's recommendations on consolidating financial regulation and authorizing the creation of financial holding companies, but the government rejected the commission's recommendation to lift the ownership cap for commercial banks. The cap would remain at 4 percent, though the financial reform package included measures to enhance the rights of bank shareholders, allowing foreign investors to take part in the management of South Korean banks as nonstanding board members.[35]

The proposed bills were presented to the National Assembly, where the legislature's Finance and Economy Committee approved them that November. However, the legislation died a quiet death shortly thereafter, to the government's great consternation. As in Mexico and Indonesia, the advent of democratic rule in Korea meant that the executive could no longer rely on the legislature to rubber-stamp its proposals. President Kim's ruling New Korea Party (NKP) had lost its absolute majority in the National Assembly three years into the president's term (in the

---

33. Presidential Commission for Financial Reform, "Financial Reform in Korea: The Final Report" (unofficial translation of executive summary), November 1997, p. 4.

34. Ibid., p. 6.

35. "Foreigners May Be Non-standing Board Members in Korean Banks," *Asia Pulse,* June 26, 1997.

April 1996 parliamentary elections), and the president had suffered major political setbacks since then, including student protests, major labor unrest, and a string of corruption scandals.[36]

In addition, Kim's financial reform package met with fierce resistance from the Bank of Korea, which would lose its powers over banking supervision and regulation to the proposed new agency and from labor unions representing the four government agencies targeted for elimination under the government's reorganization plan. The unions threatened immediate strikes. At the National Assembly, a majority of the legislators calculated it was more advantageous to do nothing than to pass highly unpopular reforms.[37] Thus, the bill was not sent to the full assembly for discussion before the body adjourned. The legislature would not meet again until after the presidential elections on December 18, and by then the country would be on the brink of financial collapse.

Crisis and Critical Juncture (1997–1998)

Korea's experiment with managed opening came to an end in the second half of 1997, when the country was enveloped by the financial crisis that had already caused chaos in Southeast Asia. As in the cases of Mexico and Indonesia, Korea was hit simultaneously by a banking crisis and a capital account crisis. The twin shocks triggered total de jure banking-sector opening and led to a degree of foreign entry into the banking system unprecedented in postwar Korea. The dual nature of the shock was critical: the banking shock compelled Korean policymakers to seek out foreign capital to recapitalize troubled financial institutions, while the capital account crisis magnified the leverage of external actors interested in liberalizing Korea's banking regime.

Korea's Banking Shock

The financial panic that began in Thailand in the late spring of 1997 spread to South Korea in the second half of that year, triggering a crisis in that country. There is voluminous literature on the causes of Korea's 1997 financial crisis; here, I highlight only the factors behind its banking shock.[38] The financial system suffered from

---

36. On the government's political weakness during this period, see B. C. Koh, "South Korea in 1996: Internal Strains and External Challenges," *Asian Survey* 37 (January 1997), 1–9.

37. Stephan Haggard and Andrew MacIntyre, "The Political Economy of the Asian Financial Crisis: Korea and Thailand Compared," in *The Asian Financial Crisis and the Architecture of Global Finance*, ed. Gregory W. Noble and John Ravenhill (Cambridge: Cambridge University Press, 2000), p. 75.

38. On the financial crisis in Korea, see David T. Coe and Se-Jik Kim, eds., *Korean Crisis and Recovery* (Washington, D.C.: IMF; Seoul, Korea: KIEP, 2002), and Heather Smith, "Korea," in *East Asia in Crisis: From Being a Miracle to Needing One?* ed. Ross H. McLeod and Ross Garnaut (London: Routledge, 1998),

several vulnerabilities. Korean conglomerates had accumulated large amounts of foreign-currency-denominated liabilities by the late 1990s, mostly in the form of loans from banks and nonbank institutions. Unlike Indonesian conglomerates, Korea's corporate giants were not allowed to own banks, but the *chaebol* acquired dozens of nonbank financial institutions, to which ownership restrictions did not apply.[39] Also, the *chaebol* were very heavily leveraged compared with their peers in Latin America and East Asia; they had debt-to-equity ratios in excesses of 400 and sometimes 500 percent, which rendered them (and their financiers) highly vulnerable to cash-flow shocks.[40] At the same time, commercial and merchant banks borrowed extensively abroad in order to lend at home, often at short maturities. Even before the crisis, some of the *chaebol* were already experiencing severe financial difficulties.[41]

Second, financial supervision and regulation in precrisis Korea was weak.[42] Rules for loan classification and provisioning were lax by OECD standards, as were regulations concerning risk concentration and large exposure. Supervision of merchant banks, where some of the riskiest lending was taking place, was especially weak. Regulators had placed no limits on how much a merchant bank could borrow abroad, and there was no effective monitoring of merchant banks' potential borrowers.[43] These failures of financial surveillance and regulation meant that key vulnerabilities were not managed until it was too late.

As in Indonesia, the Korean crisis was triggered by a financial panic that led to massive, rapid outflows of capital. The value of the won began to fall in late October 1997, when the bankruptcy of Kia, one of Korea's three major automakers, unsettled the markets. The decline in the won quickly multiplied the burden of the private sector's foreign debt. Foreign creditors began to refuse to roll over loans to Korean banks and corporations, inducing further depreciation. The government, in an attempt to stabilize the won's value, intervened extensively in foreign-exchange

---

pp. 57–72. For useful analyses of Korea's banking crisis, see Tomás J. T. Baliño and Angel Ubide, "The Korean Financial Crisis of 1997—A Strategy of Financial Sector Reform," IMF Working Paper WP/99/28, March 1999, and Takatoshi Ito and Yuko Hashimoto, "Bank Restructuring in Asia: Crisis Management in the Aftermath of the Financial Crisis and Prospects for Crisis Prevention—Korea," REITI Discussion Paper 07-E-038, February 5, 2007.

39. By the end of 1998, the seventy largest *chaebol* owned 140 nonbank financial institutions. Joon-Ho Hahm, "The Government, the *Chaebol* and Financial Institutions before the Economic Crisis," in Haggard et al., *Economic Crisis and Corporate Restructuring in Korea*, p. 87.

40. Baliño and Ubide, "Korean Financial Crisis," p. 20.

41. In January 1997, Hanbo Steel, the fourteenth-largest *chaebol*, collapsed with debts of some US$6 billion. In April 1997, the Jinro Group, ranked nineteenth among conglomerates, required a bailout to stay solvent. In July 1997, Daewoo—one of the very largest *chaebol*—narrowly avoided bankruptcy by pledging US$8.6 billion in assets to persuade its creditors to roll over debts it could not service. Ito and Hashimoto, "Bank Restructuring in Asia," p. 18.

42. Baliño and Ubide, "Korean Financial Crisis," pp. 16–19.

43. Kim and Lee, "Political Economy," p. 30.

markets, to little effect.[44] By the end of September, some 14 percent of Korean commercial bank loans had turned nonperforming, profits had dried up, and a sharp decline in stock prices had vaporized a large fraction of the banks' net worth.[45]

To avert bank runs, the authorities extended a blanket guarantee on all deposits of financial institutions until 2000. At the same time, the central bank began providing emergency liquidity to merchant banks and to the worst-affected commercial banks. Some institutions (including ten commercial banks) were closed by the authorities; others—too systemically important to be closed—were taken over by the authorities and recapitalized.

On December 29, 1997, the Kim government succeeded in pushing through the National Assembly a revised version of the financial reform package that had died in the legislature a few weeks before. This time, however, it included measures to strengthen the government's capacity to take over, close, or rehabilitate financial institutions. Among the measures approved by the legislature was a provision that amounted to the total de jure opening of the Korean banking sector. Under the amended Banking Act, the old ownership cap of 4 percent could be breached by foreign investors interested in merging with or acquiring a Korean commercial bank, subject to approval from regulators at the 10, 25, and 33 percent thresholds. Also, the authorities accelerated the timetable that had been provided to the OECD, allowing foreign banks and securities firms to set up fully owned subsidiaries in Korea subject to the same entry rules as Korean financial institutions as of March 1998. To understand this dramatic change in regulation, we must first examine the role of the Bretton Woods institutions.

Korea and the IMF

Before the Asian financial crisis, the last time Korea undertook an IMF program was in the 1980s, when the Korean authorities sought help to stabilize the economy.[46] The Fund extended to Seoul two one-year standby arrangements, disbursing about US$750 million.[47] For the next decade, Korea's relationship with the IMF was limited to regular Article IV surveillance and policy dialogue.

During the 1997 crash, the Korean authorities first approached the Fund in mid-November 1997. An IMF mission arrived in Seoul on November 26 to negotiate the

---

44. During the last week of November, the central bank spent one to two billion dollars in reserves *per day*, draining usable international reserves to US$5 billion. The won was allowed to float on December 16, 1997.

45. "Financing Operations in South Korea," *Economist Intelligence Unit*, February 1998, p. 18.

46. For details on the program, see Bijan B. Aghevli and Jorge Márquez-Ruarte, "A Case of Successful Adjustment: Korea's Experience during 1980–84," Occasional Paper 39, International Monetary Fund, August 1985.

47. "Korea: Transactions with the Fund from May 1, 1984 to July 31, 2008," available at www.imf.org (accessed August 2008).

program, the Letter of Intent was signed on December 3, and approval from the IMF's Executive Board came two days later. Korea was extended an assistance package of loans and guarantees totaling, in theory, US$55 billion. The IMF's contribution was US$21 billion—more than the organization had ever lent to a single country, and more than six times the maximum amount Korea would normally have been able to borrow under Fund rules. The rest of the money came from the World Bank (US$10 billion) and the Asian Development Bank (US$4 billion), and the remaining US$20 billion was in the form of a so-called second line of defense—nonbinding bilateral commitments from the G7 countries to provide supplementary assistance should it be required. However, the credibility of these commitments was always questionable given domestic political constraints in the G7 capitals, particularly in Washington.[48]

The program failed to restore confidence in the Korean economy. After December 8, the won's value resumed its decline, falling by 10 percent every day for five days. The program simply did not provide sufficient resources to cover Korea's enormous financing gap, and market participants never believed that the second line of defense was real.[49] Stability was not restored until the end of December, when the timetable for IMF disbursements to Korea was accelerated and when the U.S. government, in coordination with other G7 capitals, pressured international banks to keep their credit lines open and roll over Korean debt.[50] In the end, Seoul would receive some US$14.4 billon in Fund disbursements.[51]

As in Indonesia, total de jure opening of Korea's commercial banking sector was part of the IMF program from the very first Letter of Intent. Among the Korean government's commitments to the Fund on capital account liberalization, the authorities promised that

> the schedule for allowing foreign entry into the domestic financial sector will be accelerated. Foreign financial institutions will be allowed to participate in mergers and acquisitions of domestic financial institutions in a friendly manner and on equal principles. By mid-1998, foreign financial institutions will be allowed to establish bank subsidiaries and brokerage houses. Effective immediately foreign banks will be allowed to purchase equity in domestic banks without restriction, provided that the acquisitions contribute to the efficiency and soundness of the banking sector.[52]

---

48. Blustein, *Chastening*, p. 179.

49. The Fund's evaluation office would later report that IMF staff was instructed to rewrite its projections of Korean debt rollover to show that the program could be fully financed without relying on the second line of defense. It also concluded that "the program as presented was clearly underfinanced, although this fact was not explicitly acknowledged." "The IMF and Recent Capital Account Crises," p. 19.

50. For details on the "bail-in," see Blustein, *Chastening*, chap. 7.

51. "Korea: Transactions with the Fund from May 1, 1984 to July 31, 2008."

52. "Korea: Memorandum on the Economic Program," December 3, 1997.

Subsequent Letters of Intent translated these commitments into more precise and time-bound measures. In the February 7 document, the Korean government pledged to issue, by February 1998, a presidential degree providing transparent guidelines for foreign investment in domestic financial institutions. It also promised to allow foreign banks to establish subsidiaries by March 31 of the same year.[53] This last condition was designated a performance criterion in the February document, which meant that disbursement of IMF resources could not be authorized until it was implemented.[54]

To increase the probability of compliance, IMF conditionality linked together the IMF program, Korea's commitments to the OECD, and Korea's negotiations on trade in services at the WTO. Under the February 1998 Letter of Intent, the Korean authorities agreed to revise their financial services offer under the GATS to make it consistent with the Korea's OECD commitments, which as we have seen included the authorization of foreign-bank subsidiaries.[55] This was a significant concession because Korean negotiators in Geneva had refused to make this link earlier when pressed to do so in trade negotiations. By linking Korea's OECD and WTO commitments, the IMF program aimed to use the WTO's relatively robust compliance mechanisms to turn Korea's more liberal but hard-to-enforce OECD commitments into more enforceable rules.[56] The Korean authorities submitted the revised GATS offer in 1999.

The Importance of External Pressure

In the absence of ideological support for banking-sector opening, external pressure became the single most important force pushing the reform through the Korean political system. This pressure was exercised in an environment in which Korea's

---

53. "Korea: Memorandum on the Economic Program," February 7, 1998.

54. Performance criteria are conditions approved by the IMF's Executive Board that need to be met before disbursements are made under an arrangement. If a country has not complied with a performance criterion at the time of disbursement, the board must grant a waiver before the funds can be released. The decision to grant a waiver is based on whether the board has received adequate assurances that the program is on track or that remedial action has been taken.

55. "Korea: Memorandum on the Economic Program," February 7, 1998.

56. Legally, the IMF may not impose "cross-conditionality" as part of its programs—it may not make the disbursement of its resources contingent on the rules or decisions of other international organizations. It can, however, require a country to make commitments that overlap with those it may have made in the context of other international organizations or agreements. In this case, Korea undertook an IMF program to make binding the commitments under one agreement (with the OECD) through a second agreement (the GATS). This action was legally questionable, even though the IMF was clear that its performance criterion was the authorization of foreign-bank subsidiaries, not the binding of OECD commitments. Ambiguous cases such as this one led the IMF Executive Board to approve in September 2002 new guidelines emphasizing the need for program documents to distinguish clearly between the conditions on which IMF financial support depends and other elements of the borrowing country's economic program.

dependence on external resources was at its peak. Under these conditions of extreme pressure, the Korean political system responded by temporarily overcoming internal opposition to banking-sector opening and acceding to total de jure opening. To see this, we must revisit the final days of 1997.

After the initial IMF arrangement failed to restore confidence, Korea's economy entered what appeared to be an unstoppable downward spiral. On December 8, the finance ministry revealed that short-term debt was about US$100 billion, nearly double the amount it had claimed during negotiations with the IMF, while usable reserves had fallen to only US$6 billion.[57] Korea's banking authorities took over two major commercial banks about to collapse and began to inject emergency capital. The won continued to plummet; by December 10, it had lost almost half its early-1997 value. Meanwhile, the stock market fell to its lowest level since 1987, and major brokerage houses began to file for bankruptcy protection. On December 22, Moody's downgraded Korean corporate bonds, including those of twenty banks, to "junk bond" status, and the next day, Standard & Poor's downgraded Korea's long-term foreign currency rating by four notches, putting the country's risk of default on overseas debt on par with that of the Dominican Republic. By then eight of the top thirty *chaebol* had already gone bankrupt.[58]

To meet its short-term debt obligations coming due at the end of December, the Korean authorities requested on December 24 that the IMF accelerate its disbursement schedule and release about US$2 billion ahead of the original disbursement dates. Along with that request was a promise to undertake more specific structural reforms, including allowing foreign banks and brokerage houses to establish subsidiaries by March 31, 1998.[59] The IMF Executive Board agreed to the release of funds, but only if structural performance criteria were met. Key among the conditions to accelerate disbursement were some of the financial reforms contained in the legislative package that had died in the legislature in November. This time, however, the package also had to include provisions for total de jure opening of the banking system.

The National Assembly met on Monday, December 30, to discuss the thirteen financial reform bills submitted by the government. The legislators were under enormous pressure: the meeting took place just hours before Korea's most important international creditors were to meet in New York to decide whether to roll over up to US$15 billion in loans and other financial contracts coming due on December 31. The Fund's Executive Board would meet the following day to decide whether to accelerate the disbursement schedule and release the first tranche. This time, President Kim's government managed to impress upon the legislature that failing to approve the reform bills would have catastrophic consequences for the economy,

57. "International Macroeconomic Chronology," Barclays Bank, December 1997.

58. Kim and Lee, "Political Economy," p. 31.

59. "Korea: Letter of Intent," December 24, 1997.

as it would lead to the loss of support from the IMF and international creditors and to certain default. This, in turn, would damage the country's creditworthiness for years. The president managed to build a winning coalition, with his own party at the core, and almost all the bills were approved, including the one removing barriers to foreign bank entry (the legislators refused to approve a bill that would have made it easier for banks to fire employees). Korea's IMF executive director recalls the game-changing impact of the crisis on the government's ability to push reform through the legislature: "Thanks to the crisis, we were able to restructure the whole economy very quickly. Camdessus, the IMF's Managing Director, said when he came to Korea that it was a blessing in disguise. He was badly criticized for it. But, of course, he was right. Without the crisis, we would still be lingering."[60]

It is difficult to overestimate the importance of Washington's intervention with Korea's private creditors as an element of external pressure. The resources involved in that operation far exceeded what the Fund could make available to Seoul, and no other government aside from the United States could convene all the key players on such short notice and exert the necessary pressure to secure the rollovers. Years later, one of Korea's most senior economic officials during the crisis remembered, "What really mattered during the Korean crisis was U.S. government intervention to persuade major international banks not to pull their credit lines in exchange for a U.S. government offer to negotiate the outstanding debt. This was far more important than IMF resources."[61]

In contrast to the actions of Brazilian president Cardoso and Indonesian president Habibie, this was not the act of a president struggling for political survival. Kim Young Sam was a lame duck in his last days in office; his successor (from a different political party) had already been elected on December 18 and was waiting to take office in February 1998. Rather, this was the legacy of a president who understood that resisting foreign pressure at this juncture would have a calamitous impact on his country. Politically, President Kim had nothing to lose.

Washington's Hand

A long-running debate over the IMF's role in Korea is whether the U.S. Treasury, acting on behalf of the U.S. financial community, used its political muscle at the IMF to introduce banking-sector-opening measures into the Korean program. That U.S. and other advanced-economy banks wanted access to the Korean banking market is beyond doubt. Foreign banks had been making massive profits in Korea for years,

---

60. Interview with Okyu Kwon, IMF alternative executive director (1997–1999), secretary to the president for finance and economy (2000–2001), deputy minister of finance and economy (2001–2002), senior secretary to the president for national policy (2003–2004), and deputy prime minister and minister of finance and economy (2006–2007), Seoul, June 6, 2008.

61. Comments delivered at confidential forum, London, January 23, 2007.

outperforming local banks by considerable margins.[62] In 1997 alone, in part thanks to the soaring exchange rate, foreign banks saw their profits triple to some US$620 million, up from US$208 million in 1996.[63] And because the Korean government guaranteed all foreign loans to domestic enterprises, these profits were (largely) risk-free. It is not surprising that both U.S. and European banks focused much of their attention on lobbying the Korean government during the GATS negotiations.

According to an influential account of the crisis, the U.S. government played a key role in the design and negotiation of Korea's standby arrangement with the IMF, deploying David Lipton, a top Treasury official, to Seoul to "monitor" the negotiations between the Korean authorities and Fund staff. According to Blustein, "lobbying by American financial services firms, which wanted to crack the Korean market, was the driving force behind the Treasury's pressure on Seoul.... Much of Lipton's effort was concentrated on obtaining firm, specific Korean commitments to speed up liberalization of the country's financial system."[64]

The Fund's Independent Evaluation Office, on the other hand, has argued that Washington did not slip banking-sector-opening measures into the program—banking-sector opening was the IMF staff's idea all along. Fund staff had recommended to the Korean authorities that they relax restrictions on foreign ownership of domestic banks prior to the crisis, and this recommendation also appeared in the briefing paper prepared by the staff on the eve of the negotiations in Seoul.[65] According to this view, "what the IMF did in terms of financial sector restructuring was to tip the balance of power in Korea in favor of advancing the homegrown agenda."[66]

These two arguments are not mutually exclusive. While it is clear that banking-sector-opening measures were not introduced into the program, ex nihilo, by the U.S. Treasury, it is also clear that the U.S. authorities wanted to ensure that the IMF program went as far as possible in pushing the Korean government to liberalize the financial sector. Treasury's relatively heavy-handed approach to the negotiations was consistent with that goal. Lipton's participation at the negotiations must have helped the Fund extract concessions from the Korean authorities, especially given Washington's leverage in cobbling together the "second line of defense" and, more importantly, in putting pressure on U.S. banks to keep rolling over Korean debt. Also, U.S. officials kept up the pressure for banking-sector opening through the IMF Executive Board once the program was up and running. For example, at the first review of the standby agreement in February 1998, the U.S. executive director

62. Sang In Hwang and In-Seok Shin, "Banking Sector Liberalization in Korea: Impact on the Korean Economy," in *Financial Market Opening in China and Korea*, ed. Young-Rok Cheong et al. (Seoul: KIEP, 2003).

63. "Profit of Foreign Bank Branches in Korea Tripled in 1997," *Korean Industry Update*, March 16, 1998.

64. Blustein, *Chastening*, pp. 143 and 145.

65. "The IMF and Recent Capital Account Crises," p. 110.

66. Ibid., p. 109.

reminded the Korean authorities that "we look for further steps to be taken quickly—particularly binding the OECD financial services commitment in the WTO."[67]

But what is also clear is that, in contrast to Mexico and Indonesia, total de jure opening of the banking sector was not a "homegrown" reform; it lacked a domestic constituency in Korea, even among otherwise liberal government technocrats. To be sure, the Korean government was getting used to the idea of admitting foreign-bank subsidiaries, as it promised the OECD, but beyond that, de jure banking-sector opening did not enjoy domestic support. The Presidential Commission on Financial Reform's idea of competition involved raising the bank-ownership limits for *residents* to 10 percent; it did not entail allowing foreigners to purchase controlling stakes in Korean banks or accelerating the authorization of foreign-bank subsidiaries. Similarly, the legislation the Kim government prepared on the basis of the commission report did not envision de jure opening of this kind. Those measures were introduced by the IMF and ran counter to the preferences of the Korean policy elite.

Korea and the World Bank

Compared with the IMF, the World Bank played a secondary role in the opening of Korea's banking sector. Historically, relations between the Korean authorities and the Bank were somewhat chilly, as the Bank was a vocal skeptic of President Park's program of state-led development and promotion of heavy industry.[68] During the early 1980s, Korea turned to the Bank for a bread-and-butter Structural Adjustment Loan to help it cope with balance-of-payments difficulties. Save for a small loan in 1993 to help train financial policy personnel, there was little Bank involvement with Korea's financial policy until the late 1990s.

When the 1997 crisis struck, the World Bank was called on to participate in the giant assistance package being put together for Korea; the Bank agreed to contribute up to US$10 billion. The funds were disbursed to Korea in three, single-tranche loans—a US$3 billion Economic Reconstruction Loan in 1997 and two Structural Adjustment Loans of US$2 billion each in March and October 1998. The conditionality attached to these loans focused on financial- and corporate-sector restructuring, labor market reform, and social safety nets.

However, banking-sector opening was never mentioned explicitly. The March 1998 loan did require, in rather general terms, that the Korean government pledge to "take active steps to reduce public and private barriers to entry and exit of firms."[69] The October 1998 loan dealt with the issue of banking-sector opening

---

67. EBM/98/58, Minutes of Executive Board Meeting 98/58 (May 29, 1998), IMF Archives, p. 29.

68. Woo, *Race to the Swift*, pp. 131–132.

69. "Loan Agreement (Structural Adjustment Loan) between Republic of Korea and International Bank for Reconstruction and Development," Loan Number 4302 KO, March 27, 1998. The 1997 loan agreement remains classified.

only indirectly, requiring the government to make progress toward the reprivatization of Korea First Bank and Seoul Bank "through a bidding process satisfactory to the Bank."[70] It is not clear, however, if such a process would necessarily allow foreign bidders to participate. In sum, the Bank loans helped to support the general thrust of IMF conditionality, but the detailed prescriptions that drove Korea's de jure banking-sector opening through external pressure were only to be found in the Fund program.

Did Trade Negotiations Make a Difference?

Korea was one of the main targets of U.S. and European governments during the GATS negotiations. The intensity of this pressure was matched only by the recalcitrance of Korean negotiators in Geneva. As was the case with Indonesia, Korea's real concessions in banking-sector opening came only later, after the conclusion of the Financial Services Agreement and in the context of the IMF arrangement. Therefore, it is difficult to argue that the trade negotiations exerted an independent impact on banking-sector opening in Korea. The GATS did provide a lock-in device to keep policies from reverting to protectionism. The evolution of South Korea's GATS offers is shown in Appendix 2.

The offer Korea presented at the start of the negotiations in April 1994 reflected its de jure position at the time. Korea's traditional restrictions on foreign banks were all there—the ban on foreign-bank subsidiaries, the 8 percent cap on individual ownership of bank shares, the need for special permissions to move into noncore lines of business, and a generic right to retaliate against discriminatory treatment by other countries.[71] Korea's second submission, in July 1995, made no new concessions in banking but clarified existing rules, such as aggregate and individual foreign ownership ceilings and the treatment of branch capital.[72] The 8 percent cap on individual ownership did not change. The offer did express a liberal but vague intention to allow foreign financial institutions equity participation in existing banks by 1996–1997 but did not say how much. Under the offer, Korea also undertook a "standstill" for limitations on national treatment and market access, promising not to adopt new measures inconsistent with the commitments it had made so far. So far, however, the Korean authorities had not committed to anything beyond the status quo.

Once it started accession negotiations with the OECD, Korea was pressed to bind its OECD commitments to open its banking, securities, and insurance industries

---

70. "Loan Agreement (Structural Adjustment Loan) between Republic of Korea and International Bank for Reconstruction and Development," Loan Number 4399 KO, October 23, 1998.

71. GATS/SC/48, April 15, 1994.

72. GATS SC/48/Suppl. 1, July 28, 1995.

to foreign competition, a link Korean negotiators resisted. They put forward one more offer in October 1995, which did not make any substantive changes to the July position.[73] After that, Korea's position in the GATS negotiations did not change until 1998, after the Financial Services Agreement had been inked and dried. The third Korean offer was presented in February 1998, only weeks after the legislature's approval of the financial reform package, which brought about total de jure opening. The submission did not reflect any of those momentous changes.[74] It raised the aggregate shareholding ceiling for portfolio investors in most sectors to 6 percent, but this measure was rendered moot by the *lowering* of the individual shareholding ceiling in banking from 8 to 4 percent. Clearly, Korea's position at the trade-in-services negotiations was lagging far behind the rapid deregulation of the banking sector taking place at the same time.

Korea's most recent offer was made in November 1999.[75] Under this offer, the authorities bound their OECD commitments, authorizing commercial presence to foreign banks through subsidiaries as well as branches. With this submission, the Korean government complied with its pledge to the IMF. In sum, there is no evidence that the GATS negotiations pushed Korean negotiators to make any concessions beyond the status quo until 1999, when more liberal commitments were finally presented. Those liberal commitments, in turn, were the product of parallel but unrelated events, namely, the crisis and the IMF package.

The Politics of De Facto Opening (1999–2007)

Having legally opened the banking sector to foreign capital, Korean policymakers began to consider implementation. As in Mexico, Brazil, and Indonesia, de facto openness unfolded in the context of a massive restructuring of the banking sector as foreign and domestic groups vied for ownership and control of the postcrisis financial system. In Korea, the executive kept a strong grip on the process and the legislature played no significant role in the sale of banks to foreign investors as it did in Indonesia. However, the government did have to contend with a powerful and active labor movement.

In early 1998, the Korean authorities turned their attention to the rescue and restructuring of the banking system. While nonbank financial institutions such as merchant banks played a big role in the precrisis lending boom, it was the commercial banks that were saddled with the bulk of the system's nonperforming loans.

---

73. GATS/SC/48/Suppl. 1/Rev. 1, October 4, 1995.
74. GATS/SC/48/Suppl. 3, February 26, 1998.
75. GATS/SC/48/Suppl. 3/Rev. 1, November 18, 1999.

Commercial banks held almost 80 percent of the financial system's NPLs as of late 1997, putting them at the epicenter of the financial crisis.[76] After hastily establishing a new institutional framework to implement the restructuring, the banking authorities proceeded to take over, recapitalize, merge, and in some cases, close troubled financial institutions.[77] By the time the recapitalization and restructuring process was over, the government had spent some W168 trillion of public funds, or 25 percent of Korea's GDP in 2002.[78] With the restructuring, Korea's financial landscape changed rapidly in the space of a few years. By October 2006, the financial authorities had ordered the suspension or permanent closure of 893 financial institutions.[79] Of the sixteen nationwide commercial banks in Korea at the start of the crisis, only eight survived.

The two most important banks to come under government control—and those that would first test the new policy of banking-sector opening—were Korea First Bank (KFB) and Seoul Bank. These two were among the largest commercial banks, and they were critically wounded by the collapse of some of their largest *chaebol* borrowers. Under its December 24 Letter of Intent with the IMF, the government pledged to take control of both institutions and to remove the management responsible for the losses. In January 1998, both banks were nationalized: the MOFE and the Korean Deposit Insurance Corporation (KDIC) injected W1.5 trillion into each one, giving the government a 94 percent stake in each institution. By early 1999, the government would become a major shareholder in five nationwide banks: KFB, Seoul, Chohung, Hanvit, and Korea Exchange Bank (KEB). As part of its agreement with the IMF, the Korean authorities put KFB and Seoul Bank on a separate track for restructuring and privatization, and both were earmarked to be sold to foreign investors.

Two Lines of Defense

As the restructuring of the banking sector got under way, policymakers in the Blue House and the finance ministry tried to envision what the postcrisis banking sector might look like. For top officials, recapitalization was not the only reason for allowing foreign capital into the banking system. It was also an opportunity to introduce greater competition and improve the banks' human capital and technology.[80]

---

76. Ito and Hashimoto, "Bank Restructuring in Asia," p. 18.

77. In addition to the new consolidated regulator, the Financial Supervisory Commission (FSC), two other government institutions were put in place to assist with bank restructuring. First was the Korean Asset Management Corporation (KAMCO), which like Indonesia's IBRA would purchase and dispose of NPLs. The second was the Korean Deposit Insurance Corporation (KDIC), designed to provide financial assistance to troubled banks as well as protect depositors.

78. Kim and Lee, "Political Economy," p. 32.

79. Ibid.

80. Interviews with Lee Kyu Sung; Lee Dong-Gull, vice-chairman, Financial Supervisory Commission (2003–2004), Seoul, June 5, 2008; and Okyu Kwon, Seoul, June 6, 2008.

However, key decision makers still believed that foreign entry should remain limited, just as they had before the crisis—proof that the banking shock did not change their causal beliefs. Okyu Kwon, then the president's top adviser on financial issues and later deputy finance minister and finance minister, described the government's guiding principles during the restructuring in this way:

> We wanted the dominant banks to remain in the hands of Koreans. We wanted foreigners to take over some of the minor nationwide banks. And third, we wanted the government to keep control of banks where policy loans are still necessary—the IBK [Industrial Bank of Korea] and the KDB [Korea Development Bank]. When inviting foreigners to come in, we adhered to two principles: the separation of industrial and financial capital, and equal treatment for domestic and foreign capital.[81]

The Korean approach to de facto opening was thus a hybrid of the Brazilian and Indonesian strategies. Like the Brazilians, Korean policymakers preferred to merge weak domestic banks into other domestic institutions, ensuring that the very largest banks would remain in domestic hands. But in contrast to their Brazilian counterparts, the Korean authorities did not try to delay the entry of foreign investors and treat them as a second line of defense. Instead, they sought out foreign buyers from the beginning of the restructuring process, at least for some of the smaller nationwide commercial banks. The authorities were primarily interested in attracting major international banks, which would in theory be willing to inject capital, technology, know-how, and skills into weak domestic institutions. Yet despite the government's best efforts, the first wave of foreign entrants interested in acquiring controlling stakes in domestic banks was composed exclusively of hedge and private equity funds with relatively short time horizons. All of them were based in the United States.

The arrival of the nonbank foreign entrants began with the hedge fund Newbridge Capital, which acquired Korea First Bank in 1999. Although the British bank HSBC had initially shown an interest, it was the hedge fund that ultimately acquired a controlling interest in KFB and installed the first foreign CEO of a Korean bank.[82] Then, in 2000, a consortium headed by the Carlyle Group, one of the world's largest private equity funds, acquired a 40.7 percent stake in the domestic commercial bank KorAm. Carlyle, which put up most of the cash for the deal, gained indirect control

---

81. Interview with Okyu Kwon, Seoul, June 6, 2008.
82. Newbridge and the government entered into a 51–49 percent joint venture in which Newbridge had complete management control. Newbridge paid W500 billion for the controlling stake. The Korean government, through KDIC, gave Newbridge full protection against the old loan portfolio for a maximum of three years.

of seven of the thirteen seats on the bank's board.[83] In 2003, Lone Star, another U.S.-based private equity fund, acquired 51 percent of Korea Exchange Bank for about US$1.2 billion in what was then the largest single instance of foreign investment in Korea's banking sector.[84]

Also consistent with the principles outlined above, the government arranged key mergers among domestic banks when it came to strengthening some of the very largest Korean institutions. In June 2001, the government forced a merger of the two largest and healthiest banks—Kookmin Bank and Housing & Commercial Bank—forming Korea's largest commercial bank with over 1,100 branches nationwide.[85] At the same time, regulators merged four nonviable banks into Woori Financial Holdings to form another top-three institution. The troubled Seoul Bank was merged with Hana Bank to create another major Korean-owned bank.[86] By the time the restructuring was complete, the top four banks, representing some 70 percent of the system's total assets, were the product of mergers among domestic banks.

Consistent with the government's pledge to keep financial and industrial capital separate, none of the reprivatized banks was sold directly to *chaebol*. No doubt with *chaebol* support, a proposal was floated to the authorities to set up a fund composed of pooled resources from Korean industrial conglomerates and pension funds. The fund would acquire some of the reprivatized banks but would ensure that the industrial conglomerates would have only an arm's-length relationship with the banks. This proposal gained little traction in the Blue House.[87] In early 2002, the government introduced an important regulatory change affecting the *chaebol*; it raised the cap on the maximum stake a nonfinancial firm could own in a commercial bank from 4 to 10 percent, just as the Presidential Commission on Financial Reform had recommended earlier. Holdings of voting shares remained capped at 4 percent. Rather than successful lobbying by the *chaebol*, this change reflected an attempt by the government to bring regulations into line with reality.[88] A government study of the ownership structure of the reprivatized banks found that the conglomerates had in fact acquired holdings that exceeded the government's 4 percent cap. It made little sense to hold on to this regulatory fiction for much longer.

---

83. Moon Ihlwan and Mark L. Clifford, "The Bank That Almost Got Away," *Business Week* No. 3705 (October 30, 2000), 58. Carlyle was forced by the Korean authorities to bring U.S. investment bank JP Morgan into its consortium to ensure that the acquiring group had experience in the banking business.

84. Lone Star bought out Germany's Commerzbank, which had purchased a stake of 32.55 percent, as well as the Export-Import Bank of Korea.

85. "Country Finance: South Korea," *Economist Intelligence Unit*, November 2002, p. 15.

86. HSBC was interested in acquiring Seoul Bank and entered into negotiations with the government for its acquisition. However, the talks fell through over unbridgeable differences over the valuation and classification of the bank's portfolio. For details, see Chungwon Kang, "From the Front Lines at Seoul Bank: Restructuring and Reprivatization," IMF Working Paper WP/03/235, December 2003.

87. Interview with Lee Kyu Sung, Seoul, June 9, 2008.

88. Interview with Okyu Kwon, Seoul, June 6, 2008.

The Second Wave: Foreign Banks

International banks eventually took part in a second wave of foreign entry into the Korean banking sector, usually by buying the shares of the hedge and private capital funds as the latter cashed out of the market. In 2004, Citigroup became the first foreign bank to acquire an indigenous commercial bank, in a deal worth about US$2.7 billion. The U.S. bank bought Carlyle's stake in KorAm and tendered an offer for additional shares, bringing its stake to 80 percent of the bank's total stock. As in Mexico, Citi later acquired virtually all of the bank's stock, combined it with Citi's small, preexisting bank network, and delisted KorAm from the Korean Stock Exchange. Shortly after that, the United Kingdom's Standard Chartered Bank purchased Newbridge Capital's stake in Korea First Bank, as well as the rest of the stock, bringing the bank into its global network. Finally, HSBC seriously considered purchasing Lone Star's controlling stake in Korea Exchange Bank to establish a major presence in the Korean market. However, in September 2008, the global financial meltdown forced HSBC to put those plans on hold indefinitely.

That foreign banks chose to take over the shares of foreign hedge and private equity funds in Korean banks is not coincidental; it made sense for the banks, the hedge funds, and the Korean regulators. Those domestic banks were already foreign-owned and operated, and one foreign owner replacing another was a politically less controversial proposition than a foreign bank trying to acquire a Korean-owned and operated institution. The replacement of funds with banks was also consistent with the authorities' hopes to attract international banks that could help in the modernization of the system. Second, the funds had been largely successful at cleaning up their banks and taking them to profitability. Third, government influence was likely to be more muted in the banks that had been owned by foreigners for several years; this was attractive from the point of view of the new foreign entrants. Finally, the foreign banks' interest in entering the Korean retail banking market coincided with the hedge and private equity funds' desire to cash out of the same market.

Foreign investors also began to acquire smaller stakes in the rest of Korea's domestic banks. These shares did not give foreigners management control of the institutions, but they did contribute to overall foreign presence in the sector. By 2003, foreign stakes in Korean commercial banks averaged 26 percent, provoking a public debate about its merits and implications.[89] By the middle of the decade, foreigners held well over 50 percent of the equity of most private commercial banks. At the same time, the majority-foreign-owned banks accounted for one-fifth of the system's total assets (see Figures 6.1 and 6.2).

---

89. Rafael Nam, "Foreign Stakes in Banks Top 26%; Overseas Ownership Improved Financial Services but Gave Rise to Discord," *Korea Herald,* December 2, 2003.

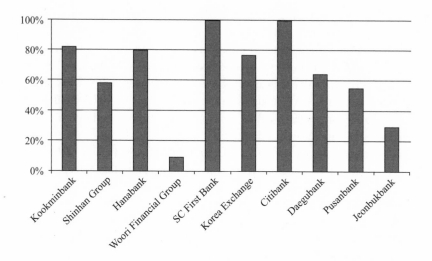

FIGURE 6.1. Foreign equity participation in major Korean banks (as of December 2006).

Source: Joon-Kyung Kim and Chung H. Lee, "The Political Economy of Government, Financial System, and the *Chaebols* before and after the 1997 Financial Crisis in Korea," CCAS Working Paper No. 11, Center for Contemporary Asian Studies, Doshisha University, April 2008, p. 75.

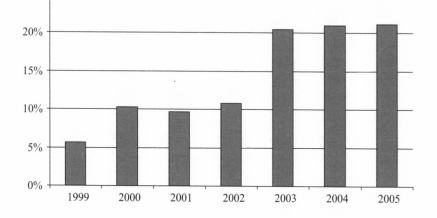

FIGURE 6.2. Share of foreign-majority-owned banks in total banking-system assets.

Source: Joon-Kyung Kim and Chung H. Lee, "The Political Economy of Government, Financial System, and the *Chaebols* before and after the 1997 Financial Crisis in Korea," CCAS Working Paper No. 11, Center for Contemporary Asian Studies, Doshisha University, April 2008, p. 76.

Foreign Banks and Organized Labor

Bank workers were among the most severely affected groups during the economic crisis.[90] Nine major commercial banks agreed to fire 32 percent of their workforce, some 17,000 workers, immediately.[91] Korea First Bank alone fired half of its nearly 8,000 employees.[92] In a country where job security had been taken for granted, where unemployment had been running at less than 3 percent in the years preceding the crisis, and where no bank had ever been closed or merged, televised images of weeping bank workers leaving their jobs for the last time caused public outrage and galvanized the unions into action.

With Korea's transition to democracy, labor unions emerged as one of the country's most powerful political groups; of the four countries studied here, Korea had the strongest bank unions. In the financial-services industry, labor was organized under the Korea Financial Industry Union (KFIU), an umbrella group that in 1998 represented the unions of twenty-seven banks and had about 130,000 members.[93] The KFIU was established in 1960, but it did not acquire enough political space to become an independent player until after the transition to democracy and the privatization of the banks. During the crisis, the KFIU and its unions actively resisted the bank mergers, sometimes resorting to strikes.

The KFIU and its labor leaders were not instinctively opposed to all foreign acquisitions. Their stance was pragmatic, as is clear from the thinking of the KFIU's former vice-president:

> The unions did not think negatively about foreign investment coming into the country. We believed that the country needed foreign investment to revive the collapsed economy. We saw foreign investment as positive financial help at a time of need, and not as something largely negative. The unions were aware that the country suffered the financial crisis because the country's financial industry was failing, and we believed that Korean banks needed to adopt the practice and policies of foreign banks, of the banks of developed countries.[94]

For the unions, the priority was minimizing job losses, and to the degree that foreign entry could help reduce or prevent job losses, the unions were willing to support it. To the government's alarm, the bank unions organized a massive, one-day strike on July 11, 2000—the first in the KFIU's forty-year history. Blocking foreign

90. On the impact of the crisis on the labor movement, see Yong Cheol Kim and Chung-in Moon, "Globalization and Workers in South Korea," in Kim, *Korea's Globalization*, pp. 54–75.

91. Kongdan Oh, ed., *Korea Briefing, 1997–1999: Challenges and Change at the Turn of the Century* (Armonk, N.Y.: M.E. Sharpe, 2000), p. 19.

92. "Chief Faces New Battle Front at Korea First Bank," *Banker* 150:890 (April 1, 2000).

93. Interview with Yook Tae Soo, former KFIU vice-president and former head of Choheung Bank Union, Seoul, June 11, 2008 (translation by Julie Yang).

94. Ibid.

acquisitions was not the goal. Rather, the unions wanted to minimize the number of bank mergers, which inevitably resulted in restructuring and massive job losses.

It is telling that after the July 11 strike, the most dramatic episode of union resistance was not about a foreign takeover but about a merger between two Korean banks, Kookmin and Housing & Commercial. That strike, in December 2000, involved some 16,000 workers.[95] Also revealing is the fact that in some cases, the unions preferred foreign takeovers to domestic mergers because they thought the former would produce fewer layoffs. For example, when Lone Star was looking to sell its controlling stake in KEB, labor leaders preferred an acquisition by HSBC to one by the local Kookmin, reckoning that because of its much smaller presence in the Korean market, HSBC was far more likely to retain KEB workers than the giant Kookmin.[96]

In a few notable cases, the labor movement mounted resistance to foreign control of Korean banks. The most dramatic example was a June 2004 strike following Citigroup's acquisition of KorAm, when an indefinite walkout shut down nearly 80 percent of the bank's branches. However, strikes like this one were motivated by fears of specific actions by the foreign management rather than by opposition to foreign management per se. In this case, the strike against Citigroup was sparked not by its acquisition of KorAm but by announced plans to delist the bank from the stock market and to absorb it into its global network.[97] The union leaders felt their members would become more exposed to potential downsizing if the bank lost all local ownership and became fully dependent on management decisions at Citi's New York headquarters. Ultimately, the labor movement did not stop the de facto opening of Korea's banking sector, but it did raise the cost of entry to foreign investors. Foreign investors were forced to deal with work disruptions and to reduce the workforce in their acquisitions to a smaller extent than they would have done in the absence of a strong labor movement.

Aside from the political challenges posed by the unions, the government faced little opposition from other domestic political groups during de facto opening. The National Assembly had no legal right to intervene in the sales, and other than occasional posturing against foreign interests for the sake of their constituents, the legislators stayed out of the process.[98] Similarly, domestic bankers were conspicuously silent. In the banks taken over by the authorities, the old management had been removed and replaced with government bureaucrats. In the banks that remained nominally independent, the government had enormous leverage because

95. For a week, union members from the two commercial banks staged a sit-in at a Kookmin's training center in the suburbs of Seoul until the gathering was forcibly broken up by riot police. "Economy Needs Win-Win-Win Strategy," *Business Korea,* January, 2001.

96. Interview with Stefan James, managing director and regional executive, Bank of America, Seoul, June 11, 2008.

97. "Concern Looms over Citigroup's Report Plan to Delist KorAm," *Asia Pulse,* February 25, 2004.

98. Interview with Okyu Kwon, Seoul, June 6, 2008.

as guarantor of the banks' foreign loans, it was in charge of negotiating directly with the banks' international creditors. Under these circumstances, bank management had few incentives to antagonize the government by resisting its restructuring plans.

Rethinking Control?

For the government, perhaps the biggest political challenge of de facto opening involved coming to terms with the dilution of government control over finance that foreign entry inevitably entailed. This realization came to the government through two episodes. In 2004, LG Card—one of Korea's largest credit-card companies—experienced severe financial distress. In practiced form, the finance ministry orchestrated a bailout of LG Card, herding commercial banks into a W5 trillion (US$4.2 billion) rescue operation. However, KEB, controlled by Lone Star, scaled back its contributions, arguing, "In a capitalist world, it's just natural for investors to avoid any decision to bring them losses."[99] A second episode involved a government-led rescue of the Korean chipmaker Hynix. Citigroup, which was leading the syndication to save Hynix, pulled out before the operation was complete; the MOFE was not impressed.

The feeling that the Korean government was losing its grip on an increasingly foreign-owned banking system led some bureaucrats and legislators to propose new regulatory tools to keep the power of foreign-owned and controlled banks in check. After the LG Card incident, the central bank's think tank proposed introducing a system of "golden shares" through which the government could exercise veto power on changes to a bank's charter.[100] The following year, members of the National Assembly drafted legislation that would have imposed nationality and residency requirements for members of the boards of directors of banks operating in Korea. None of these measures has been adopted as of 2008, but these proposals suggest that Korea's political establishment is still coming to terms with a new era in which the state no longer has unfettered influence over the banking system.

Since the early 1990s, Korea's financial policymakers consistently embraced a set of ideas about how the commercial banking system should be run. It should become more modern and globally competitive, direct government intervention in lending should diminish, it should stay separate from industrial capital and especially from *chaebol* control, and it should remain, at its core, Korean-owned and controlled. The evidence suggests that this consensus did not change throughout the period under

---

99. Anonymous KEB senior executive, qtd. in "LG Card Deal Rekindles Skepticism; Foreign-Owned Banks' Defiance Renews Criticism of Privatization Policy," *Korea Herald,* February 9, 2004.
100. "LG Card Deal Rekindles Skepticism."

study despite one change in administration and a long parade of finance ministers. Ideational change was not responsible for the opening of Korea's banking sector.

The imperative of political survival, so important in Brazil and Indonesia, was also not a major factor in Korea's decision to liberalize. After all, the key reforms were introduced by a lame duck president, and they were implemented by a single-term president from a different party, whose hold on power was never in jeopardy. Domestic politics also had little to do with the opening: indigenous, private-sector bankers were a politically feeble group before, during, and after the opening process, so changes in their lobbying power do not explain the radical change in the banking regime.

The most persuasive explanation of Korea's radical shift to de jure opening is external pressure induced by a twin banking and capital account crisis. The banking crisis forced Korean policymakers to seek foreign resources to recapitalize a handful of weak institutions. It also permitted the IMF to include banking-sector policy in its conditionality. At the same time, the capital account crisis greatly magnified Seoul's dependence on the resources and political support of the IMF, the G7 governments, and international banks. This uniquely intense episode of external pressure is what broke the deadlock in the Korean legislature, and by linking Korea's OECD and WTO commitments, it ensured that the Korean government would make credible and enforceable promises to open its banking sector.

7

CONCLUSION
Learning to Live with Barbarians

This book has provided an account of how an important dimension of financial globalization was constructed during the late twentieth and early twenty-first centuries in four different corners of the emerging world. That dimension is the opening of the domestic commercial banking sector to foreign investment, competition, and ownership. For each of the four countries studied here, I performed an autopsy of the liberalization process by dissecting its many policy dilemmas, negotiations, and political battles. Above all, the four narratives are about the struggle of different groups to control the financial pipelines of an economy and to capture the riches and influence that flow from such control.

At the heart of the political struggles portrayed in this book was an idea, the notion that a country's financial institutions should be controlled by that country's nationals, and that governments should erect regulatory barriers to keep foreigners—"the barbarians"—out. That idea proved remarkably resilient in all four countries, and it refused to die even among otherwise committed practitioners of economic liberalism. The idea's persistence was tied to the notion that banks are special, that along with a handful of other sectors of an economy these financial institutions are too important to be controlled by foreigners, even when they can be left in the hands of the private sector. The idea was buttressed sometimes by postcolonial aspirations for independence, sometimes by politicians' xenophobic nationalism, sometimes by bankers' attempts to reap the fruits of protectionism, and other times by technocratic concerns about the stability of the financial system and the need to preserve informal regulatory powers. The main argument of the book is that in all four countries it took a major crisis—a systemic shock—for those subscribing to that idea to put it aside or to be themselves pushed aside, leading governments to open their banking systems fully to global capital.

In this chapter, I draw from the case studies a few conclusions about the political economy of financial reform. I also explore the limits of the crisis argument and consider how it might be applied to other cases.

On the Political Economy of Banking Reform

The conclusions that emerge from the case studies challenge some conventional views about how and why financial globalization has been constructed by politicians, bureaucrats, and bankers. The insights fall into three categories: those related to the period of managed opening, those related to the critical juncture, and those related to the implementation of openness.

Managed Opening

One of the most striking findings about the period described here as "managed opening" in all four countries is how circumscribed was the power of foreign bankers, their governments, and the international financial institutions to bring about banking-sector opening. The instruments used to generate pressure for opening—multilateral trade negotiations, policy advice from international financial institutions, government-to-government lobbying, and OECD accession talks—all had a modest impact in producing opening. This conclusion qualifies accounts of financial globalization that emphasize the coercive aspect of its construction by a handful of "hegemonic" players; it runs against popular portrayals of Wall Street and City of London bankers, U.S. negotiators, and the IMF as hugely powerful groups wielding very large carrots and sticks and able to use them to get what they want at any time. This book suggests that during noncrisis times, "hegemonic powers" in international finance actually have surprisingly few effective instruments to pry open foreign banking markets, at least regarding relatively large emerging-market countries.[1]

The second conclusion qualifies accounts of financial globalization that stress the importance of the spread of ideas. These are narratives about cadres of U.S.-educated technocrats who, having fully bought into a "hegemonic ideology" of

---

1. Beth A. Simmons argues that the United States and the United Kingdom are hegemonic powers in the international financial system because of their enormous weight in global financial markets. Together the two countries exported on average during the 1990s US$12.6 billion worth of financial services—only slightly less than the rest of the OECD countries combined. The two countries also enjoy a dominant position in global equity markets and occupy a central position in the international payments system. Simmons, "The International Politics of Harmonization: The Case of Capital Market Regulation," *International Organization* 55 (Summer 2001), 593–594.

neoliberal economics, imported those ideas back into their native countries and proceeded to liberalize, privatize, and globalize all of them in very similar ways. On one hand, this book does lend support to the idea that U.S.-educated economists-turned-policymakers were an immensely influential force behind the adoption of liberal economic policies by countries in very different corners of the world. In all four countries studied here, U.S.-educated technocrats played a decisive role in domestic political debates about financial policy; the late 1980s and 1990s truly marked the apogee of liberal technocracy in the emerging world. On the other hand, the book shows that those technocrats did not fully buy into everything they learned in graduate school, and that perhaps nowhere was their divergence from textbook liberalism more evident than in the financial sector.

The most dramatic case is that of the Salinas technocrats in Mexico, who were zealous globalizers in almost every area except banking. Brazilian and Korean technocrats were always more skeptical students of neoliberal economics, but their thinking on banking-sector policy stands out as particularly heterodox. Of the four sets of policymakers studied here, Indonesian technocrats, by political necessity, were by far the most liberal, sometimes outdoing even the IMF in terms of financial liberalization. Indeed, Indonesia's was the only economic team studied here that consistently advocated the total opening of the banking sector, primarily because they saw liberalization as the only instrument at their disposal to keep nationalist and crony interests from wreaking economic havoc.

The third insight is about the strategic use of financial globalization for domestic political ends. In all four countries studied here, policymakers tried to administer small and carefully controlled doses of financial globalization to achieve specific policy goals, all of them related to strengthening the domestic economy. Mexican officials wanted to exchange a measure of banking-sector opening for access to valuable U.S. export markets. Brasilia attempted to use managed opening to privatize the state government banks and eliminate a major source of fiscal indiscipline. Indonesian technocrats turned to managed opening to reduce the market share of government-owned banks, limiting their financial excesses and the fiscal risk they posed. Finally, the Korean authorities saw managed opening as a means to modernize a sclerotic banking system and keep the Korean economy competitive in an age of cutthroat globalization. In short, policymakers during this period were neither victims of globalization nor doctrinaire enforcers of liberal dogma: they tried to make financial globalization work for them and their countries, and that required a measure of control over the scope, pace, and form of opening.

Critical Juncture

During the critical juncture phase of the liberalization process, policymakers were forced to reconsider their banking-sector access policy and invariably decided to embrace some form of large-scale removal of entry barriers. The main insight here is the importance of systemic banking shocks in triggering a chain of events that led to full-scale opening. In three of the four countries, the shock led to total de jure opening and extensive de facto liberalization; only in Brazil did it lead to an idiosyncratic opening involving the latter without the former. To return to the "crisis causes reform" hypothesis discussed in chapter 1, why did large-scale banking-sector opening require an "extremely bad" economic situation rather than just a "medium bad" one?

Most bureaucrats and politicians in all four countries were not reflexively opposed to all banking-sector opening, but they were convinced that it should take place gradually and within certain predetermined limits. Extensive opening was feared because it might lead to the "denationalization" of the banking system, making the system less responsive to local needs and government control. For some, it also meant the loss of valuable rent flows. As long as only a few banks failed and the system itself was not threatened, the authorities had no reason to consider rapid, full-scale opening. During such periods of nonsystemic banking distress, the government could easily recapitalize those institutions, close them down, or allow their owners to keep operating while regulators turned a blind eye, all without putting depositors or the payments system at risk.

During systemic crises, however, the government's options became severely constrained: closing down banks could trigger runs and a collapse of the payments system, while the amount of resources needed for recapitalization could quickly escalate beyond the capacity of the government or private sector to absorb. To cope with such a crisis, governments sought to maximize their room to maneuver and the amount of resources available for recapitalization. Only full opening of the banking sector could provide both. In short, the special status assigned to banking in domestic politics ensured that extensive liberalization would be contemplated only when the entire system was at risk and policymakers needed to maximize their policy options in short order. This is different from, say, trade liberalization, in which barriers can be lowered gradually and shocks do not force governments to liberalize with the same urgency. (If anything, shocks tend to induce the reimposition of protectionist barriers in trade.)

Did the magnitude of the crisis, not just its incidence, make a difference to the speed or depth of opening? While all four crises meet the Demirgüç-Kunt-Detragiache definition of a banking crisis employed in this book, the indicators vary considerably, with Indonesia suffering the most severe banking crisis in the sample and Brazil the least. In addition, Mexico, Indonesia, and Korea suffered from twin crises while Brazil suffered from only a banking crisis. No simple conclusions can be drawn from this analysis. Brazil experienced the mildest shock and also displays the lowest levels of foreign participation. Yet Indonesia and Korea suffered banking crises that were more severe than Mexico's, but Mexico exhibits a much higher level of foreign participation than those other two countries. Thus, we cannot conclude that more severe shocks necessarily lead to greater de facto liberalization. What we can conclude is that all four countries engaged in de facto liberalization on a scale that deviated markedly from historical trends, and that the incidence of the shocks, rather than their intensity, is what accounted for those large deviations.

A third conclusion relates to the role of external pressure on liberalization in the three countries that suffered twin crises. In those countries, the banking crisis forced a revision of banking-sector access rules, while the capital account crisis rendered governments dependent on outside financing and magnified external political pressure to reform. Yet the role of external pressure varied considerably. It proved critical for opening in Indonesia and Korea, but in Mexico, it actually inhibited, rather than facilitated, the opening.

The difference has to do with the power and attitudes of legislators. In the two Asian countries, the executive was able to persuade or strong-arm congressional majorities into approving radical banking-sector opening legislation, thanks to a mix of party discipline, political pressure, and persuasion about the dire consequences that would follow if IMF prescriptions were not followed in this area. In Mexico, perceived IMF (and especially U.S.) pressure provoked a violent nationalist response, including from the president's own party. The Mexican president conceded to a limited opening, at least until elections and the Serfin crisis produced a more liberally minded legislature.

A final insight in this section is about a dog that did not bark. The case studies offer little support for the "domestic power shift" hypothesis, at least as it is presented in popular political economy models. In the four countries, liberalization did not happen because incumbents lost their capacity to buy protection. In all four countries, domestic bankers did not have to bribe officials or lobby for protection in the first place, largely because politicians and bureaucrats already believed in extending that protection as a matter of national policy. Then, during the critical junctures, when government preferences changed in favor of opening, the incumbents either did not have adequate channels to lobby for protection or chose not to use them.

In Indonesia, those political channels could not be used because of ethnic sensitivities and because the incumbents exited the sector early in the crisis. In Korea, close government control over the banks and weak cohesion among private bankers created an environment that simply was not conducive to lobbying. Brazilian bankers and their (unreliable) allies in the legislature were shut out of the policy process by the executive, thanks to the latter's use of presidential decrees to implement the opening. And in Mexico, the biggest bankers eschewed lobbying, resigned themselves to the fact that some degree of opening was inevitable, and hoped that their size and the government's recapitalization efforts would help them survive in an open market. These four cases suggest that models seeking to explain liberalization based on the presence or absence of "Washington-style" lobbying have limited usefulness outside very particular settings. Cultural attitudes toward lobbying, institutional constraints, regime type, and the preferences of incumbents—which cannot automatically be assumed to be in favor of protection—have to be taken into account as we apply these models.

De Facto Opening

The first conclusion here is that banking crises are better at changing rules than altering practices. The shocks were very effective at compelling countries to adopt de jure opening, but the cases in this book show that once crisis conditions subside, a struggle begins at the implementation stage, as foreign and domestic capital, politicians, and bureaucrats try to shape de facto opening to their advantage. In three of the four cases, in spite of a legal framework of total de jure opening, domestic actors succeeded in delaying or restricting foreign entry, often in ways that diluted the ability of foreigners to translate their ownership of financial institutions into management control. Domestic authorities were able to do this through informal practices and procedural rules applied during the sale of banks.

Nowhere was this phenomenon more evident than in Brazil, where the authorities favored domestic over foreign capital whenever possible through their "second line of defense" approach. They also required foreign entrants to pay a *pedágio* or buy state banks as a price for entry, and the authorities did their best to keep the largest banking institutions in the hands of nationals. In Indonesia, the legislature required that banks be sold in pieces, opening room for domestic capital to compete in the battle for ownership and control of the banks. Meanwhile, the Korean authorities limited foreign acquisitions to second-tier institutions and, through caps on individual shareholding, ensured that while foreigners could buy shares in top banks, they would always remain minority shareholders. Only in Mexico did the authorities refrain from limiting foreign entry.

The second insight is that while the pressures on all four countries to open their markets were similar, the politics of de facto opening produced different structures of financial ownership and control. If we plot these cases on an imaginary continuum ranging from total domestic control to total foreign control of the banking sector, we would find Brazil, South Korea, Indonesia, and Mexico approximately in the positions depicted in Figure 7.1, with the Latin American countries closer to either end of the spectrum.

Moving one level deeper, Figures 7.2 through 7.5 provide snapshots of the ownership structures of the top six commercial banks in each country in 2007—about a decade after the banking shocks. To understand the changes in the financial landscape, we must look beyond the *levels* of foreign participation and examine its *form*.

Brazil's banking structure, illustrated in Figure 7.2, shows the result of Brazil's "second line of defense" strategy during the process of de facto banking-sector opening. Two of the top six banks remain firmly in government hands. In three others—Itaú, Bradesco, and Unibanco—a majority of the controlling shares are

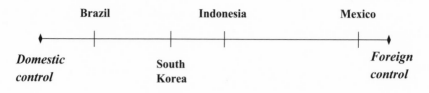

FIGURE 7.1.   Domestic v. foreign control of banks in the case countries.

owned by the founding families or their foundations.[2] These three banks absorbed most of the weak banks in need of recapitalization during the 1995 banking crisis. Only one bank of the top six—Banco Real, accounting for 7 percent of the system's assets—is foreign-owned. Brazil's implementation of openness produced a banking system whose core remains very much under national ownership and control.

The structure of Korea's top banks, illustrated in Figure 7.3, shows how Seoul's approach to de facto opening produced a banking sector that paradoxically exhibits a high degree of foreign ownership but low levels of foreign control. Of the top four banks—which together hold over two-thirds of total assets—one has the government as its controlling shareholder and in the rest, foreigners hold the majority of the shares. However, these are minority, portfolio shareholders, usually with stakes of less than 10 percent. Though this ownership structure has made Korea's top banks more attuned to profit maximization, minority shareholders remain passive actors. At the same time, the government also retains considerable influence over the selection of bank CEOs, even in institutions in which it does not own a majority stake.[3] The two banks that are both owned and controlled by single foreign investors (SC First Bank and KEB) are the two smallest of the group and account for just over a tenth of total assets. In sum, Korea's style of opening has proved adept at attracting foreign capital into the system while keeping control in local hands.

Indonesia's post-opening banking structure, shown in Figure 7.4, has a lower level of foreign participation than Korea's, but until recently, it had higher levels of foreign control. The government retains a large presence with controlling stakes in three of the top six banks, or about 35 percent of the system's assets. Until recently, consortia led by foreign investment companies held controlling stakes in the other three banks. In contrast to Korea, individual foreigners in Indonesia both owned and controlled these banks through majority stakes. Over time, the local partner in Indonesia's largest private bank (BCA) has taken over the foreign stake, so that a decade after the

---

2. In February 2009, as this book was going to press, the Central Bank of Brazil approved the merger of Itaú and Unibanco. The merged institution will become Brazil's largest bank and one of the largest financial institutions in the Americas. The bank remains a domestically owned, private institution.

3. According to a senior foreign-bank executive in Seoul, "If the government does not want you to run a bank because there is something in your record they don't like, you won't run the bank, regardless of what shareholders want." Confidential interview.

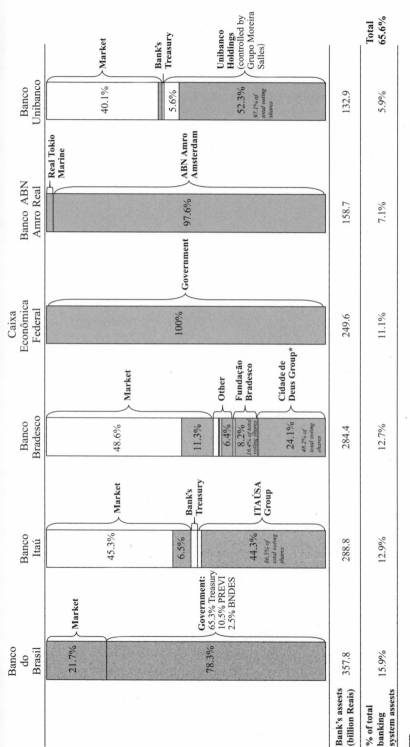

FIGURE 7.2. Brazil: Ownership structure of the top six commercial banks, 2007.

Note: Fundação Bradesco exercises control over Cidade de Deus through two channels: directly, through the ownership of 33.15 percent of its shares; and indirectly, through control over Nova Cidade de Deus, which in turn is the control group of Cidade de Deus.

Source: Economist Intelligence Unit—Country Finance 2008; banks' Web sites as of August 2008; and CVM—Comissão de Valores Mobiliários (Itaú, Bradesco, ABN, and Unibanco).

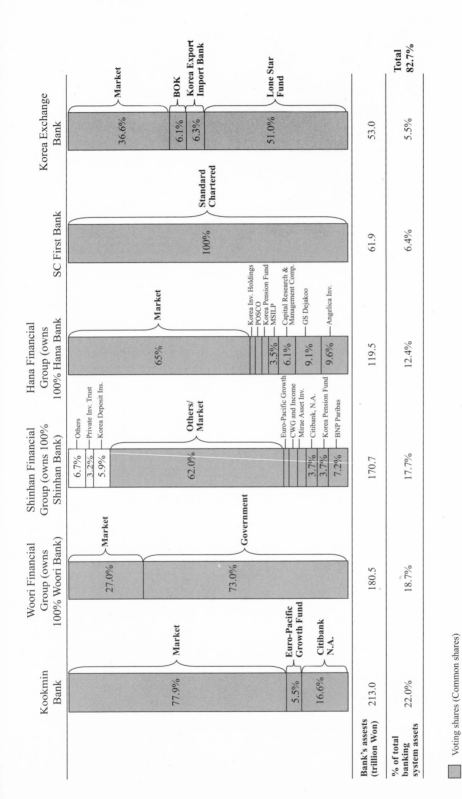

FIGURE 7.3. Korea: Ownership structure of the top six commercial banks, 2007.

Source: Economist Intelligence Unit—Country Finance 2008; SEC Report May 2008 (Kookmin, Shinhan); banks' Web sites as of August 2008 (Woori, Hana, SC, KEB).

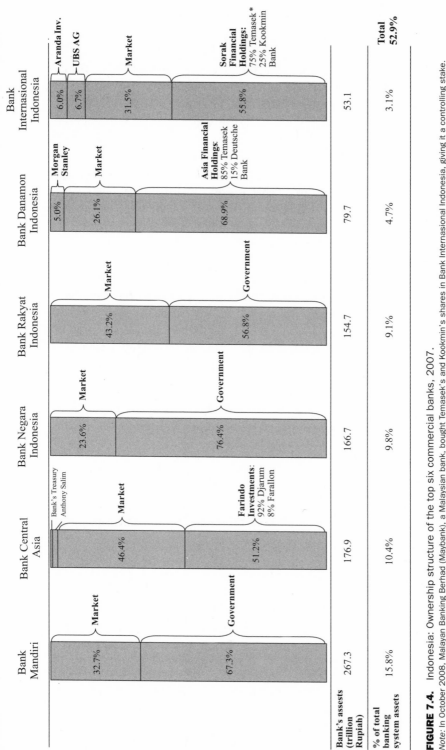

FIGURE 7.4. Indonesia: Ownership structure of the top six commercial banks, 2007.

Note: In October 2008, Malayan Banking Berhad (Maybank), a Malaysian bank, bought Temasek's and Kookmin's shares in Bank Internasional Indonesia, giving it a controlling stake.

Source: Economist Intelligence Unit—Country Finance 2008; banks' Web sites as of August 2008 (BCA, Danamon); Indonesia Stock Exchange—Company Report January 2008 (Mandiri, Negara Indonesia, and Rakyat); Annual Report 2007 (BII).

crisis, de facto opening in Indonesia seems to have kept the largest banks in the hands of the government or local investors.

Figure 7.5 shows the ownership structure of Mexico's banking system. The sector remains as concentrated as ever: the top six banks account for just over 82 percent of the system's total assets, similar to the situation in postcrisis Korea. Here the pattern of ownership and control is very clear: five of the top six banks are fully owned subsidiaries of Spanish, U.S., Canadian, and British banks, accounting for just under 80 percent of total assets. They mostly kept their old names, but several were delisted from the stock market, raising concerns about transparency and market discipline. Integrated into the foreign banks' global networks, these banks are fully controlled by their head offices abroad.[4] Only one bank, Banorte, continues to have a Mexican owner.

These are merely snapshots of the banking sector of each country at a certain point in time. These structures are fluid and are constantly changing. However, a decade after the shock that triggered opening, we have enough perspective to appreciate the distinct balance of domestic and foreign capital that has emerged in each country. This balance in part reflects policymakers' beliefs about the appropriate role for foreign and domestic capital in the domestic banking system, as well as the struggles among domestic and foreign groups to own and control a piece of each country's postcrisis financial system.

Pushing the Argument: Alternative Cases

To what extent is the finding that banking shocks produced opening applicable to other cases? To probe this question, I divide the major emerging-market economies into four categories: (1) countries that suffered banking shocks and subsequently displayed extensive banking-sector opening, (2) countries that experienced banking shocks but opened little or not at all, (3) countries that did not suffer a shock but nevertheless displayed extensive banking-sector opening, (4) and countries that neither experienced a shock nor opened their banking markets to foreign investment. When judging whether opening was "extensive" or not, I used as the key criteria whether governments removed restrictions on the ability of foreign banks to establish a presence through branches and subsidiaries *and* restrictions on the ability of foreign investors to acquire controlling stakes in domestic banks.

---

4. In 2008 and 2009, Citigroup suffered massive losses as a result of the crisis triggered by the collapse of the U.S. housing market. In its efforts to save this systemically significant institution, the U.S. authorities were actively considering the de facto nationalization of the banking giant. U.S. government ownership of Citigroup (and therefore of Banamex) would raise a dilemma, as Mexican legislation forbids foreign governments from owning domestic banks.

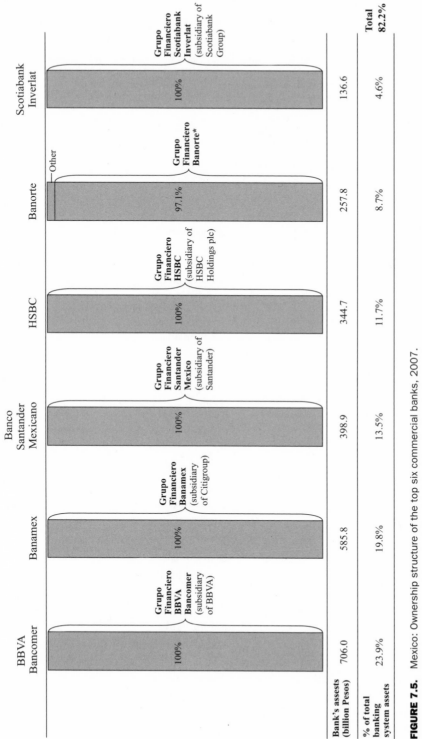

FIGURE 7.5. Mexico: Ownership structure of the top six commercial banks, 2007.

Note: Grupo Financiero Banorte is controlled by Roberto González Barrera, He and his sons own approximately 16 percent of the group's shares.

Source: Economist Intelligence Unit—Country Finance 2008; Annual Report 2007 (BBVA Bancomer, Banorte, Scotiabank); banks' Web sites as of August 2008 (Banamex, Santander, HSBC).

Table 7.1 Banking crises and de jure and de facto opening in selected emerging economies

	EXTENSIVE OPENING	NO/LITTLE OPENING
Banking crisis	**South Korea** **Mexico** **Brazil** **Indonesia** Turkey Thailand Venezuela Philippines Colombia *Quadrant 1*	Malaysia Russia *Quadrant 2*
No banking crisis	Argentina South Africa *Quadrant 3*	China (PRC) India *Quadrant 4*

Table 7.1 shows this categorization for a sample of fifteen emerging economies. "Banking crisis" is defined using the standard definition employed throughout this book. Of the fifteen countries in the sample, nine—including Mexico, Brazil, Indonesia, and South Korea—are best described as having undertaken extensive banking-sector opening in the aftermath of a banking shock, while two others, China and India, have experienced neither a shock nor extensive opening. These quadrants (1 and 4) are consistent with the argument of this book—that banking-sector shocks are a necessary trigger for extensive banking-sector opening and that during noncrisis periods, emerging economies have significant latitude to resist foreign pressure and to engage in managed opening, which usually means continued protection against foreign takeovers of domestic banks.

Four countries—Malaysia, Russia, Argentina, and South Africa—fall into two unexpected quadrants (quadrants 2 and 3). These are countries that have either opened extensively without a shock or have undergone a shock but opened little or not at all. Table 7.2 provides more detail on the crisis countries, showing the date of the shock, some indicators of its magnitude, and the dates of major banking-sector-opening reforms.

Table 7.2 Banking crises, noncrises, and changes in banking regime, 1997–2002

	COUNTRY	DATE(S) OF BANKING CRISIS	FISCAL AND QUASI-FISCAL COST OF CRISIS (AS % GDP)	NPLs (% TOTAL LOANS)	DATE(S) OF MAJOR REFORMS	MAJORITY ACQUISITIONS BY FOREIGNERS ALLOWED?
Crisis & no/little opening	Argentina	1980–82, 1995, 2001–2	55 (1980–82), 2 (1995)	14 (2001–2)	Minor reform in 1994, but already open	Yes
	Russia	1998–99	5–7	n/a	2002	Yes
	Malaysia	1997–98	17	25–35	Remains closed	No
Crisis & major opening	Indonesia	1997–98	50–55	65–75	1998	Yes
	Venezuela	1994–95	18	n/a	1994	Yes
	Philippines	1998–99	7	n/a	2000	Yes
	South Korea	1997–98	34	30–40	1998	Yes
	Colombia	1982–87	5	25	1991	Yes
	Thailand	1997–98	42	46	1997	Yes
	Turkey	2000–2001	31	n/a	2001	Yes
	Mexico	1994–95	20	11	1995, 1998	Yes
	Brazil	1994–96	5–10	15	1995–2000	Yes

Source: Columns 3–5: Glen Hoggarth, Ricardo Reis, and Victoria Saporta, "Costs of Banking System Instability: Some Empirical Evidence," *Journal of Banking and Finance* 26 (2002), 830–831; Gerard Caprio Jr. and Daniela Klingebiel, "Cases of Systemic and Borderline Financial Crises"(mimeo.), World Bank, 2003, p. 2; and "Argentina: Financial Services," *Economist Intelligence Unit,* November 22, 2005.

To go a step further, below I provide brief sketches of six country experiences, two from each of the quadrants that challenge the argument (quadrants 2, 3, and 4). These sketches are used to test, in a preliminary way, whether the banking-sector-opening experiences of other middle-income countries are consistent with the findings of this book. Where they are not, this exercise can help us identify the limits of this argument and open avenues for future research.

Quadrant 4: No Banking Crisis and Little Opening

Quadrant 4 includes the major economies of India and China. Consistent with what we would expect based on the findings of this book, these two countries have avoided major banking shocks in the past two decades and also retain protected banking sectors.

INDIA

With one of the largest underbanked populations and fastest-growing economies in the globe, it is not surprising that India has one of the most coveted banking markets in the emerging world. India's strongly nationalist governments, protectionist tradition, and extensive government presence in the banking sector have not produced a welcome environment for foreign investors, however. Just before the GATS negotiations were completed in 1997, India barred foreign banks from entering the market through subsidiaries (though branches were allowed). Foreign shareholding in individual Indian banks was limited to 20 percent, and the aggregate share of total system assets that foreign banks could control was capped at 15 percent. Despite considerable pressure during the GATS negotiations, India bound commitments consistent with the status quo. Foreign banks also faced a variety of other barriers in India, including higher tax rates than local competitors and complex procedures for opening branches.

Over time, Indian policymakers introduced more liberal policies, but the regime remains highly restrictive compared with those of the countries we have examined in this book. In 2002, the authorities allowed foreign banks to establish subsidiaries as well as branches, but the numbers of both were restricted. Three years later, the Indian authorities signaled that they would permit foreign investors to enter by acquisition *only* through the purchase of weak private banks preselected by the regulators. But in a move reminiscent of Brazil's approach to de facto opening, when a troubled Indian bank was put up for sale, Indian banking authorities chose a domestic bidder over a foreign one.

According to the Indian central bank's "roadmap" for banking-sector opening, foreigners will have to wait until at least 2009 before restrictions on foreign acquisitions of domestic banks are relaxed. As of early 2006, foreign banks controlled only 6.9 percent of the Indian banking sector's assets, a figure similar to foreign participation in the advanced economies.[5] In early 2009, the Committee on Financial Sector Assessment—a high-level advisory group chaired by the deputy governor of the Reserve Bank of India—issued an extensive report arguing that foreign entry into India's banking system should be "gradual and consistent with the overall financial policy strategy and the transition [to a more open banking regime] should happen smoothly and without causing serious imbalances."[6] In short, India's movement toward gradual opening is reminiscent of the managed-opening experiments in Brazil, Mexico, and Korea before their respective banking shocks. India has not suffered a shock of this kind in recent memory.

CHINA (PEOPLE'S REPUBLIC)

With over a trillion dollars in household savings, China remains the single most attractive financial-services market in the developing world. The Chinese government began to open its highly protected banking system in the mid-1980s as part of an experiment in managed openness. Beijing allowed foreign and joint-venture

---

5. "Foreign Banks Will Get to Open 20 Branches a Year," *Financial Express,* January 3, 2006.

6. Committee on Financial Sector Assessment, *India's Financial Sector: An Assessment,* vol. 1 (New Delhi: Foundation Books, March 2009), executive summary.

banks to engage in a wide variety of banking services but only in four legally separate enclaves (the Special Economic Zones), ensuring that foreign banks would not compete against domestic institutions for local-currency deposits. The sector was opened another notch in 1994, when Chinese authorities allowed foreign banks to engage in renminbi-denominated banking activities "on a limited and experimental basis."[7] However, foreign entry into the sector was tightly controlled—by the turn of the century, foreign banks accounted for a mere 2 percent of total financial assets in China.[8]

According to our definition, the PRC has not suffered a banking shock in recent decades (very high NPLs and fiscal costs, but no runs or emergency measures). However, there is little doubt that the Chinese banking system has been under strain since the late 1990s. In 1998, the four government-owned banks that account for 68 percent of China's banking system assets were deemed insolvent. The authorities injected some US$33 billion to recapitalize the four banks, and more cash injections followed in 2003, 2004, and 2005.[9] But because the "Big Four" are state-owned and enjoy a government guarantee, and because so far the government has been able to afford the recapitalization bills, the institutions have avoided runs, none has collapsed, and a banking crisis as we define it has been avoided. China's capital controls also support the domestic banking sector by denying exit options to domestic savers.

Starting in the 1990s, Beijing came under considerable political pressure to open its banking sector. Pressure from the U.S. government peaked in 1999, when banking-sector opening became a central issue in the bilateral talks between Washington and Beijing over China's accession to the WTO. Under the final agreement, the Chinese agreed to allow foreign banks full access to the banking sector within five years of China's accession. However, Chinese regulators retained a variety of regulations to discourage foreign bank entry: individual foreign investors are limited to a 20 percent stake in Chinese banks, and total foreign investment in the banking sector is capped at 25 percent.[10] Despite vigorous lobbying efforts by the U.S. Treasury to persuade Beijing to raise these ceilings, the Chinese government has not budged.[11]

---

7. "China: Banking Liberalisation," *Oxford Analytica Daily Brief,* February 4, 1994.

8. "China: Banks Brace for WTO," *Oxford Analytica Daily Brief,* June 22, 2000.

9. Charlene Chu et al., "China: Taking Stock of Banking System NPLs," *Fitch Ratings Special Report,* May 30, 2006, p. 2.

10. In addition, regulators retain a "one city, one branch" rule that was not addressed in the WTO negotiations. This rule will be watered down only slowly, preventing foreign banks from deploying their networks to compete for local deposits. Despite some liberalization, Chinese authorities also retain the power to set the interest rates that banks may offer and charge. Because foreign banks may enter only as branches, not as subsidiaries, they must set aside 8 percent of capital for each branch, raising the costs of doing business.

11. "Cautious Praise for Paulson over Access," *Financial Times,* May 24, 2007.

Desperate to enter the market on any terms, major advanced-economy banks, including Citigroup, HSBC, Goldman Sachs, and Standard Chartered, bought stakes in large and medium-sized Chinese banks.[12] Also, investors have participated eagerly in initial public offerings by Chinese banks. As of mid-2007, foreigners had invested in some twenty-nine Chinese banks, although foreigners collectively hold only a small fraction of the system's total assets.[13]

Compared with the scale of opening in Mexico, Brazil, Indonesia, and Korea, China's opening remains qualitatively different: foreigners can compete in the local market, but they cannot acquire management control of major banking institutions. If the experiences of the countries studied here are any guide, the Chinese authorities will make de facto opening highly discretionary and gradual despite their WTO commitments. Unless Beijing becomes unable to support the four big state banks and suffers a major banking shock, it seems unlikely that the Chinese government will engage in the type of opening that would allow advanced-economy banks to acquire major Chinese banking institutions.

In conclusion, despite intense external political pressure, India and China have retained a significant degree of control over the opening process and enough room to engage in managed opening. The experience of these countries confirms the basic intuition of this book—that for large emerging economies, external pressure in the absence of a banking shock is not enough to bring about extensive opening. Opening does take place under these conditions, but it is gradual, limited, and undertaken for narrowly tailored purposes.

Quadrant 2: Banking Crisis but Little Opening

The second quadrant includes countries whose experiences challenge the findings of this book. These are countries that suffered a banking crisis but did not respond by opening their banking sectors to foreign capital. This situation has proved quite rare in practice among emerging-market countries. Of the sample of fifteen countries, only Malaysia fits neatly into quadrant 2; the Russian case is less clear-cut.

MALAYSIA

After it gained its independence from Britain in 1957, Malaysia introduced policies designed to push foreigners out of the local banking market and "indigenize" the Malaysian banking sector. These policies worked as intended; foreign banks

---

12. Only one foreign entity, U.S. private equity fund Newbridge Capital, has been allowed to acquire a controlling stake in a Chinese institution, in this case the medium-sized Zhenzhen Development Bank.

13. Foreign banks in China operate out of some 250 branches and hold 1.7 percent of total system assets. Even if we add foreign acquisitions in existing Chinese banks, total foreign holdings remain less than 15 percent of total system assets. Peter Tebbutt et al., "Foreign Banks' Expansion into China, with a Focus on Hong Kong's Banks," *Fitch Ratings Special Report,* May 2, 2007.

held over 90 percent of the Malaysian banking market in 1957, but by 1997 they accounted for only 16.7 percent of total banking assets.[14] Foreign banks were forbidden to establish new branches in the early 1970s, and no new banking licenses were granted to foreign banks after 1973. With de novo entry effectively blocked, the only way foreigners could enter the local banking market was through the purchase of shares in existing institutions, but foreign stakes in local banks were limited to 10 percent for individual investors and 30 percent for foreigners as a whole. At the GATS negotiations, Malaysia made only marginal concessions.

With the Asian financial crisis, Malaysia's banking sector suffered a severe crisis. Two major public banks, accounting for 14 percent of financial system assets, were declared insolvent. Major finance companies were taken over by the central bank, and 25 to 35 percent of all loans turned nonperforming.[15] The crisis would eventually cost the government some 16 percent of GDP, a modest amount by regional standards, but well within our definition of a banking shock.[16]

Nevertheless, no major banking-sector-opening initiatives followed, and the government retained the same level of precrisis restrictions on foreign participation in the sector. Even today, a decade after the crisis, the Malaysian banking system remains highly restrictive. (The government's Financial Sector Master Plan calls for the removal of some discriminatory regulations that affect foreign banks and for a gradual, if limited, opening of the market starting in 2007.)

Why did Malaysia resist opening in the face of a major banking shock? Three factors stand out. Malaysia did not seek assistance from the IMF during the crisis, closing down a key channel for external pressure that proved decisive in many countries where banking shock led to extensive opening. Second, Prime Minister Mahathir's attitude about the role of the state in banking was aggressively interventionist, so the central bank and finance ministry had no reservations about taking over troubled financial institutions and felt little urgency to return them to private hands, foreign or domestic. Finally, the Malaysian government was in better shape fiscally than its neighbors, as the state oil company, Petronas, had generated comfortable surpluses that could be used to recapitalize the banking sector with domestic resources.

RUSSIA

The Russian case does not fit quite as neatly as Malaysia into this quadrant; some elements suggest it could also fit in quadrant 1. Nevertheless, its experience with banking-sector opening offers some useful insights about the limits of banking shocks as drivers of opening.

The banking system that emerged in Russia in the decade after the fall of communism was highly idiosyncratic. It was populated by an extraordinarily large number

---

14. Detragiache and Gupta, "Foreign Banks in Emerging Market Crises," p. 5.
15. Caprio and Klingebiel, "Episodes of Systemic and Borderline Financial Crises," p. 2.
16. Ibid.

of banks—in 1994, there were over 2,500 banks in Russia[17]—but the majority were either "dwarf banks," which were vehicles for tax evasion or money laundering, or "pocket banks," which were not profit-oriented entities but vehicles for financing the activities of a single company or business group.[18] Meanwhile, the state retained majority stakes in twenty-three banks, including Sberbank, the largest commercial bank.[19] Unlike many countries in Eastern and Central Europe, Russia kept its banking sector closed to foreign participation through a ban on all foreign-bank branches and a cap of 12 percent on foreign shareholdings in any individual domestic bank. Foreign banks also faced discriminatory capital requirements and limitations on expatriate staff. These prohibitions reflected in large measure the protectionist preferences of the leading Moscow banks.[20]

A capital account crisis triggered a banking shock in Russia in August 1998. Nearly 720 banks—about half of those operating at the time and representing 4 percent of assets and 32 percent of deposits—became insolvent.[21] The costs of rescuing the banking sector were estimated at 5 to 7 percent of GDP.[22] Unlike Kuala Lumpur, Moscow turned to the IMF for assistance. But despite the shock and the IMF package, the Russian authorities retained the ban on foreign branching. The 12 percent cap on foreign ownership was maintained until November 2002, when ceilings on foreign ownership were lifted entirely, subject to approval by the government. This measure may have been a delayed response to the shock, but more research is required to answer this question.

Yet Moscow's lifting of the shareholding cap was of little practical significance, for two reasons. Russia's most important commercial banks remained in government hands, and Moscow had no intention of privatizing them. And second, unlike most other countries in the sample, there was little for foreigners to buy in the Russian banking sector: foreign investors saw the vast majority of Russian banks as unsuitable for acquisition.[23] This is partly because, with the exception of the government-owned Sberbank, no other commercial bank had a branch network of any significance.[24] Given the structure of the Russian banking system, for foreign investors real opening meant lifting the ban on branching; through de novo

---

17. Juliet Johnson, *A Fistful of Rubles: The Rise and Fall of the Russian Banking System* (Ithaca: Cornell University Press, 2000), p. 19.

18. William Tompson, "Banking Reform in Russia: Problems and Prospects," OECD Economics Department Working Paper No. 410 (Paris: OECD Publishing, 2004), pp. 5–6.

19. Ibid., p. 7.

20. On the political power of Russian banks, see Juliet Johnson, "Carving up the Bear: Banks and the Struggle for Power in Russia," *Post-Soviet Prospects,* Center for Strategic and International Studies, March 1997.

21. Caprio and Klingebiel, "Episodes of Systemic and Borderline Financial Crises," p. 5.

22. Ibid.

23. "Russia Industry: Foreign Banks Seeking a Way In," *Economist Intelligence Unit,* January 20, 2006.

24. See Johnson, *Fistful of Rubles,* p. 224.

entry, foreign banks were confident they could make deep inroads into the Russian market.

Seeking to end the ban on branching, the U.S. government put considerable pressure on Moscow during bilateral talks for Russia's accession to the WTO and were met by ferocious resistance from Russian officials, who at one point threatened to link the issue with the ability (or inability) of foreign companies to compete for natural gas infrastructure projects in Russia. In July 2006, U.S. negotiators backed off and dropped their demand that foreign banks be allowed to open branches.[25] As of April 2009, the ban on branching remained in the books.

How has Russia managed to keep its banking sector effectively closed despite the 1998 banking shock? A superficial analysis suggests two factors. First, the Russian central bank simply incurred the massive costs of injecting emergency liquidity support into the banking system without turning to foreign capital. To raise cash, the government borrowed huge amounts abroad, increasing its foreign debt by US$18.5 billion in just seven months.[26] Inflation tripled between 1997 and 1999. Also, the government simply took over troubled private banks, resigned to the prospect that the state would have to nurse them back to health without assistance and that those banks might have to remain state-owned for the indefinite future.

Like the Malaysian case, the Russian experience suggests that countries can retain protectionist policies in the aftermath of a banking shock, but at very high costs to the state and to the public. This case suggests a new line of inquiry for future research: Under what conditions do governments deem it preferable to retain barriers to foreign participation in banking, even when it means potentially ruinous costs to the state? Another factor are policymakers' attitudes about the role of the state in finance. In contrast to policymakers in the four countries covered in this book, Malaysian and Russian authorities felt no need to privatize the banks taken over during the crisis (or indeed, those that were in already state hands before the crisis). Without privatizations, the question of foreign participation in existing institutions became a moot point.

Quadrant 3: No Banking Crisis but Extensive Opening

Countries in the third quadrant also challenge the argument of this book, but in a different way. In this quadrant lie the relatively rare cases of emerging-market countries in which meaningful banking-sector opening emerged in the absence of banking crises. The two cases—Argentina and South Africa—highlight some of the argument's limitations and point to the role of initial conditions and historical legacies in producing liberal banking regimes.

---

25. "Russia Politics: Russia Claims Breakthrough with US on WTO," *Economist Intelligence Unit*, July 13, 2006.

26. Johnson, *Fistful of Rubles*, p. 213.

ARGENTINA

Argentina is an unusual case, as it embraced liberal banking long *before* it experienced banking crises in 1980–1982, 1995, and 2001–2002. Since at least 1957, Argentine banking laws have provided for equal treatment for both foreign and domestic banks, while entry has been granted on the condition of reciprocity. Aside from brief interruptions in the 1960s and 1970s, Argentina consistently maintained a liberal banking regime in law and in practice, allowing for de novo entry and extending to foreigners the same rights for merging with or acquiring local banks as those enjoyed by domestic investors. Under 1994 regulations, the reciprocity condition was dropped entirely, and in the 1990s, this liberal regime was locked into place through the GATS and through a U.S.-Argentina bilateral investment treaty.

Foreign banks enjoyed a significant presence in Argentina, accounting for half of total banking sector assets, before the 2001–2002 banking shock. Citibank alone had fifty-four branches in Argentina in 2002, compared with only thirty-four in neighboring Brazil, which has an economy that is five times as large.[27] When this twin crisis hit Argentina, foreign banks had to decide whether to expand their operations or scale back. They chose to retrench and, in some cases, to exit the market completely. Public outrage turned against the foreign banks, and several had their offices vandalized. Yet the government stood by its commitment to a liberal banking regime, though foreign participation after the crisis fell to about a quarter of banking system assets (see Figure 1.2.)

What might account for this outcome? The literature suggests that the nature of Argentine economic development may be largely responsible. With the rise of a powerful agro-exporting elite dependent for credit on foreign banks since the nineteenth century, an influential domestic constituency emerged that was willing to defend the liberal banking regime. At the same time, a strong indigenous banking elite never developed, and therefore demands for banking-sector protectionism never materialized.[28] A key element of Argentina's resilient liberal banking regime, then, may be rooted in the historical development of the links between the real sector and international banks.

SOUTH AFRICA

Like Argentina, South Africa in the nineteenth century had a banking sector that was highly integrated with foreign capital, and unlike most other countries in the sample, it did not experience a period of prolonged financial protectionism. British and Dutch capital dominated the South African banking system from the late 1800s onward; by the 1970s, two of the top four banks in South Africa were headquartered in London and Amsterdam (Barclays and Nedbank, respectively), while a

---

27. Del Negro and Kay, "Global Banks, Local Crises," 2002, p. 2.
28. Thorburn, "Political Economy of Foreign Banks," 2004.

third (Standard Bank) broke away from its London-based parent only in the 1960s.[29] During the 1980s, under intense pressure from civil society to participate in the embargo against the apartheid government, the leading foreign banks operating in South Africa sold or closed down their operations. By 1987, all the major foreign banks, including Citibank and Standard Chartered, had left the country.

With the end of apartheid and the repeal of international sanctions in the early 1990s, the government moved to normalize its international financial relations. Under the 1990 Banks Act, foreigners were allowed to acquire equity in South African banks without restrictions, other than to purchase the equity in staggered intervals and receive permission from the minister of finance. In 1995, the central bank lifted restrictions on the establishment of foreign-bank branches (only subsidiaries and representative offices had been allowed previously). By 2000, all the remaining discriminatory regulations had been removed, so that foreign banks were treated on a par with their local counterparts. There were no banking crises throughout this period; South Africa's banking sector proved stable and well regulated, even in the wake of crises in other emerging economies. In 2005, Pretoria approved the acquisition of one of South Africa's "big four" domestic banks by the U.K.-based Barclays. The transaction was the single biggest FDI injection into the country and the first time that a foreign bank took a controlling interest in an existing domestic bank. Foreign participation increased to 16 percent of total banking-system assets.[30]

Like the Argentine story, the South African experience appears to be one characterized by unusually strong historic links between a local commodity-exporting elite and foreign banking institutions. Foreign banks had been deeply involved in financing South Africa's gold-mining operations since the late nineteenth century, just as they had bankrolled Argentina's agro-exporters. The foreign banks' dominant presence prevented the rise of an indigenous banking elite, and in the absence of a strong nationalist movement with antiforeign overtones, the foreign banks and the liberal banking regime that supported their operations remained intact well into the twentieth century. In this context, post-apartheid opening should be seen as a return to South Africa's long tradition of liberal banking rather than as a historical aberration. In sum, the Argentine and South African cases suggest that future research should focus on why and how banking-sector protectionism failed to take root in developing countries with historically high levels of integration between export industries and foreign banks.

As work on this book was coming to an end, the world was experiencing its worst economic slowdown since the Great Depression. The crisis began in the United

---

29. On the history of foreign banks in South Africa, see Stuart Jones, ed., *Banking and Business in South Africa* (New York: St. Martin's Press, 1988).

30. International Monetary Fund, "South Africa: Selected Issues," IMF Country Report No. 05/345, September 2005, p. 40.

States, where a massive housing-price bubble caused extensive damage to the balance sheets of global financial institutions, many of which were exposed through mortgage-backed securities they held in their portfolios. Top investment banks collapsed or were absorbed by other institutions. The U.S. government injected hundreds of billions of dollars to recapitalize some of the largest financial institutions in the system, including some of the commercial banking giants that had featured prominently in the wave of global expansion just years earlier, such as Citigroup and Bank of America. There was even talk that the government might have to nationalize some of these institutions. European banks, some of which had extensive operations in Central and Eastern Europe, were also reeling as the crisis spread to that region of the world.

In an ironic twist, foreign capital rushed in to help recapitalize some of America's largest banks, including Citigroup. The Korea Development Bank seriously considered acquiring a large stake in Lehman Brothers, a U.S. investment bank that later collapsed. Brazil's largest private banks, including the giant Itaú-Unibanco, pondered whether the crisis would give them an opportunity to penetrate the U.S. and other markets through cheap acquisitions.

Behind closed doors and in the opinion pages of newspapers, U.S. policymakers began to ask whether the entry of foreign capital into banking and other sensitive sectors would threaten U.S. national security and its strategic interests. Legislators called for heightened scrutiny of foreign investments in areas deemed "critical infrastructure," which refers to "system and assets, whether physical or virtual, so vital to the United States that the incapacity or destruction of the particular systems or assets…would have a debilitating impact on national security."[31] Though the Treasury has yet to issue a detailed list of what sectors are considered "critical infrastructure," major commercial banks were widely expected to be on the list.

The global crisis served to highlight that governments everywhere still regard banks as special because they confer power over financial resources vital to a nation's economic health. Ownership and control of domestic banks by foreigners is still viewed with suspicion, even in the most globalized of times and in the richest and most open economies. As a result, the process of opening the banking sector to foreign participation will remain controversial and intensely political. Understanding what forces drive that process and with what implications for the distribution of wealth and power will remain an enduring question at the heart of international political economy.

---

31. U.S. Department of the Treasury, 31 CFR Part 800, Office of Investment Security, RIN 1505-AB88, "Regulations Pertaining to Mergers, Acquisitions, and Takeovers by Foreign Persons."

Bibliography

Abdelal, Rawi. *Capital Rules: Institutions and the International Monetary System.* Cambridge, Mass.: Harvard University Press, 2007.

Abdullah, Burhanuddin, and Wimboh Santoso. "The Indonesian Banking Industry: Competition, Consolidation and Systemic Stability." In "The Banking Industry in the Emerging Market Economies: Competition, Consolidation, and Systemic Stability." BIS Working Paper No. 4, August 2001, pp. 80–92.

Agenor, Pierre-Richard. "Benefits and Costs of Financial Integration: Theory and Facts." Policy Research Working Paper 2699, World Bank, October 2001.

Aghevli, Bijan B., and Jorge Márquez-Ruarte. "A Case of Successful Adjustment: Korea's Experience during 1980–84." Occasional Paper 39, International Monetary Fund, August 1985.

Aguilar Zínser, Adolfo. "Authoritarianism and North American Free Trade: The Debate in Mexico." In *The Political Economy of North American Free Trade,* ed. Ricardo Grinspun and Maxwell A. Cameron, pp. 205–216. London: Macmillan, 1993.

Andrews, David M. "Capital Mobility and State Autonomy: Toward a Structural Theory of International Monetary Relations." *International Studies Quarterly* 38 (1994), 193–218.

Armijo, Leslie Eliott. "Brazilian Politics and Patterns of Financial Regulation, 1945–1991." In *The Politics of Finance in Developing Countries,* ed. Stephan Haggard, Chung H. Lee, and Sylvia Maxfield. Ithaca: Cornell University Press, 1993.

Arndt, Heinz. "Banking in Hyperinflation." *Bulletin of Indonesian Economic Studies* 5 (October 1966), 45–70.

Auerbach, Nancy N. *States, Banks, and Markets: Mexico's Path to Financial Liberalization in Comparative Perspective.* Boulder, Colo.: Westview Press, 2001.

Babb, Sarah. *Managing Mexico: Economists from Nationalism to Neoliberalism.* Princeton, N.J.: Princeton University Press, 2001.

Baer, Werner. *The Brazilian Economy: Growth and Development.* London: Praeger, 2001.

Baer, Werner, and Edmund Amann. "The Illusion of Stability: The Brazilian Economy under Cardoso." In Werner Baer, *The Brazilian Economy: Growth and Development,* pp. 199–219. London: Praeger, 2001.

Baer, Werner, and James T. Bang. "Privatization and Equity in Brazil and Russia." *Kyklos* 55 (2002), 495–522.

Baliño, Tomás J. T., and Angel Ubide. "The Korean Financial Crisis of 1997—A Strategy of Financial Sector Reform." IMF Working Paper WP/99/28, March 1999.

Barajas, Adolfo, Roberto Steiner, and Natalia Salazar. "The Impact of Liberalization and Foreign Investment in Colombia's Financial Sector." *Journal of Development Economics* 63 (2000), 157–196.

Barker, Wendy J. "Os bancos, a indústria e o Estado no Brasil." *Revista de Economia Política* 10 (April–June 1990), 132–146.

Baron, David P., and David Besanko. "Strategy, Organization, and Incentives: Global Corporate Banking at Citibank." *Industrial and Corporate Change* 10, 1 (2001), 1–36.

Basave Kunhardt, Jorge. *Los grupos de capital financiero en México (1974–1995).* Mexico City: Instituto de Investigaciones Económicas, UNAM, y Ediciones El Caballito, 1996.

Bates, Robert H., Avner Greif, Margaret Levi, Jean-Laurent Rosenthal, and Barry R. Weingast. *Analytic Narratives.* Princeton, N.J.: Princeton University Press, 1998.

Batunanggar, Sukarela. "Indonesia's Banking Crisis Resolution: Lessons and the Way Forward." Paper prepared for the Financial Stability Research Project at the Centre for Central Banking Studies, Bank of England, December 2, 2002.

Bennett, Andrew, and Alexander L. George. "Case Studies and Process Tracing in History and Political Science: Similar Strokes for Different Foci." In *Bridges and Boundaries: Historians, Political Scientists, and the Study of International Relations,* ed. Colin Elman and Miriam Fendius Elman. Cambridge, Mass.: MIT Press, 2001.

Bennett, Robert L. *The Financial Sector and Economic Development: The Mexican Case.* Baltimore: Johns Hopkins University Press, 1965.

Benston, George J., and George G. Kaufman. "Is the Banking and Payments System Fragile?" *Journal of Financial Services Research* 9 (December 1995), 209–240.

Berger, Allen N., Leora F. Klapper, and Gregory F. Udell. "The Ability of Banks to Lend to Informationally Opaque Small Businesses." *Journal of Banking and Finance* 25 (2001), 2127–2167.

Bevilaqua, Alfonso S. "State-Government Bailouts in Brazil." Discussion Paper, Department of Economics, Catholic University of Rio de Janeiro (PUC-Rio), March 2000.

Bevilaqua, Alfonso S., and Eduardo Loyo. "Openness and Efficiency in Brazilian Banking." Discussion Paper No. 390, Catholic University of Rio de Janeiro (PUC-Rio), September 1998.

Bhattacharya, Joydeep. "The Role of Foreign Banks in Developing Countries: A Survey of the Evidence." Cornell University, mimeo., 1994.

Biersteker, Thomas. "The 'Triumph' of Liberal Economic Ideas in the Developing World." In *Global Change, Regional Response: A New International Context of Development,* ed. Barbara Stallings, pp. 174–196. New York: Cambridge University Press, 1995.

Binhadi. *Financial Sector Deregulation, Banking Development, and Monetary Policy.* Jakarta: Institut Bankir Indonesia, 1995.

Bird, Graham, and Dane Rowlands. "Do IMF Programmes Have a Catalytic Effect on Other International Capital Flows?" *Oxford Development Studies* 30, 3 (2002), 229–249.

Blustein, Paul. *The Chastening: Inside the Crisis That Rocked the Global Financial System and Humbled the IMF.* New York: Public Affairs, 2001.

Bodin de Moraes, Pedro. "Foreign Banks in the Brazilian Economy in the 1980s." Department of Economics, Catholic University of Rio de Janeiro (PUC-RJ), August 1990.

Boediono. "The International Monetary Fund Support Program in Indonesia: Comparing Implementation under Three Presidents." *Bulletin of Indonesian Economic Studies* 38, 3 (2002), 385–391.

Boito, Armando, Jr. "Neoliberal Hegemony and Unionism in Brazil." *Latin American Perspectives* 25 (January 1998), 31–93.

Bresnan, John. *Managing Indonesia: The Modern Political Economy.* New York: Columbia University Press, 1993.

British Invisibles. "Barriers to Financial Services Trade in Key Markets (First Revise)." Document prepared by British Invisibles for the Financial Leaders Working Group, London, June 9, 1997.

Burki, Shahid Javed. "A Fate Foretold: The World Bank and the Mexican Crisis." In *Mexico 1994: Anatomy of an Emerging-Market Crash,* ed. Sebastian Edwards and Moisés Naím. Washington, D.C.: Carnegie Endowment for International Peace, 1997.

Calvo, Guillermo A., and Enrique G. Mendoza. "Petty Crime and Cruel Punishment: Lessons from the Mexican Debacle." *American Economic Review* 86 (May 1996), 170–175.

Camdessus, Michel. "Address at the Annual Meeting of the Union of Arab Banks." New York, May 20, 1996.

Cameron, Lisa. "Survey of Recent Developments." *Bulletin of Indonesian Economic Studies* 35 (April 1999), 3–41.

Camp, Roderic A. *Entrepreneurs and Politics in Twentieth-Century Mexico.* New York: Oxford University Press, 1989.

Caprio, Gerard, Jr., and Daniela Klingebiel. "Episodes of Systemic and Borderline Financial Crises." Mimeo., World Bank, 2003.

Cardero, María Elena, José Manuel Quijano, and José Luis Manzo. "Cambios recientes a la organización bancaria y el caso de México.", In *La banca: Pasado y presente,* ed. José Manuel Quijano, pp. 198–199. Mexico City: CIDE, 1983.

Cardoso, Fernando Henrique. *A arte da política: A história que vivi.* Rio de Janeiro: Civilização Brasileria, 2006.

———. *Mãos à Obra, Brasil: Proposta de governo.* Brasilia, 1994.

Carvalho, Carlos Eduardo, and Guiliano Contento de Oliveira. "Fragilização de grandes bancos no início do Plano Real." *Nova Economia* 12 (January–June 2002), 69–84.

Carvalho, Fernando J. Cardim de. "Price Stability and Banking Sector Distress in Brazil after 1994." Institute of Economics, Federal University of Rio de Janeiro, Discussion Paper No. 388, March 1996.

Castañeda, Jorge G. *Perpetuating Power.* New York: New Press, 2000.

———. *Sorpresas te da la vida: México 1994.* Mexico City: Aguilar Nuevo Siglo, 1994.

Centeno, Miguel Angel. *Democracy within Reason: Technocratic Revolution in Mexico.* University Park: Pennsylvania State University Press, 1997.

Chalmers, Ian, and Vedi R. Hadiz. *The Politics of Economic Development in Indonesia: Contending Perspectives.* London: Routledge, 1997.

Chamon, Marcos, Paolo Manasse, and Alessandro Prati. "Can We Predict the Next Capital Account Crisis?" Paper presented at the 7th Jacques Polak Annual Research Conference, International Monetary Fund, November 9–10, 2006.

Charlesworth, Harold K. *The Banking System in Transition.* Jakarta: New Nusantara Publishing Co., 1959.

Cheng, H., ed. *Financial Policy and Reform in Pacific-Basin Countries.* Lexington, Mass.: Lexington Books, 1986.

Choi, Byung-Sun. "Financial Policy and Big Business in Korea: The Perils of Financial Regulation." In *The Politics of Finance in Developing Countries,* ed. Stephan Haggard, Chung H. Lee, and Sylvia Maxfield. Ithaca: Cornell University Press, 1993.

Chu, Charlene, L. Lin, K. Lin, and D. Marshall. "China: Taking Stock of Banking System NPLs." *Fitch Ratings Special Report,* May 30, 2006, p. 2.

Claessens, Stjin, Asli Demirgüç-Kunt, and Harry Huizinga. "How Does Foreign Entry Affect the Domestic Banking Market?" *Journal of Banking and Finance* 25 (2001), 891–911.

Clarke, George, Robert Cull, Maria Soledad Martinez Peria, and Susana M. Sánchez. "Foreign Bank Entry: Experience, Implications for Developing Economies, and Agenda for Further Research." *World Bank Research Observer* 18 (Spring 2003), 25–59.

Clarke, George, Robert Cull, Laura D'Amato, and Andrea Molinari. "The Effect of Foreign Entry on Argentina's Domestic Banking Sector." World Bank Policy Research Working Paper 2158, August 1999.

Clarke, George, Robert Cull, and María Soledad Martínez Peria. "Does Foreign Bank Penetration Reduce Access to Credit in Developing Countries? Evidence from Asking Borrowers." World Bank Policy Research Working Paper 2716, November 2001.

Coe, David T., and Se-Jik Kim, eds. *Korean Crisis and Recovery.* Washington, D.C.: IMF; Seoul: KIEP, 2002.

Cohen, Benjamin J. "Phoenix Risen: The Resurrection of Global Finance." *World Politics* 48, 2 (1996), 268–296.

Cole, David C., and Betty F. Slade. *Building a Modern Financial System.* Cambridge: Cambridge University Press, 1996.

Cole, David C., and Yung C. Park. *Financial Development in Korea, 1945–1978.* Cambridge, Mass.: Harvard University Press, 1983.

Collier, Ruth Berins, and David Collier. *Shaping the Political Arena: Critical Junctures, the Labor Movement, and Regime Dynamics in Latin America.* Princeton, N.J.: Princeton University Press, 1991.

Concheiro Bórquez, Elvira. *El gran acuerdo.* Mexico City: Ediciones Era, 1996.

Corazza, Gentil. "Crise e reestruturação bancária no Brasil." *Revista Análise,* Porto Alegre, 12, 2 (2001), 21–42.

Crystal, Jennifer S., B. Gerard Dages, and Linda S. Goldberg. "Does Foreign Ownership Contribute to Sounder Banks in Emerging Markets? The Latin American Experience." Federal Reserve Bank of New York, May 29, 2001.

del Angel-Mobarak, Gustavo, Carlos Bazdresch Parada, and Francisco Suárez Dávila. *Cuando el estado he hizo banquero.* Mexico City: Fondo de Cultura Económica, 2005.

del Negro, Marco, and Stephen J. Kay. "Global Banks, Local Crises: Bad News from Argentina." *Federal Reserve Bank of Atlanta Economic Review* (Third Quarter, 2002), 1–18.

Demirgüç-Kunt, Asli, and Enrica Detragiache. "The Determinants of Banking Crises in Developing and Developed Countries." *IMF Staff Papers* 45 (March 1998), 81–109.

Demirgüç-Kunt, Asli, Ross Levine, and Hong G. Min. "Opening to Foreign Banks: Issues of Stability, Efficiency, and Growth." In *Proceedings of the Bank of Korea Conference on the Implications of Globalization of World Financial Markets.* December 1998.

Detragiache, Enrica, and Poonam Gupta. "Foreign Banks in Emerging Market Crises: Evidence from Malaysia." IMF Working Paper WP/04/129, July 2004.

Detragiache, Enrica, Poonam Gupta, and Thierry Tressel. "Finance in Lower-Income Countries: An Empirical Exploration." IMF Working Paper WP/05/167, August 2005.

Detragiache, Enrica, Thierry Tressel, and Poonam Gupta. "Foreign Banks in Poor Countries: Theory and Evidence." IMF Working Paper WP/06/18, January 2006.

Djiwandono, J. Soedradjad. *Bank Indonesia and the Crisis.* Singapore: ISEAS, 2005.

———. "Role of the IMF in Indonesia's Financial Crisis." In *Governance in Indonesia: Challenges Facing the Megawati Presidency,* ed. Hadi Soesastro, Anthony L. Smith, and Han Mui Ling, pp. 196–228. Singapore: ISEAS, 2002.

Dobson, Wendy, and Pierre Jacquet. *Financial Services Liberalization in the WTO.* Washington, D.C.: Institute for International Economics, 1998.

Domanski, Dietrich. "Foreign Banks in Emerging Market Economies: Changing Players, Changing Issues." *BIS Quarterly Review,* December 2005, 69–81.

Domínguez, Jorge I., ed. *Technopols: Freeing Politics and Markets in Latin America in the 1990s.* University Park: Pennsylvania State University Press, 1997.

Drazen, Allan, and William Easterly. "Do Crises Induce Reform? Simple Empirical Tests of Conventional Wisdom." *Economics and Politics* 13 (July 2001), 130–131.

Edwards, Sebastian, and Moisés Naím, eds. *Mexico 1994: Anatomy of an Emerging-Market Crash.* Washington, D.C.: Carnegie Endowment for International Peace, 1997.

Enoch, Charles, Barbara Baldwin, Olivier Frécaut, and Arto Kovanen. "Indonesia: Anatomy of a Banking Crisis; Two Years of Living Dangerously, 1997–99." IMF Working Paper WP/01/52, May 2001.

Enoch, Charles, Oliver Frécaut, and Arto Kovanen. "Indonesia's Banking Crisis: What Happened and What Did We Learn?" *Bulletin of Indonesian Economic Studies* 39 (April 2003), 75–92.

Euh, Yoon-Dae, and James C. Barker. *The Korean Banking System and Foreign Influence.* London: Routledge, 1990.

Fane, George, and Ross H. McLeod. "Banking Collapse and Restructuring in Indonesia, 1997–2001." *Cato Journal* 22 (Fall 2002), 277–294.

FitzGerald, Valpy, and Rosemary Thorp, eds. *Economic Doctrines in Latin America: Origins, Embedding, and Evolution.* London: Palgrave MacMillan, 2005.

Fleischer, David. "The Cardoso Government's Reform Agenda: A View from the National Congress, 1995–1998." *Journal of Interamerican Studies and World Affairs* 40 (Winter 1998), 119–136.

Focarelli, Dario, and Alberto Franco Pozzolo. "The Patterns of Cross-Border Bank Mergers and Shareholdings in OECD Countries." *Journal of Banking and Finance* 25 (2001), 2305–2337.

Franco, Gustavo. "The Real Plan." Remarks delivered at the seminar "Economics and Society in Brazil: New Trends and Perspectives," University of Chicago, November 2–3, 1995.

Freitas, Maria Cristina Penido de, ed. *Abertura do sistema financeiro no Brasil nos anos 90.* São Paulo: Fundap, Fapesp, 1999.

Friend, Theodore. *Indonesian Destinies.* London: Belknap Press, 2003.

Galindo, Arturo, Alejandro Micco, and Andrew Powell. "Loyal Lenders or Fickle Financiers: Foreign Banks in Latin America." Inter-American Development Bank Working Paper 529, December 2005.

Garman, Christopher, Cristiane Kerches da Silva Leite, and Moisés da Silva Marques. "Impactos das relações banco central x bancos estaduais no arranjo federativo pós-1994: Análise à luz do caso Banespa." *Revista de Economia Política* 1 (January–March 2001), 40–61.

Gerschenkron, Alexander. *Economic Backwardness in Historical Perspective.* Cambridge, Mass.: Harvard University Press, 1962.

Gil-Diaz, Francisco, and Agustin Carstens. "One Year of Solitude: Some Pilgrim Tales about Mexico's 1994–1995 Crisis." *American Economic Review* 86 (May 1996), 164–169.

Gills, Barry K., and Dongsook S. Gills. "Globalization and Strategic Choice in South Korea: Economic Reform and Labor." In *Korea's Globalization,* ed. Samuel S. Kim, pp. 29–51. Cambridge: Cambridge University Press, 2000.

Goldberg, Lawrence G., and Anthony Saunders. "The Determinants of Foreign Banking Activity in the United States." *Journal of Banking and Finance* 5 (March 1981), 17–32.

Goldsmith, Raymond W. *Brasil, 1850–1984: Desenvolvimento financeiro sob um século de inflação.* São Paulo: Harper & Row do Brasil, 1986.

Goldstein, Judith, and Robert Keohane, eds. *Ideas and Foreign Policy: Beliefs, Institutions, and Political Change.* Ithaca: Cornell University Press, 1993.

Golob, Stephanie R. "Beyond the Policy Frontier: Canada, Mexico, and the Ideological Origins of NAFTA." *World Politics* 55 (April 2003), 361–398.

——. "'Making Possible What Is Necessary': Pedro Aspe, the Salinas Team, and the Next Mexican 'Miracle.'" In *Technopols: Freeing Politics and Markets in Latin America in the 1990s,* ed. Jorge I. Domínguez, pp. 95–143. University Park: Pennsylvania State University Press, 1997.

Gomes de Almeida, Júlio Sérgio, and Maria Cristina Penido de Freitas. "A regulamentação do sistema financeiro." IE/UNICAMP, Campinas, Discussion Paper No. 63, March 1998.

Gourevitch, Peter A. *Politics in Hard Times: Comparative Responses to International Economic Crises.* Ithaca: Cornell University Press, 1986.

Graf, Pablo. "Policy Responses to the Banking Crisis in Mexico." In "Bank Restructuring in Practice," BIS Policy Paper No. 6, pp. 164–182. Bank for International Settlements, August 1999.

Grossman, Gene M., and Elhanan Helpman. "Protection for Sale." *American Economic Review* 84 (September 1994), 830–850.

Group of Ten. "Report on Consolidation in the Financial Sector." January 2001.

Gruben, William C., and Robert McComb. "Liberalization, Privatization, and Crash: Mexico's Banking System in the 1990s." *Federal Reserve Bank of Dallas Economic Review* (First Quarter, 1997), 21–30.

———. "Privatization, Competition, and Supercompetition in the Mexican Commercial Banking System." *Journal of Banking and Finance* 27 (2000), 229–249.

Guillén, Mauro F., and Adrian E. Tschoegl. "At Last the Internationalization of Retail Banking? The Case of the Spanish Banks in Latin America." Working Paper 99-41, Financial Institutions Center, Wharton School of Business, September 1999.

Guimarães, Pedro. "How Does Foreign Entry Affect the Domestic Banking Market? The Brazilian Case." *Latin American Business Review* 3, 2 (2002).

Haas, Peter M. "Introduction: Epistemic Communities and International Policy Coordination." *International Organization* 46 (Winter 1992).

Haber, Stephen. "Mexico's Experiments with Bank Privatization and Liberalization, 1991–2002" (mimeo.), Stanford University, March 23, 2004.

———. "Mexico's Experiments with Bank Privatization and Liberalization, 1991–2003." *Journal of Banking and Finance* 29 (2005), 2325–2353.

Haggard, Stephan, Chung H. Lee, and Sylvia Maxfield, eds. *The Politics of Finance in Developing Countries.* Ithaca: Cornell University Press, 1993.

Haggard, Stephan, Wonhyuk Lim, and Euysung Kim, eds. *Economic Crisis and Corporate Restructuring in Korea: Reforming the Chaebol.* Cambridge, Mass.: Harvard University Press, 2003.

Haggard, Stephan, and Andrew MacIntyre. "The Political Economy of the Asian Financial Crisis: Korea and Thailand Compared." In *The Asian Financial Crisis and the Architecture of Global Finance,* ed. Gregory W. Noble and John Ravenhill. Cambridge: Cambridge University Press, 2000.

Haggard, Stephan, and Sylvia Maxfield. "The Political Economy of Financial Internationalization in the Developing World." *International Organization* 50 (Winter 1996), 35–68.

Hahm, Joon-Ho. "The Government, the *Chaebol* and Financial Institutions before the Economic Crisis." In *Economic Crisis and Corporate Restructuring in Korea: Reforming the Chaebol,* ed. Stephan Haggard, Wonhyuk Lim, and Euysung Kim. Cambridge, Mass.: Harvard University Press, 2003.

Hall, Peter, ed. *The Political Power of Economic Ideas: Keynesianism across Nations.* Princeton, N.J.: Princeton University Press, 1989.

Halsenbalg, Carlos, and Clovis Brigagão. "Formação do empresario financeiro no Brasil." *Dados* 8 (1971).

Hamilton-Hart, Natasha. *Asian States, Asian Bankers: Central Banking in Southeast Asia.* Ithaca: Cornell University Press, 2002.

Harada, Kimie, and Takatoshi Ito. "Rebuilding the Indonesian Banking Sector—Economic Analysis of Bank Consolidation and Efficiency." *JBICI Review* 12 (August 2005), 32–59.

Harinowo, Cyrillus. *IMF: Penanganan Krisis dan Indonesia Pasca-IMF.* Jakarta: PT Gramedia Pustaka Utama, 2004.

Harris, Stephen L. "South Korea and the Asian Crisis: The Impact of the Democratic Deficit on OECD Accession." In *International Financial Governance under Stress,* ed. Geoffrey R. D. Underhill and Xiaoke Zhang, pp. 140–159. Cambridge: Cambridge University Press, 2003.

Hawkins, John, and Dubravko Mihaljek. "The Banking Industry in the Emerging Market Economies: Competition, Consolidation, and Systemic Stability; An Overview." BIS Paper No. 4, Bank for International Settlements, August 2001.

Hernández Rodríguez, R. *Empresarios, banca, y estado: El conflicto durante el gobierno de José López Portillo.* Mexico City: Miguel Angel Porrúa Editores, 1988.

Higgins, Benjamin H., and William C. Hollinger. "Central Banking in Indonesia." In *Central Banking in South and East Asia,* ed. S. G. Davies. Hong Kong: Hong Kong University Press, 1960.

Hill, Hal. *The Indonesian Economy.* Cambridge: Cambridge University Press, 2000.

Hjartarson, Joshua. "Foreign Bank Entry and Financial Sector Transformation in Hungary and Poland." Ph.D. dissertation, University of Toronto, 2005.

Hoggarth, Glen, Ricardo Reis, and Victoria Saporta. "Costs of Banking System Instability: Some Empirical Evidence." *Journal of Banking and Finance* 26 (2002), 825–855.

Hutchcroft, Paul D. *Booty Capitalism: The Politics of Banking in the Philippines.* Ithaca: Cornell University Press, 1998.

Hwang, Sang In, and In-Seok Shin. "Banking Sector Liberalization in Korea: Impact on the Korean Economy." In *Financial Market Opening in China and Korea,* ed. Young-Rok Cheong, Doo Yong Yang, and Wang Tongsan. Seoul: KIEP, 2003.

"International Macroeconomic Chronology," Barclays Bank, December 1997.

Ito, Takatoshi, and Yuko Hashimoto. "Bank Restructuring in Asia: Crisis Management in the Aftermath of the Financial Crisis and Prospects for Crisis Prevention—Korea." REITI Discussion Paper 07-E-038, February 5, 2007.

Johnson, Chalmers A. *MITI and the Japanese Miracle: The Growth of Industrial Policy, 1925–1975.* Stanford, Calif.: Stanford University Press, 1982.

Johnson, Juliet. "Carving up the Bear: Banks and the Struggle for Power in Russia." *Post-Soviet Prospects,* Center for Strategic and International Studies, March 1997.

———. *A Fistful of Rubles: The Rise and Fall of the Russian Banking System.* Ithaca: Cornell University Press, 2000.

Johnson Ceva, Kristin. "Business-Government Relations in Mexico since 1990: NAFTA, Economic Crisis, and the Reorganization of Business Interests." In *Mexico's Private Sector: Recent History, Future Challenges,* ed. Riordan Roett. Boulder, Colo.: Lynne Rienner, 1998.

Jones, Leroy, and Il Sakong. *Government, Business, and Entrepreneurship in Economic Development: The Korean Case.* Cambridge, Mass.: Harvard University Press, 1980.

Jones, Stuart, ed. *Banking and Business in South Africa.* New York: St. Martin's Press, 1988.

Joyce, Joseph P., and Ilan Noy. "The IMF and the Liberalization of Capital Flows." East-West Center Working Paper No. 84, Economics Series, August 2005.

Kahler, Miles. "Orthodoxy and Its Alternatives: Explaining Approaches to Stabilization and Adjustment." In *The Politics of Economic Adjustment: International Conflicts and the State,* ed. Stephan Haggard and Robert Kaufman, pp. 33–61. Princeton, N.J.: Princeton University Press, 1992.

Kang, Chungwon. "From the Front Lines at Seoul Bank: Restructuring and Reprivatization." IMF Working Paper WP/03/235, December 2003.

Kenward, Lloyd R. *From the Trenches: The First Year of Indonesia's Financial Crisis of 1997/98 as Seen from the World Bank's Office in Jakarta.* Jakarta: Center for Strategic and International Studies, 2002.

Kim, Joon-Kyung, and Chung H. Lee. "The Political Economy of Government, Financial System, and the *Chaebols* before and after the 1997 Financial Crisis in Korea." CCAS Working Paper No. 11, Center for Contemporary Asian Studies, Doshisha University, April 2008.

Kim, Yong Cheol, and Chung-in Moon. "Globalization and Workers in South Korea." In *Korea's Globalization,* ed. Samuel S. Kim, pp. 54–75. Cambridge: Cambridge University Press, 2000.

Kim Young Sam. "Reforms for Stronger Competitiveness." Address at the National Policy Review Conference at Chong Wa Dae, December 27, 1993.

Koh, B. C. "South Korea in 1996: Internal Strains and External Challenges." *Asian Survey* 37 (January 1997).

Krueger, Anne. "Trade Policy and Economic Development: How We Learn." *American Economic Review* 87, 1 (1997), 1–22.

Kurzer, Paulette. *Business and Banking: Political Change and Economic Integration in Western Europe.* Ithaca: Cornell University Press, 1993.

Lake, David A. *Power, Protection, and Free Trade: The International Sources of American Commercial Strategy, 1887–1939.* Ithaca: Cornell University Press, 1988.

La Porta, Rafael, Florencio López-de-Silanes, and Guillermo Zamarripa. "Related Lending." NBER Working Paper No. 8848, March 2002.

Laurence, Henry. *Money Rules: The New Politics of Finance in Britain and Japan.* Cambridge: Cambridge University Press, 2001.

Lee, Chung H. "The Government, Financial System, and Large Private Enterprises in the Economic Development of South Korea." *World Development* 20, 2 (1992), 187–197.

Leiteritz, Ralf J. "Explaining Organizational Outcomes: The International Monetary Fund and Capital Account Liberalization." *Journal of International Relations and Development* 8 (2005), 1–26.

Lensink, Robert, and Niels Hermes. "The Short-Term Effects of Foreign Bank Entry on Domestic Bank Behaviour: Does Economic Development Matter?" *Journal of Banking and Finance* 28 (March 2004), 553–568.

Levine, Ross. "Foreign Banks, Financial Development, and Economic Growth." In *International Financial Markets,* ed. E. B. Claude. Washington, D.C.: AEI Press, 1996.

Lim, Wonhyuk. "The Emergence of the *Chaebol* and the Origins of the *Chaebol* Problem." In *Economic Crisis and Corporate Restructuring in Korea: Reforming the Chaebol,* ed. Stephan Haggard, Wonhyuk Lim, and Euysung Kim, pp. 35–52. Cambridge, Mass.: Harvard University Press, 2003.

Loriaux, Michael, et al. *Capital Ungoverned: Liberalizing Finance in Interventionist States.* Ithaca: Cornell University Press, 1997.

Loser, Claudio M., and Ewart S. Williams. "The Mexican Crisis and Its Aftermath: An IMF Perspective." In *Mexico 1994: Anatomy of an Emerging-Market Crash,* ed. Sebastian Edwards and Moisés Naím. Washington, D.C.: Carnegie Endowment for International Peace, 1997.

Lukauskas, Arvid, and Susan Minushkin. "Explaining Styles of Financial Market Opening in Chile, Mexico, South Korea, and Turkey." *International Studies Quarterly* 44 (2000), 695–723.

Lustig, Nora. "Mexico in Crisis, the US to the Rescue: The Financial Assistance Packages of 1982 and 1995." Mimeo., January 1997.

Macedo Cintra, Marcos Antonio. "Negociações multilaterais e regionais sobre serviços financeiros e seu impacto doméstico." In *Abertura do sistema financeiro no Brasil nos anos 90,* ed. Maria Cristina Penido de Freitas, pp. 174–205. São Paulo: FUNDAP, 1999.

MacIntyre, Andrew J. "Political Parties, Accountability, and Economic Governance in Indonesia." In *Democracy, Governance, and Economic Performance: East and Southeast Asia in the 1990s,* ed. Jean Blondel, Takashi Inoguchi, and Ian Marsh. Tokyo: United Nations University Press, 1999.

——. "Politics and the Reorientation of Economic Policy in Indonesia." In *The Dynamics of Economic Policy Reform in South-East Asia and the South-West Pacific,* ed. Andrew J. MacIntyre and Kanishka Jayasuriya. Oxford: Oxford University Press, 1992.

——. "The Politics of Finance in Indonesia: Command, Confusion, and Competition." In *The Politics of Finance in Developing Countries,* ed. Stephan Haggard, Chung H. Lee, and Sylvia Maxfield. Ithaca: Cornell University Press, 1993.

Mackey, Michael W. "Informe sobre la evaluación integral de las operaciones y funciones del Fondo Bancario de Protección al Ahorro, FOBAPROA y la calidad de supervisión de los programas del FOBAPROA de 1995 a 1998." July 1999.

Maia, Geraldo. "Restructuring the Banking System—The Case of Brazil." In "Bank Restructuring in Practice," BIS Policy Paper No. 6, pp. 106–121. Bank for International Settlements, August 1999.

Makler, Harry M. "Bank Transformation and Privatization in Brazil: Financial Federalism and Some Lessons about Bank Privatization." *Quarterly Review of Economics and Finance* 20 (2000), 45–69.

Martínez Peria, María Soledad, and Ashoka Mody. "How Foreign Participation and Market Concentration Impact Bank Spreads: Evidence from Latin America." World Bank Policy Research Working Paper 3210, February 2004.

Martinez-Diaz, Leonardo. "Banking Sector Opening: Policy Questions and Lessons for Developing Countries." Issue Brief 2007-02, Global Economy and Development Program, Brookings Institution, February 2007.

———. "Pathways through Financial Crisis: Indonesia." *Global Governance* 12 (October–December 2006).

Mathieu, Nicolas. *Financial Sector Reform: A Review of World Bank Assistance.* Washington, D.C.: World Bank, 1998.

Maurer, Noel. *The Power and the Money: The Mexican Financial System, 1876–1932.* Stanford, Calif.: Stanford University Press, 2002.

Maxfield, Sylvia. "Bankers' Alliances and Economic Policy Patterns: Evidence from Mexico and Brazil." *Comparative Political Studies* 23 (January 1991), 419–458.

Maxfield, Sylvia. "Capital Mobility and Mexican Financial Liberalization." In Michael Loriaux et al., *Capital Ungoverned: Liberalizing Finance in Interventionist States,* pp. 92–119. Ithaca: Cornell University Press, 1997.

———. *Gatekeepers of Growth: The International Political Economy of Central Banking in Developing Countries.* Princeton, N.J.: Princeton University Press, 1997.

———. *Governing Capital: International Finance and Mexican Politics.* Ithaca: Cornell University Press, 1990.

McLeod, Ross H. "Dealing with Bank System Failure: Indonesia, 1997–2003." *Bulletin of Indonesian Economic Studies* 40 (April 2004), 95–116.

———. "Indonesia's New Banking Law." *Bulletin of Indonesian Economic Studies* 28 (December 1992), 107–122.

McQuerry, Elizabeth. "Managed Care for Brazil's Banks." *Federal Reserve Bank of Atlanta Economic Review* (Second Quarter, 2001), 27–44.

Mendonça de Barros, José Roberto, Monica Baer, and Carlos Pio. "Brazil and the IMF: Virtues and Limits of the 2002 Agreement." Paper prepared for the Asamblea General del Club de Madrid, Madrid, November 1–2, 2003.

Micco, Alejandro, Ugo Panizza, and Mónica Yañez. "Bank Ownership and Performance." Inter-American Development Bank Working Paper 518, November 2004.

Minella, Ary Cesar. *Banqueiros: Organização e poder político no Brasil.* Rio de Janeiro: Espaço e Tempo/ANPOCS, 1988.

Minushkin, Susan. "*Banqueros* and *Bolseros:* Structural Change and Financial Market Liberalization in Mexico." *Journal of Latin American Studies* 34 (2002), 915–944.

Minushkin, Susan, and Charles Parker III. "Relaciones entre la banca y el gobierno: La nueva estructura financiera en México." *Política y Gobierno* 9, (First Semester 2002), 181–223.

Mitchell, Clyde. "The New Indonesian Bill." *New York Law Journal,* March 25, 1992, p. 3.

Monteiro, Jorge Vianna. *Economia & política: Instituções de estabilização econômica no Brasil.* São Paulo: Fundação Getulio Vargas, 1998.

Montgomery, John. "The Indonesian Financial System: Its Contribution to Economic Performance, and Key Policy Issues." IMF Working Paper WP/97/45.

Montinola, Gabriella, and Ramón Moreno. "The Political Economy of Foreign Bank Entry and Its Impact: Theory and a Case Study." Federal Reserve Bank of San Francisco, Working Paper No. PB01-11, October 2001.

Montoya, José Córdoba. "Mexico." In *The Political Economy of Reform,* ed. John Williamson, pp. 232–284. Washington, D.C.: Institute for International Economics, 1994.

Moon, Chung-in. "Patterns of Business-Government Relations in South Korea." In *Business and Government in Industrializing Asia,* ed. Andrew MacIntyre, pp. 142–166. Ithaca: Cornell University Press, 1994.

Murillo, José Antonio. "La banca después de la privatización: Auge, crisis y reordenamiento." In *Cuando el estado he hizo banquero,* ed. Gustavo del Angel-Mobarak, Carlos Bazdresch Parada, and Francisco Suárez Dávila, pp. 247–290. Mexico City: Fondo de Cultura Económica, 2005.

National Institute of Economics and Research. "Capital Market Liberalization: Summary." Single Market Review Series. European Commission, August 1996.

Nelson, Joan, ed. *Economic Crisis and Policy Choice: The Politics of Adjustment in the Third World.* Princeton, N.J.: Princeton University Press, 1990.

Núñez Estrada, Héctor Rogelio. "Reforma de la administración pública del sistema bancario y su efecto en la crisis sistémica: 1990–2000 la quiebra de Banca Serfín." Paper prepared for the IX CLAD Congress on State Reform and Public Administration, Madrid, November 2–5, 2004.

Oatley, Thomas. "How Constraining Is Capital Mobility?" *American Journal of Political Science* 43 (October 1999).

Odell, John S. "Case Study Methods in International Political Economy." *International Studies Perspectives* 2 (2001), 161–176.

Oh, Kongdan, ed. *Korea Briefing, 1997–1999: Challenges and Change at the Turn of the Century.* Armonk, N.Y.: M.E. Sharpe, 2000.

Oppenheimer, Andres. *Bordering on Chaos.* New York: Little, Brown, 1996.

O'Rourke, Kevin. *Reformasi: The Struggle for Power in Post-Suharto Indonesia.* Sydney: Allen & Unwin, 2002.

Ortíz Martínez, Guillermo. *La reforma financiera y la desincorporación bancaria.* Mexico City: Fondo de Cultura Económica, 1994.

Paauw, Douglas S. *Financing Economic Development.* Glencoe, Ill.: Free Press, 1960.

Pangetsu, Mari. "The Indonesian Bank Crisis and Restructuring: Lessons and Implications for Other Developing Countries." G24 Discussion Paper No. 23, UNCTAD, November 2003.

Panglaykim, J., and D. H. Penny. "The New Banking Laws." *Bulletin of Indonesian Economic Studies* (February 1968), 75–77.

Pardede, Raden. "Survey of Recent Developments." *Bulletin of Indonesian Economic Studies* 35 (August 1999), 3–40.

Park, Yung Chul. "Financial Repression, Liberalization, and Development in Developing Countries." Working Paper, Korean Development Institute, 1987.

Patrick, Hugh. "Corporate Governance and the Indonesian Financial System: A Comparative Perspective." Discussion Paper No. 16. APEC Study Center, Columbia Business School, August 2001.

Paula, Luiz Fernando de. "Los determinantes del reciente ingreso de bancos extranjeros a Brasil." *Revista de la CEPAL* 79 (April 2003), 169–188.

Pauly, Louis. *Opening Financial Markets: Banking Politics on the Pacific Rim.* Ithaca: Cornell University Press, 1988.

Peek, Joe, and Eric S. Rosengren. "Collateral Damage: Effects of the Japanese Bank Crisis on Real Activity in the United States." *American Economic Review* 90 (March 2000), 30–45.

——. "The International Transmission of Financial Shocks: The Case of Japan." *American Economic Review* 87 (September 1997), 495–505.

Pincus, Jonathan, and Rizal Ramli. "Deepening or Hollowing Out? Financial Liberalization, Accumulation and Indonesia's Economic Crisis." In *After the Storm: Crisis,*

Recovery and Sustaining Development in Four Asian Economies, ed. K. S. Jomo. Singapore: Singapore University Press, 2004.

———. "Indonesia: From Showcase to Basket Case." *Cambridge Journal of Economics* 22 (1998), 723–734.

Pinheiro, Armando Castelar, Regis Bonelli, and Ben Ross Schneider. "Pragmatic Policy in Brazil: The Political Economy of Incomplete Market Reform." Discussion Paper No. 1035, IPEA, August 2004.

Pio, Carlos. "A estabilização heterodoxa no Brasil: Idéias e redes políticas." *Revista Brasileira de Ciências Sociais* 16 (June 2001).

Poret, Pierre. "Mexico and the OECD Codes of Liberalisation." *OECD Observer* 189 (August–September 1994), 39–43.

Power, Timothy J. "Brazilian Politicians and Neoliberalism: Mapping Support for the Cardoso Reforms, 1995–1997." *Journal of Interamerican Studies and World Affairs* 40 (Winter 1998), 51–72.

Power, Timothy J. "The Pen Is Mightier Than the Congress: Presidential Decree Power in Brazil." In *Executive Decree Authority,* ed. John M. Carey and Matthew Soberg Shugart, pp. 197–230. Cambridge: Cambridge University Press, 1998.

Prawiro, Radius. "Back to the Wisdom of the Market Economy." In *The Politics of Economic Development in Indonesia: Contending Perspectives,* ed. Ian Chalmers and Vedi R. Hadiz. London: Routledge, 1997.

———. *Pergulatan Indonesia Membangun Ekonomi: Pragmatisme Dalam Aksi.* Jakarta: PT Elex Media Komputindo, 1998.

Quarles, Randal K. "Russian Integration in the Global Financial System." Remarks to the US-Russia Banking Conference, Washington, D.C., April 15, 2005.

Rajan, Ramikishen S., and Rahul Sen. "Liberalization of Financial Services in Southeast Asia under the ASEAN Framework Agreement on Services (AFAS)." Centre for International Economic Studies Discussion Paper No. 0226, Adelaide University, October 2002.

Reich, Gary M. "The 1988 Constitution a Decade Later: Ugly Compromises Reconsidered." *Journal of Interamerican Studies of World Affairs* 40 (Winter 1998), 5–24.

Resende-Santos, João. "Fernando Henrique Cardoso: Social and Institutional Rebuilding in Brazil." In *Technopols: Freeing Politics and Markets in Latin America in the 1990s,* ed. Jorge I. Domínguez. University Park: Pennsylvania State University Press, 1997.

Robison, Richard. *Indonesia: The Rise of Capital.* Sydney: Allen & Unwin, 1986.

Robison, Richard, and Vedi R. Hadiz. *Reorganising Power in Indonesia: The Politics of Oligarchy in an Age of Markets.* London: Routledge-Curzon, 2005.

Rodrik, Dani. "Understanding Economic Policy Reform." *Journal of Economic Literature* 34, 1 (1996), 9–41.

———. "Why Is There Multilateral Lending?" NBER Working Paper No. 5160, 1995.

Rosser, Andrew. *The Politics of Economic Liberalization in Indonesia.* Richmond, U.K.: Curzon Press, 2002.

Rubin, Robert, and Jacob Weisberg. *In an Uncertain World: Tough Choices from Wall Street to Washington.* New York: Random House, 2003.

Rubio, Luis. "Coping with Political Change." In *Mexico under Zedillo,* ed. Susan Kaufman Purcell and Luis Rubio. Boulder, Colo.: Lynne Rienner, 1998.

Rueschemeyer, Dietrich, and John D. Stephens. "Comparing Historical Sequences—A Powerful Tool for Causal Analysis: A Reply to John Goldthorpe's 'Current Issues in Comparative Macrosociology.'" *Comparative Social Research* 16 (1997), 55–72.

Sadli, Mohammad. "Commemorating the Economic Policies of 3 October 1966." In *The Politics of Economic Development in Indonesia: Contending Perspectives,* ed. Ian Chalmers and Vedi R. Hadiz. London: Routledge, 1997.

Salinas de Gortari, Carlos. *México: Un paso difícil a la modernidad.* Mexico City: Plaza & Janés, 2000.

Sampaio Rocha, Fernando Alberto. "Desnacionalização bancária no Brasil, 1997–2000." Master's thesis, Institute of Economics, State University of Campinas, Brazil, 2002.

Sánchez Martínez, Hilda. "El sistema monetario y financiero mexicano bajo una perspectiva histórica: El Porfiriato." In *La banca: Pasado y presente,* ed. José Manuel Quijano, pp. 15–92. Mexico City: CIDE, 1983.

Sato, Yuri. "Post-crisis Economic Reform in Indonesia: Policy for Intervening in Ownership in Historical Perspective." IDE Research Paper No. 4. Institute for Developing Economies (IDE-JETRO), September 2003.

Schneider, Ben Ross. "Organized Business Politics in Democratic Brazil." *Journal of Interamerican Studies and World Affairs* 39 (Winter 1997–1998), 95–127.

Schuijer, Jan. "OECD Members' Experience with Capital Account Liberalization and Its Relevance to Other Countries." Comments at the Global Forum on International Investment, Shanghai, December 5–6, 2002.

Schwarz, Adam. *A Nation in Waiting: Indonesia's Search for Stability.* Boulder, Colo.: Westview Press, 2000.

Secretaría de Hacienda y Crédito Público. *FOBAPROA: La verdadera historia.* Mexico City: SHCP, 1998.

Shadlen, Kenneth C. "Continuity amid Change: Democratization, Party Strategies, and Economic Policy-Making in Mexico." *Government and Opposition* 34, 3 (1999), 397–419.

Shiraishi, Takashi. "Technocracy in Indonesia: A Preliminary Analysis." RIETI Discussion Paper Series 05-E-008, March 2006.

Sikkink, Kathryn. "Development Ideas in Latin America." In *International Development and the Social Sciences: Essays on the History and Politics of Knowledge,* ed. Frederick Cooper and Randall Packard, pp. 228–256. Berkeley: University of California Press, 1997.

Simmons, Beth A. "The International Politics of Harmonization: The Case of Capital Market Regulation." *International Organization* 55 (Summer 2001), 593–594.

Skully, Michael T. "Commercial Banking in Indonesia: An Examination of Its Development and Present Structure." *Asian Survey* 22 (September 1982), 874–893.

Smith, Heather. "Korea." In *East Asia in Crisis: From Being a Miracle to Needing One?* ed. Ross H. McLeod and Ross Garnaut, pp. 57–72. London: Routledge, 1998.

Stallings, Barbara, ed. *Global Change, Regional Response: A New International Context of Development.* New York: Cambridge University Press, 1995.

Stallings, Barbara, with Rogério Studart. *Finance for Development: Latin America in Comparative Perspective.* Washington, D.C.: Brookings Institution Press, 2006.

Stern, Joseph J. "Indonesia–Harvard University: Lessons from a Long-Term Technical Assistance Project." *Bulletin of Indonesian Economic Studies* 36 (December 2000), 113–125.

Stiglitz, Joseph. "The Role of the State in Financial Markets." In *Proceedings of the World Bank Annual Conference on Development Economics.* Washington, D.C.: World Bank, 1993.

Summers, Lawrence H. "Repairing and Rebuilding Emerging Market Financial Systems." Remarks to the Federal Deposit Insurance Corporation's International Conference on Deposit Insurance, Washington, D.C., September 9, 1998.

——. "Riding the Storm: Latin America and the Global Financial Market." Remarks to the Council of the Americas, Washington, D.C., May 3, 1999.

——. "Statement on the WTO Agreement in Financial Services." U.S. Treasury, RR-2111, December 13, 1997.

——. "Testimony before the House Committee on Banking, Finance, and Urban Affairs." U.S. House of Representatives, February 1, 1994.

Sundararajan, V., and Tomás J. T. Baliño, eds. *Banking Crises: Cases and Issues.* Washington, D.C.: IMF, 1991.

Suryadinata, Leo. *Pribumi Indonesians, the Chinese Minority and China.* Singapore: Heinemann Asia, 1992.

Suta, I Putu Gede Ary, and Soebowo Musa. *Membedah Krisis Perbankan.* Jakarta: Yayasan Sad Satria Bhakti, 2003.

Taylor, John B. "Testimony before the House Small Business Committee." U.S. House of Representatives, October 24, 2001.

Tebbutt, Peter, Charlene Chu, and Lydia Lin. "Foreign Banks' Expansion into China, with a Focus on Hong Kong's Banks." *Fitch Ratings Special Report,* May 2, 2007.

Tebbutt, Peter, and Tan Lai Peng. "Indonesian Banks—Ownership Developments, H105 Results, and Outlook. *Fitch Ratings Special Report,* October 18, 2005.

Tebbutt, Peter, and Ambreesh Srivastava. "Indonesia's Banks—Ownership Changes, Loan Book Developments, and End-2003 Results Update." *Fitch Ratings Special Report,* May 11, 2004.

Tello, Carlos. *La nacionalización de la banca en México.* Mexico City: Siglo Veintiuno Editores, 1984.

Thorburn, Diana. "The Political Economy of Foreign Banks in Latin America: Mexico and Argentina, 1990–2001." Ph.D. dissertation, School for Advanced International Studies, Washington, D.C., 2004.

Tompson, William. "Banking Reform in Russia: Problems and Prospects." OECD Economics Department Working Paper No. 410. Paris: OECD Publishing, 2004.

Topik, Steven. *The Political Economy of the Brazilian State, 1889–1930.* Austin: University of Texas Press, 1987.

Trigueros, Ignacio. "The Mexican Financial System and NAFTA." In *Mexico and the North American Free Trade Agreement: Who Will Benefit?* ed. Victor Bulmer-Thomas, Nikki Craske, and Mónica Serrano, pp. 43–57. London: Macmillan, 1994.

Triner, Gail D. *Banking and Economic Development: Brazil, 1889–1930.* New York: Palgrave/United Nations, 2000.

Tschoegl, Adrian E. "Financial Crises and the Presence of Foreign Banks." Financial Institutions Center Working Paper 03-35, Wharton School of Business, December 5, 2003.

———. "Ideology and Changes in Regulations: The Case of Foreign Bank Branches over the Period 1920–1980." In *Political Risks in International Business,* ed. Thomas L. Brewer. New York: Praeger, 1985.

———. "'The World's Local Bank': HSBC's Expansion into the US, Canada, and Mexico." *Latin American Business Review* 5, 4 (2005), 45–68.

Turczyn, Sidnei. *O sistema financeiro nacional e a regulação bancária.* São Paolo: Revista Dos Tribunais, 2005.

Turrent Díaz, Eduardo. *História del Banco de México.* Mexico City: Banco de México, 1982.

Underhill, Geoffrey R. D., and Xiaoke Zhang. *International Financial Governance under Stress.* Cambridge: Cambridge University Press, 2003.

U.S. Department of Commerce. "The Big Emerging Markets." *Business America* 115, 3 (1994).

Vansetti, M. Cilina R., Philip Guarco, and Gregory W. Bauer. "The 'Fall' of Bancomer and the Future of the Indigenous Mega-Banks in Latin America." Moody's Investors Service Special Comment, Global Credit Research, April 2000.

Vidotto, Carlos A. "Crise, PROER e desnacionalização bancária sob o Plano Real." Mimeo., 2006.

von Bertrab, Hermann. *Negotiating NAFTA: A Mexican Envoy's Account.* Washington Paper 173. Westport, Conn.: Praeger, 1997.

Walter, Andrew. "Understanding Financial Globalization in International Political Economy." In *Globalizing International Political Economy,* ed. Nicola Philips, pp. 141–164. Basingstoke, U.K.: Palgrave Macmillan, 2005.

Walter, Ingo, and H. Peter Gray. "Protectionism and International Banking: Sectoral Efficiency, Competitive Structure, and National Policy." *Journal of Banking and Finance* 7 (December 1983), 611–614.

Wardhana, Ali. "Financial Reform: Achievements, Problems, and Prospects." In Ross McLeod, *Indonesia Assessment 1994: Finance as a Key Sector in Indonesia's Development,* pp. 79–93. Singapore: ISEAS, 1994.

——. "The Indonesian Banking System: The Central Bank." In *The Economy of Indonesia: Selected Readings,* ed. Bruce Glassburner, pp. 338–358. Ithaca: Cornell University Press, 1971.

——. "Structural Adjustment in Indonesia: Export and the 'High Cost' Economy." Keynote address at the 24th Conference of Southeast Asian Central Bank Governors, Bangkok, January 25, 1989. Reprinted in *Indonesian Quarterly* 17 (Third Quarter, 1989), 207–217.

Weyland, Kurt G. "Theories of Policy Diffusion: Lessons from Latin American Pension Reform." *World Politics* 57 (January 2005), 262–295.

——, ed. *Learning from Foreign Models in Latin American Policy Reform.* Baltimore: Johns Hopkins University Press, 2004.

White, Russell N. *State, Class, and the Nationalization of the Mexican Banks.* New York: Crane Russak, 1992.

Williamson, John, ed. *The Political Economy of Reform.* Washington, D.C.: Institute for International Economics, 1994.

Winters, Jeffrey A. "The Determinants of Crisis in Southeast Asia." In *The Politics of the Asian Economic Crisis,* ed. T. J. Pempel. Ithaca: Cornell University Press, 1999.

——. "The Politics of Created Crisis: Indonesian Banking Reform in the 1980s." Mimeo., Northwestern University, June 10, 1996.

——. *Power in Motion: Capital Mobility and the Indonesian State.* Ithaca: Cornell University Press, 1996.

Woo, Jung-En (Meredith Woo-Cumings). *Race to the Swift: State and Finance in Korean Industrialization.* New York: Columbia University Press, 1991.

Woo-Cumings, Meredith. "Slouching toward the Market: The Politics of Financial Liberalization in South Korea." In Michael Loriaux et al., *Capital Ungoverned: Liberalizing Finance in Interventionist States,* pp. 57–91. Ithaca: Cornell University Press, 1997.

——, ed. *The Developmental State.* Ithaca: Cornell University Press, 1999.

Wood, Duncan R. "Business Association, Regional Integration, and Systemic Shocks: The Case of the ABM in Mexico." In *Organized Business and the New Global Order,* ed. Justin Greenwood and Henry Jacek, pp. 59–76. Basingstoke, U.K.: Macmillan, 2000.

Woods, Ngaire. *The Globalizers: The IMF, the World Bank, and Their Borrowers.* Ithaca: Cornell University Press, 2006.

Woolcock, Stephen. *The Liberalization of Financial Services.* European Policy Forum, London, October 1997.

Wu, Yuan-li, and Chun-hsi Wu. *Economic Development in Southeast Asia: The Chinese Dimension.* Stanford, Calif.: Hoover Institution Press, 1980.

Zedillo Ponce de León, Ernesto. Speech delivered at the 60th convention of the Mexican Bankers' Association, Cancún, Mexico, March 1997.

News and News Analysis

"100% Foreign Holdings OK'd in RI Banks." *Jakarta Post,* October 17, 1998.

"Argentina: Financial Services." *Economist Intelligence Unit,* November 22, 2005.

"Bamerindus: From Liability to Asset." *Emerging Markets Debt Report,* April 7, 1997.

"Bamerindus Solution Lies in the Hands of Malan." *Gazeta Mercantil Online,* March 6, 1997.

"Banamex Poll Finds Mexicans Prefer It to BBV in Merger Battle over Bancomer." *Reforma,* June 8, 2000.

BCA Sale to Go on Despite Protest." *Jakarta Post,* March 12, 2002.

"Brazil: A Winner's Bet—Pedro Malan, Brazil's New Finance Minister and the Former President of Banco Central do Brasil (Central Bank), Discusses Reform and the Financial Sector," *Banker* 245, 827 (January 1, 1995).

"Brazil: Privatization." *Cambridge International Forecasts Country Report,* March 1999.

"Brazil–World Bank Rift Widens; Ministerial Report Accuses Bank of Usury." *Latin American Weekly Report,* Finance Section, March 23, 1989, p. 7.

"Call for Limiting Share Ownership in Indonesian Banks." *Asia Pulse,* June 16, 1998.

"Cautious Praise for Paulson over Access." *Financial Times,* May 24, 2007.

"Cemex Calls It a Day." *Jakarta Post,* May 10, 2006.

"Chief Faces New Battle Front at Korea First Bank." *Banker* 150:890 (April 1, 2000).

"China: Banking Liberalisation." *Oxford Analytica Daily Brief,* February 4, 1994.

"China: Banks Brace for WTO." *Oxford Analytica Daily Brief,* June 22, 2000.

"Citibank Meets Thai PM, Interested in First Bangkok City Bank." Agence France Presse, December 4, 1997.

"Collor Plan and Financial Sector." *Latin American Markets,* April 20, 1990.

"Concern Looms over Citigroup's Report Plan to Delist KorAm." *Asia Pulse,* February 25, 2004.

"Country Finance: South Korea." *Economist Intelligence Unit,* November 2002.

"Economy Needs Win-Win-Win Strategy." *Business Korea,* January, 2001.

"Financing Operations in South Korea." *Economist Intelligence Unit.* February 1998.

"Foreign Banks Will Get to Open 20 Branches a Year." *Financial Express,* January 3, 2006.

"Foreigners May Be Non-standing Board Members in Korean Banks." *Asia Pulse,* June 26, 1997.

"Franco Rebate As Seclarações de Setubal." *Folha de São Paulo,* July 10, 1998, Sec. Dinheiro, pp. 2–5.

"House against Proposal to Give IBRA Special Power." *Jakarta Post,* September 15, 1998.

"HSBC Acquired R$7 Billion in Bamerindus Assets, Says Loyola." *Gazeta Mercantil Invest News,* June 26, 1997.

"Indonesia's Banks: Grip of the Dead Hand." *Economist,* September 16, 2006, p. 86.

"LG Card Deal Rekindles Skepticism; Foreign-Owned Banks' Defiance Renews Criticism of Privatization Policy." *Korea Herald,* February 9, 2004.

"Mercosur: Breaking Brazil's Banks." *Economist Intelligence Unit,* November 11, 1996.

"Mexico Regulations: New Rules Pressure Banks to Seek Fresh Capital." *Economist Intelligence Unit,* October 4, 1999.

"Negro panorama, pronostica la agencia británica IBCA." *El Financiero,* February 21, 1995, p. 7.

"The Privatization of Semen Gresik." *Van Zorge Report on Indonesia* 3 (November 2001).

"Proer: A Soft Landing for Wayward Private Banks." *Latin Finance,* September 1997.

"PROES: Easing State Governments Out of the Banking Industry." *Latin Finance,* September 1997.

"Profit of Foreign Bank Branches in Korea Tripled in 1997." *Korean Industry Update,* March 16, 1998.

"Russia Industry: Foreign Banks Seeking a Way In." *Economist Intelligence Unit,* January 20, 2006.

"Russia Politics: Russia Claims Breakthrough with US on WTO." *Economist Intelligence Unit,* July 13, 2006.

"Sacked Golkar Legislators Protest Their Dismissal." *Jakarta Post,* October 16, 1998.

"Stakes in Banks 'Should Be Limited' to 20 Percent." *Jakarta Post,* June 16, 1998.

"Thailand Not Ready to Liberalize Finance Sector." Xinhua News Agency, June 16, 1997.

Acworth, William. "Mexico Weighs Action to Urge Foreign Banks." *American Banker* 5 (January 9, 1995), 2.

Adachi, Vanessa. "Brandão critica falta de transparência." *Folha de São Paulo,* July 10, 1998, Sec. Dinheiro, pp. 2–5.

Adachi, Vanessa, and Ricardo Grinbaum. "Política monetaria causa temor." *Folha de São Paulo,* July 9, 1998.

Aznam, Suhaini. "Banks for All Buyers: Indonesia Opens Up Important Stock Sector." *Far Eastern Economic Review* 155 (November 19, 1992), 74.

Barham, John. "Privatisation Is Succeeding Despite Awkward Episodes: Brazil." *Financial Times,* October 8, 1999, p. 9.

Burns, Richard. "'We've Been Trying to Get into Brazil for a Very Long Time.'" *Latin Finance,* June 1997, p. 28.

Carroll, Paul B., and Craig Torres. "Two Solid Banks Appear Set to Gain Ground on Weaker Rivals in Mexico." *Wall Street Journal,* March 6, 1995, sec. A, p. 10.

Chávez, Marcos. "Aumenta 47% su deuda en dólares; Pérdidas por 3 mil 176 mdnp." *El Financiero,* January 5, 1995, p. 8.

———. "Previsible aumento en su cartera vencida bruta de 16 mil mdnp; Bancos al borde de la insolvencia." *El Financiero,* February 27, 1995, p. 4.

Dewanto, Nugroho, and Endah W. S. "Who Will Acquire BCA?" *Tempo* 13 (December 4–10, 2001).

Dewanto, Nugroho, Agus S. Riuyanto, and Endah W. S. "The Death of SMEs' Dream Child." *Tempo* 5 (October 9–15, 2001).

Fidler, Stephen, and John Ridding. "Foreigners to Own Mexico Banks." *Financial Times,* January 2, 1995, p. 3.

Flores, Gerardo, and Alicia Salgado. "Beneplácito de la SHCP por BBVA-Bancomer." *El Financiero,* June 14, 2000, p. 1.

Foster, Angus. "Red Faces over a Pink Folder." *Financial Times,* December 9, 1995, p. 3.

Franco, Gustavo H. B. "Bancos estrangeiros, bancos estaduais e o pedágio." *Boletim da Tendências,* February 16, 2000.

Fucs, José. "O que significa a venda do Real." *Exame,* July 29, 1998, p. 50.

González, Víctor, and Gerardo Flores. "El capital foráneo no afectará el sistema de pagos." *El Financiero,* January 21, 1995, p. 4.

Graham, George. "Serfín Troubles Cut HSBC Price by $126m." *Financial Times,* December 31, 1997.

Group of Seven. "Finance Minister Paul Martin Chosen as Inaugural Chairperson of New Group of Twenty." Press release of the G7 finance ministers' meeting, September 25, 1999.

Guest, Ian. "Rambo Factor Brazil: A Major World Bank Project Has Turned into a Salutary Lesson about the Pitfalls of Financing Multilateral Aid for the Environment." *Guardian,* February 2, 1990.

Howard, Georgina. "Divide a banqueros eventual control del sistema de pagos." *El Financiero,* January 26, 1995, p. 9.

———. "'Entrampados' bancos mexicanos por el vencimiento de 8 mil 700 mdd en Cedes." *El Financiero,* February 6, 1995, p. 7.

Howard, Georgina, and Marcos Chávez M. "Bajas las utilidades de los bancos." *El Financiero,* February 3, 1995, p. 1.

Howard, Georgina, and Gerardo Flores. "Chase Manhattan, la excepción; pospone proyectos la banca extranjera hasta julio." *El Financiero,* January 6, 1995, p. 6.

Howard, Georgina, Armando Torres, and Gerardo Flores. "Prepara Hacienda una mayor apertura financiera; Autorizará México 100% de participación extranjera en intermediarios nacionales." *El Financiero,* January 4, 1995, p. 7.

Ihlwan, Moon, and Mark L. Clifford. "The Bank That Almost Got Away." *Business Week* No. 3705 (October 30, 2000), 58.

Kagda, Shoeb. "Reflections on a Clean-Up Campaign." *Business Times Singapore,* March 13, 2004.

Lingga, Vincent. "BCA: Major Deal of the Year." *Jakarta Post,* September 3, 2001.

Lowell, Anne, and Ed Paisley. "Proud Seoul." *Institutional Investor* 31 (December 1997).

Martinez Aznárez, César. "Maquillaje contable en bancos." *La Jornada,* September 1999.

McLeod, Ross H. "Lessons from Crisis Management." *Jakarta Post,* March 18, 2004.

Nam, Rafael. "Foreign Stakes in Banks Top 26%; Overseas Ownership Improved Financial Services but Gave Rise to Discord." *Korea Herald,* December 2, 2003.

Ocampo, Rafael, and Fernando Ortega Pizarro. "Los grandes empresarios se dicen engañados; sólo Azcárraga y Slim renegociaron a pesos, antes de la devaluación, parte de su deuda." *Proceso,* January 2, 1995.

Patú, Gustavo. "BC utilizou reservas para socorrer Banespa." *Folha de São Paulo,* May 15, 1995, Sec. Dinheiro, pp. 2–3.

Patú, Gustavo, and Marta Salomon. "Bancos aplicam R$3,6 mi no Congresso." *Folha de São Paulo,* October 8, 1995.

Pereira Filho, Arthur. "HSBC Bamerindus marca a nova fase." *Folha de São Paulo,* September 28, 1997.

Pinto, Celso. "Mais bancos estrangeiros." *Folha de São Paulo,* August 26, 1997.

——. "O risco dos bancos externos." *Folha de São Paulo,* December 21, 1997.

Praginanto. "Indonesia Moves to Trim Its Bloated Banking Sector." *Nikkei Weekly,* March 22, 1999.

Rico, Salvador. "Aceptarán banqueros el control extranjero de la banca; Eficiencia, el requisito: ABM." *El Financiero,* February 25, 1995, p. 7.

Rico, Salvador, and Georgina Howard. "Acelerada apertura financiera despreocupa a la banca nacional." *El Financiero,* January 25, 1995, p. 1.

Salgado, Alicia. "Condicionará la CFC la fusión entre Bancomer y Banamex-Accival." *El Financiero,* June 12, 2000, p. 4.

——. "Envía Banamex-Accival a Bancomer propuesta no solicitada de fusión." *El Financiero,* May 4, 2000, p. 4.

——. "Exentan de restricciones a filiales extranjeras 'salvadoras'; Retrasar el apoyo a bancos obligará a un ajuste mayor del sistema: CNBV." *El Financiero,* May 31, 1995, p. 4.

Smith, Tony. "Flush from Sell-Offs, Brazil Is Privatization's Poster Child." BC cycle, Associated Press, January 16, 2001.

Tangeman, Michael. "Right Place, Right Time." *Latin Finance* (May 1998), 38.

Tesoro, Jose Manuel. "How Vested Interests Tried to Derail Gresik Privatization." *Asiaweek,* January 22, 1999.

Tricks, Henry. "BBVA Cast as Conquistador: Unsolicited Bid Stands in Way of Spanish Bank's Latin American Expansion Strategy." *Financial Times,* May 5, 2000, p. 32.

World Bank Sources

"Loan Agreement (Structural Adjustment Loan) between Republic of Korea and International Bank for Reconstruction and Development." Loan Number 4302 KO, March 27, 1998.

"Loan Agreement (Structural Adjustment Loan) between Republic of Korea and International Bank for Reconstruction and Development." Loan Number 4399 KO, October 23, 1998.

World Bank. "Brazil: An Assessment of the Private Sector." Report No. 11775-BR, June 24, 1994, Vol. 1.

——. "Brazil: An Assessment of the Private Sector." Report No.11775-BR, June 24, 1994, Vol. 2.

——. "Brazil: Central Bank Modernization Technical Assistance Project." Project Appraisal Document, World Bank Report No. 16867. October 23, 1997.

——. "Brazil: Forging a Strategic Partnership for Results—An OED Evaluation of World Bank Assistance." Operations Evaluation Department, 2004.

——. "Brazil: Selected Issues of the Financial Sector." Report No. 7725-BR, March 1990.

——. "The Development of Brazilian Capital Markets." Country Operations Division, Report No. 11581-BR, March 1993.

——. *Finance for Growth: Policy Choices in a Volatile World.* New York: Oxford University Press for the World Bank, 2001.

——. "Financial Sector Reform: A Review of World Bank Assistance." Report No. 17454, Vol. 1. Operations Evaluation Department, March 6, 1998.

——. *Global Development Finance: Financing the Poorest Countries.* Washington, D.C.: World Bank, 2002.

——. *Global Development Finance: The Role of International Banking.* Washington, D.C.: World Bank, 2008.

——. *IEG Review of World Bank Assistance for Financial Sector Reform.* Washington, D.C.: Independent Evaluation Group, World Bank, 2006.

——. "Indonesia Country Assistance Note." Report No. 19100. Operations Evaluation Department, March 29, 1999.

——. "Indonesia in Crisis: A Macroeconomic Update." Washington, D.C., July 16, 1998.

——. "Indonesia's Financial Sector: A Strategy for Development." Report No. 15735-IND, June 14, 1996.

——. "Mexico Country Assistance Evaluation." Operations Evaluation Department, Report No. 22498, June 28, 2001.

——. *OED Review of Bank Assistance for Financial Sector Reform.* Washington, D.C.: Operations Evaluation Department, World Bank, July 22, 2005.

——. "World Bank Relations with Mexico." Operations Evaluation Department, *OED Précis* No. 71, June 1994.

——. *World Development Finance Database.* April 2006 edition.

——. *World Development Indicators Database.* 2006.

IMF Sources

"Bolivia: Enhanced Structural Adjustment Facility Policy Framework Paper, 1998–2001." August 25, 1998.

"Brazil Letter of Intent." April 20, 2000.

"Brazil Letter of Intent." March 14, 2001.

"Brazil Letter of Intent." March 4, 2002.

"Brazil Letter of Intent." November 3, 2000.

"Brazil Letter of Intent." November 30, 2001.

"Brazil: Letter of Intent and Memorandum of Economic Policies." March 4, 2002.

"Brazil: Letter of Intent and Memorandum of Economic Policies." November 13, 1998.

"Ethiopia: Letter of Intent and Memorandum on Economic and Financial Policies." December 31, 2001.

"Georgia: Enhanced Structural Adjustment Facility Policy Framework Paper, 1998–2000." July 10, 1998.

"Indonesia: Letter of Intent." January 20, 2000.

"Indonesia: Letter of Intent." July 22, 1999.

"Indonesia: Letter of Intent and Memorandum of Economic and Financial Policies." January 15, 1998.

"Indonesia: Letter of Intent and Memorandum of Economic and Financial Policies."
    October 31, 1997.
"Indonesia: Letter of Intent and Memorandum on Economic and Financial Policies."
    January 15, 1998.
"Indonesia: Second Supplementary Memorandum of Economic and Financial Policies."
    June 24, 1998.
"Indonesia: Supplementary Memorandum of Economic and Financial Policies." April 10, 1998.
"Korea: Letter of Intent." December 24, 1997.
"Korea: Letter of Intent." February 7, 1998.
"Korea: Memorandum on the Economic Program." December 3, 1997.
"Korea: Memorandum on the Economic Program." February 7, 1998.
"Korea: Transactions with the Fund from May 1, 1984 to July 31, 2008." Available at www.
    imf.org (accessed August 2008).
"Mexico: Letter of Intent and Memorandum of Economic Policies." January 26, 1995.
"Thailand: Letter of Intent and Memorandum of Economic Policies." August 14, 1997.
"Ukraine: Letter of Intent: Memorandum on Economic and Financial Policies."
    August 11, 1998.
International Monetary Fund. "The IMF and Recent Capital Account Crises: Indonesia,
    Korea, Brazil," Independent Evaluation Office, September 12, 2003.
——. *IMF Annual Report, 1996—World Economic Outlook.* Washington, D.C.: IMF, Sep-
    tember 27, 1996.
——. "The IMF's Approach to Capital Account Liberalization." Independent Evaluation
    Office, April 20, 2005.
——. *International Capital Markets: Developments, Prospects, and Key Policy Issues.* Wash-
    ington, D.C.: IMF, September 2000.
——. *International Financial Statistics Database,* 2006.
——. Press Release No. 95/59, "IMF Approves Stand-By Credit for Costa Rica." November
    29, 1995.
——. "South Africa: Selected Issues." IMF Country Report No. 05/345, September 2005.
EBM/96/103, Minutes of Executive Board Meeting 96/103 (November 15, 1996). IMF
    Archives.
EBM/98/58, Minutes of Executive Board Meeting 98/58 (May 29, 1998). IMF Archives.
SM/96/262, Korea—Staff Report for the 1996 Article IV Consultation, October 22, 1996.
    IMF Archives.

WTO Documents

GATS/SC/13, April 15, 1994.
GATS/SC/13/Suppl. 1, July 28, 1995.
GATS/SC/13/Suppl. 3, February 26, 1998.
GATS/SC/43, April 15, 1994.
GATS/SC/43/Suppl. 1, July 28, 1995.
GATS/SC/43/Suppl. 3, February 26, 1998.
GATS/SC/48, April 15, 1994.
GATS SC/48/Suppl. 1, July 28, 1995.
GATS/SC/48/Suppl. 1/Rev.1, October 4, 1995.
GATS/SC/48/Suppl. 3, February 26, 1998.
GATS/SC/48/Suppl. 3/Rev.1, November 18, 1999.
GATS/SC/56, April 15, 1994.
GATS/SC/56/Suppl. 1, July 28, 1995.
GATS/SC/56/Suppl. 3, February 26, 1998.

Other Official Documents

Act of the Republic of Indonesia No. 7 of 1992 Concerning Banking (unofficial translation).

Act of the Republic of Indonesia No. 10 of 1998 Concerning the Amendment to Act No. 7 of 1992 Concerning Banking.

Annual Report, Indonesian Bank Restructuring Agency, Jakarta, 2000.

BACEN Communiqué No. 5,796, Central Bank of Brazil, Brasilia.

BACEN Communiqué No. 5,798, Central Bank of Brazil, Brasilia.

Comisión Nacional Bancaria. *Memoria 1993.* Mexico City: CNB, 1993.Committee on Financial Sector Assessment. *India's Financial Sector: An Assessment Volume 1.* New Delhi: Foundation Books, March 2009.

Committee on Financial Sector Assessment. *India's Financial Sector: An Assessment,* vol.1 (New Delhi: Foundation Books, March 2009).

"Declaración del Gobierno de los Estados Unidos Mexicanos sobre la aceptación de sus obligaciones como miembro de la Organización de Cooperación y Desarrollo Económicos." April 14, 1994.

"Dictamen de la Comisión de Hacienda y Crédito Público, con proyecto de decreto por el que se expide la Ley de Protección al Ahorro Bancario, y se reforman, adicionan y derogan diversas disposiciones de las Leyes del Banco de México, de Institutciones de Crédito, del Mercado de Valores y Para Regular las Agrupaciones Financieras, Cámara de Diputados." *Gaceta Parlamentaria* 2, 178 (December 12, 1998).

"Framework Agreement between the United States and Mexico for Mexican Economic Stabilization," February 21, 1995.

"Korea's Quest for Reform and Globalization." Selected Speeches of President Kim Young Sam. Presidential Secretariat, Republic of Korea, 1995.

Malan, Pedro Sampaio. *Exposição de Motivos No. 89.* Ministry of Finance, Brasilia, March 7, 1995.

——. *Exposição de Motivos No. 311.* Ministry of Finance, Brasilia, August 23, 1995.

Office of the United States Trade Representative. *National Trade Estimate—Korea.* 1997.

Presidential Commission for Financial Reform. "Financial Reform in Korea: The Final Report." Unofficial translation of executive summary, November 1997.

Senado de la República (Mexico). *Diario de los debates,* No. 3. January 17, 1995.

——. *Diario de los debates,* No. 10. January 27, 1995.

"Statement by the Government of the Republic of Korea Concerning the Acceptance by the Republic of Korea of the Obligations of Membership in the Organization for Economic Co-operation and Development." October 9, 1996.

Appendix 1

LIST OF INTERVIEWEES

INTERVIEWEE	POSITION/INSTITUTION	PLACE AND DATE
	UNITED STATES	
Ariel Buira	Former Deputy Governor, Bank of Mexico	Washington, DC, February 28, 2005
Charles Dallara	Managing Director, Institute for International Finance	Washington, DC, March 2, 2005
Dennis de Tray	Director for Country Office Staff (1994–97) and Country Director (1997–99), World Bank Indonesia Office	Washington, DC, October 4, 2006
Greg Fager	Director, Asia Pacific Department, Institute for International Finance	Washington, DC, March 2, 2005
Daniel Fineman	International Economist, Office of International Banking and Securities Markets, US Treasury	Washington, DC, March 4, 2005
Mary Goodman	Financial Services Negotiations Team (1994–95), Special Assistant to the Assistant Secretary for International Affairs (1995–96), US Treasury	Washington, DC, March 10, 2005
Katie Klingensmith	International Economist, Office of International Banking and Securities Markets, US Treasury	Washington, DC, March 4, 2005
Carl Johan-Lindgren	Former Assistant Director, Banking Supervision and Regulation Division, Monetary and Exchange Affairs Department, IMF	Washington, DC, March 2, 2005
Claudio Loser	Former Director of the Western Hemisphere Department, IMF (1994–2002)	Washington, DC, July 31, 2007
Meg Lundsager	Deputy Assistant Secretary for Trade and Investment Policy, US Treasury	Washington, DC, March 8, 2005
José de Luna Martínez	Senior Financial Economist, World Bank	Washington, DC, March 3, 2005
Donald Mathieson	Division Chief, Emerging Markets Surveillance Division, International Capital Markets Department, IMF	Washington, DC, March 1, 2005

(Continued)

INTERVIEWEE	POSITION/INSTITUTION	PLACE AND DATE
Nader Nazmi	Deputy Director, Latin America Department, Institute for International Finance	Washington, DC, March 2, 2005
Michael Pomerleano	Lead Financial Specialist, Financial Sector Development Department, World Bank	Washington, DC, March 2, 2005
Liliana Rojas-Suarez	Former Deputy Chief, Capital Markets and Financial Studies Division, Research Department, IMF	Washington, DC, March 3, 2005
Whittier Warthin	Director, Office of Financial Services Negotiations, US Treasury	Washington, DC, March 4, 2005
MEXICO		
Patricia Armendáriz	Former Vice-President of Banking Supervision, National Banking and Securities Commission	Mexico City, March 31, 2005
Gabriel Díaz Leyva	Chief Supervisor of Financial Institutions C-1, National Banking and Securities Commission	Mexico City, March 29, 2005
Sergio Kurczyn Bañuelos	Director, Economic Studies, Citigroup-Banamex	Mexico City, March 16, 2005
Mauricio Naranjo González	Former Vice-President of Banking Supervision (VP-1), National Banking and Securities Commission	Mexico City, March 15, 2006
Pascual O'Dogherty Madrazo	Director, Financial System Analysis, Bank of Mexico	Mexico City, April 4, 2005
José Quijano León	Director General, Financial System Analysis, Bank of Mexico	Mexico City, April 4, 2005
Carlos Sales Gutiérrez	Carlos Sales Gutiérrez, President, Fiscal Affairs Commission, Mexican Senate (1995–98)	Mexico City, December 27, 2005
Jaime Serra Puche	Undersecretary of Finance (1986–88); Secretary of Commerce and Industry (1988–94); Secretary of Finance and Public Credit (1994)	(Correspondence) January 4, 2006
José Sidaoui	Deputy Governor, Bank of Mexico	Mexico City, April 5, 2005
Francisco Suárez Dávila	President, Fiscal Affairs Commission, Chamber of Deputies (Mexico) (1994–97)	Mexico City, December 16, 2005
Anatol von Hahn	Managing Director, Scotiabank Inverlat, SA	Mexico City, April 8, 2005

INTERVIEWEE	POSITION/INSTITUTION	PLACE AND DATE
Guillermo Zamarripa Escamilla	Former Vice-President of Banking Supervision (VP-2), National Banking and Securities Commission	Mexico City, April 8, 2005
BRAZIL		
Luiz Carlos Alvarez	Former Director of Bank Supervision, Central Bank of Brazil	(Telephone) May 5, 2005
Pérsio Arida	President, Central Bank of Brazil (1994)	São Paulo, April 19 2005, and Oxford, November 9, 2005
Arminio Fraga	President, Central Bank of Brazil (1999–2003)	Rio de Janeiro, May 3, 2006
Gustavo Loyola	President, Central Bank of Brazil (1995–97)	São Paulo, May 5, 2005
Márcio Issao Nakane	Analyst, Central Bank of Brazil	São Paulo, April 18, 2005
Paulo Guilherme Monteiro Lobato Ribeiro	Former President of Banco Real and Director of FEBRABAN	May 22, 1995, São Paulo (interviewed by Ben Ross Schneider)
Fernando Alberto Sampaio Rocha	Analyst, Central Bank of Brazil	(Telephone) April 15, 2005
Paolo Zaghen	Former Director for the Restructuring of the State Financial System, Central Bank of Brazil	April 27, 2005, São Paulo
INDONESIA		
Sukarela Batunanggar	Senior Analyst, Bank Indonesia	Jakarta, April 13, 2006
Soedradjad Djiwandono	Governor, Bank Indonesia (1993–98)	Oxford, March 16, 2006
Gene Galbraith	President Commissioner, Bank Central Asia	Jakarta, April 3, 2006
Hamden Handoko	Former Vice-President, Indonesian Bank Restructuring Agency	Jakarta, March 29, 2006
Cyrillus Harinowo	Former Alternate Executive Director, IMF; Independent Commissioner, Bank Central Asia	Jakarta, April 5, 2006

(Continued)

INTERVIEWEE	POSITION/INSTITUTION	PLACE AND DATE
Don Johnston	Former advisor to Bank Rakyat Indonesia, Harvard Institute for International Development	Jakarta, March 27, 2006
Lloyd Kenward	IMF Resident Representative in Indonesia (1987–89) and Senior Economist, World Bank Indonesia office (1994–98)	Jakarta, March 22, 2006
Richard McHowat	Chief Executive Officer, HSBC Indonesia	Jakarta, April 6, 2006
Adrianus Mooy	Governor, Bank Indonesia (1988–93)	Jakarta, April 5, 2006
Raden Pardede	Vice-President Director, State-Owned Asset Management Company	Jakarta, March 29, 2006
Stephen Schwartz	Senior Resident Representative, IMF Jakarta Office; Former Deputy Division Chief, IMF Asia and Pacific Department	Jakarta, March 28, 2006
Rusli Simanjundtak	Former assistant to Soedradjad Djiwandono; Director, Directorate of Bank Supervision 2, Bank Indonesia	Jakarta, April 4, 2006
Djauhari Sitorus	Financial Analyst, World Bank, Indonesia office	Jakarta, April 7, 2006
P. S. Srinivas	Lead Financial Economist, World Bank, Indonesia office	Jakarta, March 24, 2006
Ali Wardhana	Finance Minister (1968); Coordinating Minister of Economics, Finance, and Industry (1983–88); Senior Advisor, Ministry of Finance (1989–)	Jakarta, April 11, 2006
SOUTH KOREA		
Duck-Koo Chung	Former Minister of Commerce, Industry, and Energy; Former Vice-Minister of Finance	Seoul June 10, 2008
Stefan James	Managing Director and Regional Executive, North Asia, Bank of America	Seoul June 11, 2008
Meral Karasulu	Resident Representative, Korea, IMF	Seoul June 10, 2008
Okyu Kwon	Deputy Prime Minister and Minister of Finance and Economy (2006–2007); Chief Secretary to the President for National Policy and Senior Secretary to the President for Economic Policy (2006–2007); Ambassador and Permanent	Seoul June 6, 2008

INTERVIEWEE	POSITION/INSTITUTION	PLACE AND DATE
	Representative to the OECD (2004–2006); Senior Secretary to the President for National Policy (2003–2004); Deputy Minister of Finance and Economy (2001–2002); Secretary to the President for Finance and Economy, Office of the President (2000–2001); Alternate Executive Director, IMF (1997–1999)	
Bon-Sung Lee	Chief, Financial Institutions Research Division, Korea Institute of Finance	Seoul June 9, 2008
Dong-Gull Lee	Former Vice-Chairman, Financial Supervisory Commission (2003–4)	Seoul June 5, 2008
Kyu Sung Lee	Minister of Finance and Economy (March 1998– May 1999); Minister of Finance and Economy (1988–90)	Seoul June 9, 2008
Il SaKong	Special Economic Advisor to the President; Former Minister of Finance (1987–88)	Seoul June 4, 2008
Tae-Soo Yoon	Former Vice-President, Korean Financial Industry Union; former head of Choheung Bank Union	Seoul June 11, 2008

GATS COMMITMENTS

Mexican offers at the GATS negotiations (1994–1998)

DATE OFFER PRESENTED	KEY CHANGES OR ADDITIONS MADE TO PREVIOUS OFFER
APRIL 15, 1994 (INITIAL OFFER)	• Foreigners may hold, in the aggregate, only up to 20 percent of a domestic bank's equity • Individual shareholding by foreigners capped at 2.5 percent of total equity • Effective control of the enterprise by the Mexican shareholders is required
JULY 28, 1995	• Foreign banks may establish representative offices in the country with the prior authorization of the SHCP; such offices may not act as financial intermediaries • Foreigners may hold, in the aggregate, only up to 30 percent of a domestic bank's equity
OCTOBER 4, 1995	No change
NOVEMBER 4, 1997	No change
FEBRUARY 26, 1998	• Foreign investors may hold, in the aggregate, up to 40 percent of common stock capital and up to 100 percent of the additional capital representing 40 percent of nonvoting common stock capital • Foreign investment by artificial persons exercising governmental functions is not allowed • The limit on individual holdings is 5 percent of capital stock or up to 20 percent of capital stock with authorization from the SHCP

Source: Author's summary based on Mexico's GATS submissions.

Brazilian offers at the GATS negotiations (1994–2003)

DATE OFFER PRESENTED	KEY CHANGES OR ADDITIONS MADE TO PREVIOUS OFFER
APRIL 15, 1994 (INITIAL OFFER)	• No new foreign-bank branches and subsidiaries allowed; number of foreign-bank branches in Brazil frozen at levels of October 5, 1988 • No increases in foreigners' share of the capital stock of Brazilian financial institutions allowed • Minimum paid-in capital and net worth requirements applicable to foreign-bank branches and foreign-controlled banks are twice those established for Brazilian banks
JULY 28, 1995	• Increases in foreign participation and new foreign-bank branches are allowed only in connection with the state bank privatization program
OCTOBER 4, 1995	No change
FEBRUARY 26, 1998	• New foreign-bank branches and subsidiaries, as well as increases in foreign participation in domestic banks, are permitted only "when subject to case-by-case authorization by the Executive Branch" by means of a presidential decree (and as part of the state bank privatization program) • Applying investors may be required to fulfill specific conditions

Source: Author's summaries based on Brazil's GATS submissions.

Indonesian offers at the GATS negotiations (1994–2003)

DATE OFFER PRESENTED	KEY CHANGES OR ADDITIONS MADE TO PREVIOUS OFFER
APRIL 15, 1994 (INITIAL OFFER)	• Foreign banks may open sub-branch offices in only eight cities (Jakarta, Surabaya, Semarang, Bandung, Medan, Ujung Pandang, Denpasar, and Batam Island), and they may open only one office in each of these cities
	• Acquisition of local existing banks is allowed through the purchase of up to 49 percent of the shares listed in the stock exchange
	• Except for existing branches of foreign banks, foreign services provider must be in the form of joint-venture bank; these are allowed on a reciprocity basis
	• In foreign bank branches, only executive positions can be occupied by expatriates; at least one of them shall be an Indonesian national
	• In joint-venture banks, director positions can be occupied by expatriates only in proportion to their ownership shares
	• The GOI reserves the right to establish regulations concerning the paid-up capital requirements for joint-venture banks
JULY 28, 1995	• All market access and national treatment limitations specified for banking will be eliminated by the year 2020 subject to similar commitment by other countries
	• Foreign bank and joint-venture banks may open one sub-branch and one auxiliary office in the eight cities specified above
FEBRUARY 26, 1998	• Discriminatory paid-up capital requirement to be eliminated in 1998
	• Foreign banks and joint-venture banks may open offices, without restriction on number, in the eight cities specified above
	• In the case of joint-venture banks, no transfer of ownership shall take place without the consent of all parties in the concerned bank
	• With respect to the presence of natural persons, no economic needs test will apply. A non-Indonesian employed as manager or as technical expert shall have at least two Indonesian understudies during his/her term.
JANUARY 24, 2003	No change

Source: Author's summary based on Indonesia's GATS submissions.

Korean offers at the GATS negotiations (1994–2003)

DATE OFFER PRESENTED	KEY CHANGES OR ADDITIONS MADE TO PREVIOUS OFFER
APRIL 15, 1994 (INITIAL OFFER)	• Only representative offices of branches of foreign banks are permitted • Branches may only be established one year after a representative office has been established • A maximum limit of 8 percent is applied to the equity ownership of a bank by a natural or juridical person • Permissions are required for engaging in business other than the main banking business and for engaging in trust business • Government reserves the right to take action in response to discriminatory treatment accorded to Korean financial service providers in any foreign country
JULY 28, 1995	• Portfolio investment is permitted only for stocks listed in Korean stock exchanges; foreign investors can own up to 3 percent of a (nonstate-owned) company's total stock in all sectors, including financial services • Aggregate foreign investment cannot exceed 15 percent in all sectors, including financial services • The Korean government undertakes a standstill for limitations on national treatment and market access, where specific commitments were undertaken • Foreign financial institutions will be allowed equity participation in existing banks in 1996-97 • Assets owned by foreign bank branches must be kept within Korean territory; capital of the head office is not recognized when determining the extent of funding and lending activities of branches
OCTOBER 4, 1995	No change
FEBRUARY 26, 1998	• In the context of portfolio investment, foreigners can own up to 6 percent of a (nonstate-owned) company's total stock in all sectors • Aggregate foreign investment cannot exceed 23 percent in all sectors • A person may own up to 4 percent of the stocks of a bank and 15 percent of the stocks of a provincial bank without special authorization from the authorities
NOVEMBER 18, 1999	• Commercial presence is permitted to foreign banks (entry by subsidiary is bound)

Source: Author's summary based on Korea's GATS submissions.

Index

Page numbers followed by letters *f* and *t* refer to figures and tables, respectively.